READING DANCING

READING DANCING:

Bodies and Subjects in

Contemporary American Dance

SUSAN LEIGH FOSTER

UNIVERSITY OF CALIFORNIA PRESS   *Berkeley, Los Angeles, London*

University of California Press
Berkeley and Los Angeles, California
University of California Press, Ltd.
London, England
© 1986 by
Susan Leigh Foster
Printed in the United States of America
3   4   5   6   7   8   9

Photographs © Radford Bascome, Lorenzo Capellini,
Johan Elbers, Arnold Genthe, Philip Hipwell, Phyllis
Liedeker, James Klosty, Babette Mangolte, Peter Moore,
Barbara Morgan, Alan Pogue, Tony Russell, Marion
Scarborough, Martha Swope, Ellen Wallenstein, and
Tony Whitman.

Library of Congress Cataloging-in-Publication Data

Foster, Susan Leigh.
   Reading dancing.

   Bibliography: p.
   Includes index.
   1. Modern dance—United States.   2. Choreography.
3. Movement, Aesthetics of.   4. Dancing—History.
I. Title.
GV1783.F67   1986   793.3′1973   85-16530
ISBN 0-520-06333-3 (ppb.)

Frontispiece: Merce Cunningham and Carolyn Brown
in *Suite for Five* (1956). Photo by Radford Bascome.
Courtesy of the Dance Collection, New York Public
Library at Lincoln Center.

The paper used in this publication meets the minimum
requirements of American National Standard for Information Sciences—Permanence of Paper for Printed
Library Materials, ANSI Z39.48—1984.   ∞

For my parents, who drove me forty miles
each way to my first dance classes

CONTENTS

ILLUSTRATIONS

PREFACE

I remember being completely baffled the first time I saw the Merce Cunningham Dance Company: painfully bright lights, ear-piercing sounds, dancers walking matter-of-factly to random locations on the stage, beginning phraseless sequences of movement that paused in strange positions at unpredictable moments, exiting abruptly and re-entering midsequence, and then John Cage stealing the show with his champagne drinking and tart anecdotes.[1]

What were they doing? What was the dance about?

It was the summer of 1967 at the American Dance Festival. I was a midwestern teenager, who had given up ballet after ten years of intensive training to study modern dance. I wanted to be a choreographer, and at the time I thought modern dance offered far more opportunities than ballet for making and presenting original work. But Cunningham. His dances didn't mean anything. Even two years later—when the company was in Paris and I witnessed a deeply moving performance of *Field Dances* (1963)—I rushed backstage to thank Cunningham for such a profound image of how the world should be, only to have him explain that the dance was divided into sections that were repeated in a different order for each performance, as determined by chance procedures.

Was there no meaning to his dances at all?

Over the years I came to love Merce Cunningham's dances, to appreciate his extraordinary arrangements of human bodies moving in space and time. But it was only once I began making dances of my own and studying dance history that I came to value Cunningham's dances not only for themselves but also for what they allow us to understand about dance in general. In 1953 Cunningham premiered his *Suite by Chance*, a dance that decisively broke with contemporary choreographic methods by using chance procedures to compose and then sequence dance movement.[2] And this extraordinary gesture of ordering movement randomly was only part of his choreographic agenda. Cunningham intended to call into question and even to sever the intimate relationship that then existed between music, human feeling, and movement. All three, he asserted, could and should be seen as separate realms of events, whose correspondences were haphazard at best. By disassociating dance movement from its musical and emotional sources, Cunningham gave it a new independence as the material, tangible substance out of which the dance could be constructed as an entirely autonomous event. This objectification of dance movement contravened prevailing assumptions about dance composition not only because it acknowledged no "natural" connection between movement and feeling but also because it suggested that the dance could simply be about human bodies moving and nothing more.

The quest for a natural way of moving, a natural body, and a natural, organic choreographic process dominated American concert dance in the early part of this century, and it continues today.[3] Typically, those engaged in this quest accord dance a role as the most appropriate medium of expression for primal, emotional, and libidinal dimensions of human experience. Dance is seen as an outlet for intuitive or unconscious feelings inaccessible to verbal (intellectual) expression. Based on this model, dancers often cultivate a sanctimonious mutism, denying what is verbal, logical, and discursive in order to champion the physical and the sensate. At the same time, they are oppressed by the inferior status of their accomplishments within a society that esteems the verbal or the mathematical over all other forms of discourse. Nonetheless, this role for dance—as the spontaneous, graceful, erotic, and, above all, fervent use of the body—offers dance a clear place and function in society.

As long as dance participates in the pursuit of the "natural," however, little can be said about the art of choreography. The "natural" creative process, an intensely private search for inspiration and appropriate expression, cannot be learned but only assimilated by rehearsing and performing in a choreographer's dances. One of the major theoretical works on dance composition of the last fifty years, Doris Humphrey's *The Art of Making Dances*, testifies to the unwillingness of choreographers to articulate compositional methods. In her final chapter, Humphrey summarizes her advice to the novice dance maker as follows:

Symmetry is lifeless
Two-dimensional design is lifeless
The eye is faster than the ear
Movement looks slower and weaker on stage
All dances are too long
A good ending is forty percent of the dance
Monotony is fatal; look for contrasts
Don't be a slave to, or mutilator of, the music
Listen to qualified advice; don't be arrogant
Don't intellectualize; motivate the movement
Don't leave the ending to the end.[4]

This impoverished set of instructions for making good dances could never result in the complex manipulation of thematic material, the eloquent spatial organization, and the powerful, symbolic bodily shapes that are the hallmarks of Humphrey's dances.

But dance theory, according to this model, can do no better. In the twentieth century, the most influential theories of dance composition have been formulated by philosopher Suzanne Langer, critic John Martin, and ethnologist Curt Sachs.[5] All three locate the origins of dance in early human gestural attempts at communication. They oppose these primal yearnings to express human feeling to the subsequent artificiality of civilized movement, and they look to dance as a medium that can return us to a vital energy and an unalienated sense of wholeness. For all three, as for the majority of early twentieth-century choreographers,[6] the body serves as a physical instrument for an interior subjectivity, and the dance functions as a luminous symbol of unspeakable human truths, which, because they are unspeakable, leave us little to say about the dance's organization.[7] Thus the dance remains an ephemeral event whose immediate appeal can never be captured in words. At best, criticism is able to provide a historical perspective or an aesthetic judgment for what is otherwise too fragile and fleeting for comment.

How to get at the workings of a dance. Admittedly, it is difficult for choreographers, dancers, and viewers alike to apprehend choreographic structure. Dancers undergo years of training to translate the proprioceptive sensations of movement into hypothesized images of how that movement looks and feels to another. The talent for remembering movement is difficult to cultivate and certainly not rewarded by this society. Choreographers contend with cumbersome notation systems or pale video reflections as the only documentation of the dance they have conceived and executed. And the literature describing dance historically and cross-culturally is relatively inaccessible.

Because of the fleeting nature of the medium as well as their own aesthetic concerns, twentieth-century choreographers have, in general, preferred not to talk about their dances. Even Cunningham, who rejected the choreographic methods of his contemporaries, has refrained for most of his artistic life from talking about his work.[8] Like them, he wants the dance to speak for itself in a language all its own. Yet because his dances have presented movement ranging from the balletic to the pedestrian, ordered through a variety of procedures including the aleatory, and have thereby offered up the activity of moving as their meaning, they allow us to address the question of dance composition anew. They shatter the silent organic unity of the "natural" body and of a naturally expressive creative process so that instead of grasping the choreographer's intended meaning by intuiting the body's intrinsic message, we can decipher a dance's codes and structures. We can look, on the one hand, at the choice of movement and the principles for ordering that movement and, on the other, at the procedures for referring to or representing worldly events in danced form. That is to say, we can begin to ask *how* any dance means what it does.

"Reading dancing" is the name I have given to this active and interactive interpretation of dance as a system of meaning. In the study of contemporary American concert dance that follows, I propose a set of choreographic conventions that create and convey what a dance is about. I examine these choreographic conventions first in terms of the artistic practice of the choreographer, surveying four current approaches to dance composition represented in the works of Deborah Hay, George Balanchine, Martha Graham, and Merce Cunningham. To trace the development of choreographic meaning from class and rehearsal to the dance performance itself, I compare these choreographers' views on the creative process, dance technique, and the expressive act, as well as their implicit assumptions about the role of the body and the expressive subject in their dances. At the same time, in much the same way that Cunningham's dances challenged our expectations when they were first presented, I hope to call into question our familiar beliefs about how a dance is made. All too often we attend a dance concert with unquestioned assumptions concerning the kind of body we will see or the kind of message we will receive. But choreographers do not necessarily share those assumptions, as we will see. The four choreographers examined in this study describe their approaches to composition in radically contrasting terms; they disagree about standards of technical competence; and they profess entirely different ideas about what the body is and does. And yet how each choreographer cultivates the body remains remarkably congruent with his or her overall aesthetic. As a result, the comparison of these four choreographic approaches can expand and also organize our expectations about the dancing body and the dance.

If chapter 1 disengages the dance from our familiar associations by presenting an array of contrasting ideas about the creative process, chapter 2 looks specifically at the craft of dance composition. Once the body, the subject, and the expressive act have been "de-naturalized," then the dance can be examined explicitly as a system of codes and conventions that support its meaning. Chapter 2 considers five such conventions: (1) the dance's frame—how it separates itself from the rest of the world; (2) its modes of representation—how through *resemblance, imitation, replication,* or *reflection* the dance refers to the world; (3) its style—how it creates a personal signature for itself; (4) its vocabulary—the individual movements of which dance is composed; and (5) its syntax—the principles governing the selection and combination of movements. The first three conventions allow the dance to refer to events in the world, and the last two, vocabulary and syntax, lend to dance its internal coherence and structure. The dance's meaning is, in part, a product of the tensions created between these two kinds of conventions—between the references that the dance makes to the world and to its own organization.

Chapter 3 uses the poetics of dance established in chapter 2 and the four contemporary approaches to choreography developed in chapter 1 to construct a history for contemporary concert dance. Beginning with the European court spectacles of the late Renaissance and moving through eighteenth-century neoclassicism to early twentieth-century expressionism and finally to the outgrowth of the Cunningham revolution of the 1950s, I argue that the principal method for composing dances in each of these historical periods resembles one of the four contemporary models. Thus the works of Hay, Balanchine, Graham, and Cunningham provide familiar ground on which to organize the available artifacts of dances from these four key periods in the history of Western dance. At the same time, the comparison of past and present uses of similar sets of choreographic conventions points up the historical specificity of those conventions. Such a comparison allows us to see the extent to which meaning for any given choreographic structure is to be found embedded in its social and historical setting.

Chapters 1 through 3 examine dance as a product of the choreographer's creative process, of the conventions that compose it, and of its historical situation, respectively. The fourth chapter completes this analysis by considering the experience of the dance's viewers.[9] Each of the four choreographic models outlined in chapter 1 gives viewers specific responsibilities and a unique involvement in the dance, almost as if they participated in the same cultivation of body and subject undertaken by the choreographer and dancers as a result of their "reading" of the dance. Chapter 4 reflects back on these different experiences for dance viewers by proposing a fifth model for the choreographic process, one that actually includes viewers in the making of the dance. Performances by companies like the Grand Union, Meredith Monk and the House, and Twyla Tharp Dance Company incorporate a variety of tactics for exposing and commenting on their own use of choreographic conventions. Dances created by the Grand Union and Meredith Monk, in particular, feature the conventions by which they are made. In so doing, they engage the viewer in a relationship that extends beyond the active participation of reading the dance. I have called this open-ended, playful, yet self-critical, interaction between viewer and dance "writing dancing."

My choice of "reading" and "writing" as metaphors for interpreting dance draws upon contemporary discussions of these terms in literary and cultural criticism. In particular, the works of Roland Barthes, Michel Foucault, and Hayden White support the argument that reading and writing are forms of (bodily) inscription. All three of these theorists have witnessed and written about epistemological ruptures in their respective disciplines equivalent to the impact of Cunningham's dances on the concert dance tradition. All three have attempted to rethink the issue of representation, and in doing so they have called into question the nature of the subject (and the body) who engages in the act of representation. Although my analysis is in no way intended to introduce or critique their work, it does translate many of their ideas in order to arrive at a theory of representation in dance; I have pointed to some of the correspondences in the notes.

But if *Reading Dancing* is inspired by recent cultural criticism, it is equally influenced by the work of contemporary choreographers. In the same way that Langer, Martin, or Sachs share with the choreographers of their period assumptions about the artistic process, *Reading Dancing* is a product of contemporary attitudes toward dance composition. One feature of the contemporary American concert dance tradition is its unparalleled diversity of choreographic methods; in *Reading Dancing*, I have tried to support and encourage an acceptance of these different approaches to dance making. Unlike some critics who would argue that ballet is the only enduring Western concert dance form and who see modern dance as a moment of rebellious experimentation lacking in consequence because of its failure to produce a lexicon,[10] I see the tradition's strength and vitality in its eclectic range of styles, vocabularies, and syntaxes.

Yet in addition to its pluralistic constituency, the contemporary American dance world possesses a second and equally important feature—the capacity to reflect critically on its various enterprises and to choreograph commentary about its own artistic process. And it is this reflexive impulse, initiated by Cunningham and elaborated by choreographers Yvonne Rainer, Trisha Brown, Douglas Dunn, David Gordon, Meredith Monk, and others, that inspires a book about dance composition such as this. Like Foucault and Barthes, these choreographers challenge traditional distinctions between thought and action, subject and object, artist and critic, thereby suggesting the possibility of writing about dance in a way that does not, on the one hand, reductively explain it or, on the other, despair of ever re-creating its transient meaning. *Reading Dancing*, then, gestures toward an interdisciplinary domain where writing and dancing sign in the direction of one another.[11]

For their part in making this writing dance, I would like to acknowledge my debt to Hayden White, Jim Clifford, Margaret Brose, Sharon Traweek, and Stephen Greenblatt, who taught me to "read"; and to Richard Bull and Cynthia Novack, who taught me dance composition. To them, and to my colleagues at Wesleyan Richard Stamelman, Bill Stowe, Dave Konstan, Vera Schwarcz, Anne Greene, Miriam Silverberg, Alvin Lucier, Ron Kuivila, and Cheryl Cutler, for their advice and encouragement; to choreographers and scholars Roberta Bristol, Trisha Brown, Judith Cobau, Mark Franko, Deborah Hay, and Selma Jeanne Cohen, for their invaluable comments and criticism; to my editors Andy Szegedy-Maszak, George Russell, and Stephanie Fay, for their great patience and insight; and to Alice Pomper, who did far more than the typing, my deepest thanks.

CHAPTER ONE

Reading Dance:

Composing the Choreographer,

the Dancer, and the Viewer

This reading of American concert dance first considers the choreographic projects of four artists: Deborah Hay, George Balanchine, Martha Graham, and Merce Cunningham. An eclectic group of dance makers, whose works are most often associated with different traditions and even different moments in the history of dance, the four choreographers have nonetheless presented their work contemporaneously. During the 1983–84 New York season, for example, Graham celebrated her ninetieth birthday by presenting a major new work, her version of *The Rite of Spring*, while Cunningham, appearing across town, danced in his new piece entitled *Pictures*. Despite Balanchine's death in 1983, a full complement of his dances was presented during the New York City Ballet's winter and spring performances. Less well known, Hay, an avant-garde choreographer, also performed; and like the others, she has established an enthusiastic following—an avid and learned dance audience that comes to see a particular vision of art.

I have chosen the works of these choreographers in order to consider paradigmatic types in American concert dance. The dances of each of these choreographers exhibit a unique form. Each explores a special conception both of dance movement and of the dancing body and a singular conviction about the purpose of art. Furthermore, the approach taken by each choreographer is consistent throughout; that is, the form the dances take is consonant with each choreographer's creative process, with each one's philosophy of the training and rehearsing required for dance performance, and with each one's expectations concerning viewers' responses. Because of this internal coherence as well as the distinctiveness of each choreographer's project, these four approaches to dance provide vivid illustrations of four models for the choreographic project.[1]

But is it possible to speak about the works of these choreographers, which in the case of Graham or Balanchine span a sixty-year period, as the result of a uniform creative process? And how can the choreography be separated from the changing historical and social circumstances that surround each choreographer's career? In the 1920s, for example, Graham's choice of movement vocabulary derived from a new, nonclassical conception of the relationship between emotion and kinesthetic form as one that cultivated the body's dynamic responsiveness to human feeling. Her recent work, however, privileges the visual appearance of movement, its shape and line, over these tensile connections between movement and the psyche. Where before there was a dancer suspended in torment between earth and air, now the dancer contracts with an anguished gesture, twists, falls to the ground, rises to perform a series of *bourrées* on the knees, steps into an arabesque turn, and so forth. In the same way, her much-acclaimed *Acts of Light* (1981) presents an inventory of the now well-established Graham lexicon—from simple articulations of the spine to dazzling jumps and leaps across the floor—all with a joyful exhilaration and virtuosity typically seen at the ballet. Although Graham's classic film, *A Dancer's World* (1957), shows many of the same movement motifs, in that period of her artistic development they could never stand on their own. All movement was necessarily incorporated into the dance as a vehicle for expressing some dramatic situation.

Cunningham's work has changed along similar lines. After soundly rejecting Graham's artistic premises in the late 1940s and leaving her company to formulate his own aesthetics of dance, he has in his recent dances increasingly emphasized a picture-oriented style. The choreography attends less to the transitoriness of all movement and focuses more on poses and on bodily shapes that involve maximum stretch and extension. Furthermore, Cunningham's dancers are far more uniform in their physical appearance and range of skills than in previous times, thereby enhancing the movement's visual design. At the same time, the dances in which Cunningham himself appears manifest a new allegorical significance: his compelling, idiosyncratic vocabulary of minimal steps and tiny, flickering hand gestures seems to lament his inability to move like the other dancers but also conveys his masterful command over what they do. His specterlike presence makes it impossible to say, as one once could, that Cunningham's dances are about unique bodies moving in space and time.

My purpose here, however, is not to deliver precise historical accounts of specific pieces but to articulate a theory of representation in dance that can encompass a variety of approaches to dance composition. I have chosen, therefore, to pass over the marked changes in the choreographers' careers and instead to focus on certain conceptions of dance, evident throughout their work, that permit a composite or generalized overview of their artistic concerns. I have asked the same questions of each choreographer's work to elucidate their visions of what a dance is and what it involves: the creative process of making a dance, the organization of dance classes and rehearsals, the relation between dance and the other arts, and the responsibilities and pleasures of the dance's performers and its viewers. Comparing these four distinct visions of dance expands our notions of choreographic methods and demonstrates how the processes of making a dance and making a dancer are bound together.[2] It also reveals how the dancing body as well as the dancing subject comes to be endowed with a symbolic significance that permeates its very existence.[3]

Deborah Hay in
Solo Performance (1979).
Photo by Ellen Wallenstein. ©

Deborah Hay dances with and within the world around her.[4] She communes with the natural and social landscape, sensing and manifesting its constant change. Her facial expression, her costume, the quality, shape, and timing of her movement—all reflect a calm, ethereal rapport with her surroundings. She proclaims a loving openness toward the dance, the audience, and the environment by moving with grace and dignity, completely absorbed in the dance. From the moment she walks into the performing space—a concert stage, a gallery, or a park— she works to create a sense of community among everyone present. Often she stands still for a moment in the middle of the space, acknowledging the audience and the moment; then she begins to dance.

Diverse movements compose her dance. Some are simple, like a sustained run through the space; others are complex, involving turning jumps, falls, or precarious balances accompanied by detailed gestures of the arms or head. Whether a movement is minute and delicate or sweeping and forceful, it appears full, even luscious. Movements may be repeated, becoming more vivid and acquiring a wealth or ripeness with each repetition, but they seldom recur. The dance, which may last an hour or more, consists largely of discrete phrases performed several times and then left behind. The movements do not suggest a plot or build to a dramatic or emotional climax, nor do they conform to the structure of the musical accompaniment. Instead, the dance unfolds as a continuous series of new events unified by the grace and dedication with which they are performed. Like the individual repeated movements, the dance acquires power and meaning through the simple compilation of individual images.

Music for the dance supports the ambience of communal rapport created by the choreography. Sounds repeat and then imperceptibly evolve into new textures and harmonies. Sometimes these changes coincide with the occurrence of a new movement image; sometimes the sound actively contradicts the quality of the movement. The overall effect, however, is one of music as a shimmering chordal voice singing in harmony with the melody of the dance. Program notes often function as yet another voice participating in the dance, with titles and notes for dances consisting of poetic images that sometimes label the movement being performed. The audience can look back and forth from movement to a verbal description of what the movement represents. These descriptions include images from nature—"reflecting brook," "still summer hill," "bird dance," or "gnarled trees"— interspersed with specific movement directives—"slow, well-paced run," or "large sweeping movements on the floor"—and more abstract instructions such as "the embodiment of all images," "arrival," or "preponderance of the great." The movement occasionally looks like its namesake, as in the case of "bird dance," "hair wash," or any of the movement directives such as "slow, well-paced run," "sitting up and lying down," or "rolling laboriously." More often, however, the movement approximates some quality or feature of the image such as stillness, gnarledness, or randomness.

The dances depict these various images, yet they also embody an attitude toward them to such an extent that they often seem more like rituals than concerts. The powerful impression Hay makes moving alone for an hour, or the equally forceful statement made when a group of her dancers perform, is reminiscent of that of a sacred undertaking. Although they are intended to take place in a quotidian time and space rather than an imaginary land of past or future, her dances attempt to transform their location and the viewers' perceptions into a more harmonious environment. And although they do not tell stories of archetypal or mythical significance, they allude to the world with reverence, grace, and generosity. This spirit of the dance, evoked by the dancers' performance, seems to embrace dancers, musicians, and audience alike.

According to Hay, "Everyday the whole day from the minute you get up is potentially a dance."[5] This succinct statement about the relationship between life and art summarizes many of her aesthetic concerns. Her choreography is informed by her willingness to see the world as motion, to see that movement is everywhere—in the tree branches shifting, the cars rolling by, people pausing at a street corner,

Rehearsal of Deborah Hay's *HEAVEN/below* (1980). Photo by Marion Scarborough. ©

a newspaper blowing down the sidewalk, a bird landing on the telephone wire. The fluctuations, the pulsations, the ebb and flow of this universal movement partake of some universal order, creating an empyreal rapport. Dancing is the activity of being present in and consciously aware of one's own movement as part of this flux.

To live her life as a dance, Hay cultivates her awareness of forms and rhythms in the day's mundane activities like setting the table, sipping coffee, or combing hair. She tries to establish an ease and fullness in the performance of these activities, and she encourages others to do the same:

Bring the dances with you to the lab and the A&P.
Bring 'em on the bus, into the garden, and upstairs.
Take them out walking and take them to bed.[6]

Such instructions are inspired, in part, by Hay's investigation of Asian religions and by her study of the Chinese martial art form t'ai chi ch'uan. Borrowing principles from these traditions, she intends to fashion a Taoist vision of the universe in which each human being exists as but a small part. In this universe, life's dance is available to everyone sensitive to daily movement and willing to locate personal movement within the patterns of all movement.

Hay has created a number of opportunities for people untrained in dance both to develop sensitivity to the movement of daily life and to learn how that movement relates to social and natural patterns. Her book, *Moving Through the Universe with Bare Feet*, offers a new approach to social dancing that emphasizes the vitality of simple movements and the communal experience of performing such movements with others. These scores for social dances, called *Circle Dances*, include simple verbal instructions accompanied by a set of drawings and suggestions for music taken from popular records. In a large, comfortable room, the dances begin slowly and gently, guided by a series of vivid metaphorical images—images designed to enhance a relaxed, supple, open carriage of the body and to focus the dancer's attention on the process of breathing. The dancer is asked to "Breathe into a gentle arch like a supple bow" or "Standing, relaxed, together, turn your head from facing right to facing left shoulder, breathe the movement into existence, imagine a great force of water coming out of both ears irrigating land on either side of you."[7] Many of the instructions recast the body, likening it to diverse entities or events. The dancer imagines the body as bow, as irrigation pump, as balloon, or as particles dispersing into the air. These images are complemented by descriptions of such movements as stretching forward, stepping and hopping, running, or lying down.

More structured than a typical social dance event, Hay's *Circle Dances*, supported by the changing moods of the music, alternate between quiet, meditative moments and more vigorous and socially interactive periods. The dancers are asked to feel the circle, to encounter one another's gazes, and to sense the group's energy. Participants often attain a feeling of well-being that extends into daily living because the dances nurture a sense of grace, both bodily and social.

In keeping with her commitment to a continuity between life and art, Hay sees little difference between these highly participatory social dances and the more formal dance concerts that she and her company perform. Both events depend on the same awareness of the subtleties and details of movement that Hay brings to her own daily activities. "The dance is my being here in this space, totally, and preparation for this performance is my entire life and nothing more or less," she says.[8] Thus Hay and her company prepare for a concert, in part, by ritualizing the domestic tasks of a dance production. They may even clean the room in which the dance will occur and make it warm and hospitable by obtaining flowers or fruit for the audience. These activities are performed with a sense of their importance as part of one's daily "dance," and they also help focus concentration for the special version of the ongoing dance about to take place.

Throughout the concert itself, dancers manifest an extraordinary presence, a willingness to be seen moving that results from complete commitment, even surrender, to the movement.[9] This presence makes Hay's concerts both special and specialized, requiring a strong technical foundation and competence. Hay and her dancers have developed the ability to concentrate so fully on the movement that each image seems to permeate their bodies completely. Their bodies seem porous and protean and thus capable of a delicate saturation in the movement.

To emphasize the commitment necessary to perform her dances, Hay frequently invokes as a metaphor the idea of a cellular consciousness. She asserts that every cell in the body must participate in each moment of the dance.

I dance by directing my consciousness to the movement of every cell in my body simultaneously so that I can feel all parts of me from the inside, from the

Deborah Hay Dance Company
in *The Well* (1984). Photo by
Alan Pogue. ©

very inside out moving. I dance by feeling the movement of space simultaneously all over my body so that it is like bringing my sensitivity to the very edges of my being from my head to my toe so that I can feel the movement of the air around me.[10]

Although the technique of cellular consciousness can be practiced anywhere, it is highly rigorous and specific. The dancer maintains a vigilant awareness of all areas of the body, registering any reluctance to move, invigorating any insensitive area with new energy. During this careful process of bodily renewal, a focus on breathing is crucial. By breathing consciously and fully, one can detect tense or dull areas of the body and bring them to life. Breathing also connects the body and the space around it, the dancer's specific movements and the pattern of all surrounding movement. With sufficient practice at cellular consciousness, the body becomes quiet, alert, and relaxed, capable of moving with alacrity and fullness.

When Hay teaches her technique of cellular consciousness, she begins by asking students simply to move in their own way and in their own time while focusing on the image of the body's cells. Students may spend the first hour of a three-hour class in this movement meditation. Further guidance from Hay comes in the form of more specialized instructions, such as "Today, make every cell vulnerable," or a request that a student pay more attention to a particular part of the body.[11] The sparseness of critical commentary lends a communal atmosphere to the classes but also fosters each individual's responsibility in developing the necessary concentration. Following these basic exercises in bodily awareness, students may use cellular consciousness to transform the body into imagined events by learning and performing Hay's dances as fully as possible. Thus even in the organization of her classes Hay attempts to bridge the gap between exercise or preparation and performance.

The sequence of events in Hay's dances seems haphazard, determined by chance or intuition or both. Movements strongly contrast with preceding movements and resemble others, but no narrative theme is apparent. Hay often instructs dancers to repeat each movement until they feel it has been performed completely, or until satiated with it. The dancer then proceeds to the next movement by instantaneously attuning all cells of the body to the performance of that image. Because dancers advance through the sequence of movements in their own time, the duration and number of repetitions are not synchronized, and the execution of each dancer, while similar to that of other dancers, is marked by idiosyncracies of individual interpretation. In performances by those highly skilled in Hay's technique, however, each dancer's uniqueness becomes increasingly refined. The dancers' awareness of cellular movement extends to the surrounding movements of others so that remarkable unisons frequently occur. At the same time, the dancers' full participation in the images allows the individuality of their physical structures to emerge in vivid detail.

Deborah Hay Dance Company in *Tribute to Growth* (1983). Photo by Phyllis Liedeker. ©

This striking ensemble is all the more eloquent because the choreography allows no transitions between successive movements. The dancer is fully involved in one movement and then immediately engages in the next. The piece acquires interest and meaning because of the dancers' sustained involvement in each successive activity, as though the dance were about the activity of performing movements. Yet the individual dancer does not appear to be someone who is performing movements. The dancer as a performing subject dissolves as the dance progresses, and the dancer seems to become the very movements being performed. In dancing the image of "arrival," for example, Hay does not show an individual character arriving somewhere. Instead, she embodies the act of arriving itself. Similarly, Hay approximates "gnarled trees" or "well-paced run" by resonating with those things rather than depicting them.

Hay's technique of cellular consciousness is essential in achieving this identity between the dancer's subject or self, and image. She tunes her being to the dance image by redefining her subjectivity as neither more nor less than the cells of the body. The lack of transitions between dance movements only reaffirms this discontinuous sense of self. There is no consistent being to whom the dance is happening. Hay and her dancers are simply the sum total of the body's cells, each of which participates fully in the moment of the dance. Hay emphasizes again and again that she is not "herself" when she dances. Nor is she herself impersonating someone or something else. Dance for her is "self"-transcendent. Like the world of which she is a part, Hay moves as a fluid, changing congeries of metaphorical images that consort with one another in grace and harmony.

Although Hay does not require her audiences to comprehend this vision of subject or world, she hopes they will sense her generosity and conviction, and perhaps the sacred in what she dances. And she invites them to become immersed with her and the other performers in an endeavor that is both playful and forthright. As the movement images accrete, they seem to suggest a journey through the landscape. Because of the frank, open gaze of the dancers and the simplicity of their movement, the audience, even though they remain seated, are invited along on this journey. The calm, unassuming execution and the steady pacing of the dance reveal not so much the dancer performing the dance as the dance itself. As witnesses to this process, dancers and audience together can affirm their harmonious placement as part of the world's ongoing movement.

George Balanchine

George Balanchine's dances are visual masterpieces of design, proportion, and form.[12] They progress fluidly from one elegant picture to the next. Each movement of the dance alludes to an ideal visual image—a geometrized shape the body can attain or a grouping of dancers can suggest by their arrangement in space. The opening scene on the stage signals the events to follow. Typically, the curtain rises on a breathtaking tableau—beautifully costumed dancers carefully placed against a decorous yet stimulating backdrop. This still life is put into motion by the music, which supports and sustains a kaleidoscope of color, design, movement, and, perhaps most important, virtuoso performance.

Balanchine's dances take as their format either the pantomimic story dance or the plotless, abstract divertissement. The story dances involve a simple, often familiar, plot—the adventures of a mythic hero such as Orpheus, or a fairy tale like *The Nutcracker*, or a famous play like *A Midsummer Night's Dream*. The dances follow the story line, also described in the program notes, combining pantomimed dialogue and action with more abstract movement sequences. The plotless dances focus primarily on the formal composition of movement and its correspondence to the music, although they usually retain some semblance of narrative by suggesting an active courtship or love relationship or, perhaps, the loss and recovery of love.

The narrative theme provides an important structural support for the dance, but the relationship of the music to the dance is even more compelling.[13] The dance movement parallels the structure of the music,

The New York City Ballet in George
Balanchine's *Apollo* (1928). Photo
1963 by Martha Swope. ©

often translating musical dynamics, changes in pitch, rhythmic patterns, phrasing, and orchestration into sequences of movement. New formations of dancers and movement phrases usually begin in synchrony with new musical themes; reiterations in the music accompany a recurrence of corresponding movement sequences. Out of this parallelism of music and dance comes a perfectly measured consonance of visual and aural patterns.

The dancers' execution of the movement is equally perfect. Balanchine's choreography requires extraordinary speed, strength, flexibility, and endurance; at the same time, the performance appears effortless, as if attaining a superb visual image required neither work nor strength. Women float with arched torsos, arms trailing softly behind, from one astonishing placement of the limbs to the next. Men, more forceful and grandiose in their movement, still glide coolly through gravity-defying leaps and endless turns. These extraordinary instances of virtuosity are often framed by configurations of dancers whose minimal gestures support the main action, yet even minimal actions are executed with exceptional precision and agility. Dancers who sometimes evince a total absorption in the dance can also distance themselves slightly by regarding their own bodies' effortless execution of the movement. Or they gaze up and out from the dance toward the audience, as if enjoining viewers to admire and take pleasure in their elegant rendition of exemplary movement.

Balanchine's choreography may allude to the ideal, but his sense of himself as an artist is mundane and real. Where Deborah Hay defines her role in the creative process as that of a hollow reed, blown by the winds to produce the dance, George Balanchine sees himself as a chef serving up *plats du jour* to a discriminating group of patrons. As his biographer Bernard Taper has commented,

He can seldom be trapped into speaking of ballet as an art or himself as an artist. He prefers to view himself as an artisan, a professional maker of dances. When he talks of what he does, he often compares himself to a chef (he is, incidentally, a superb cook), whose job it is to prepare for an exacting clientele a variety of attractive dishes that will delight and surprise their palates, or to a carpenter, a good carpenter with pride in his craft—a cabinetmaker, say.[14]

Balanchine "cooks" dances, experimenting with the texture, color, and design of the finest ingredients. He works within the confines set by production demands and scheduling, the budget, and his dancers' injuries to produce the best he can. As he himself observes, "I do not create. Only God creates. I only put the pieces together."[15] Balanchine begins putting the pieces together by working with dancers directly because, as he explains, ideas for a ballet come from the dancers' own technical expertise, their particular flair for moving, and their idiosyncratic mastery of specific movements. These living versions of abstract choreographic ideas serve as the catalysts for dance making. Using the structural organization of the musical score as template, Balanchine transforms the dancers' repertoire of skills into elegant spectacle.

For Balanchine the dance is consummately visual: "A ballet may contain a story, but the visual spectacle, not the story is the essential element."[16] The capacity of movement to display designs is Balanchine's central interest. While for him both dance and sight register discrete images, like those in a sequence of photographs, only dance can show pristine, well-proportioned forms in an order that highlights both their distinctiveness and their continuity. To accomplish this display of designs, the choreographer must take into account the fact that the eye focuses on only one central point of an image at a time and all events surrounding that point blur in relation to their distance from it. Balanchine cites this theory of visual perception to explain his tendency, and that of ballet in general, to arrange movements of great intricacy at one focal point, framed by a large number of simpler movements and poses.[17]

Only certain kinds of movement exhibit the visual features this approach to choreography requires. Highly specialized and nonutilitarian, this dance movement emphasizes the linear: it is crisp-edged, geo-

The New York City Ballet in George
Balanchine's *Agon* (1957). Photo
1963 by Martha Swope. ©

metrical, and axial. "Choreographic movement, used to produce visual sensations, is quite different from the practical movement of everyday life used to execute a task, to walk, to lift an object, to sit down. Choreographic movement is an end in itself, and its only purpose is to create the impression of intensity and beauty." [18] Thus Balanchine, unlike Deborah Hay, sharply distinguishes between pedestrian and dance movement. Nor does he make any attempt to work with dancers inexpert in executing this specialized vocabulary.

Training for the dance, advises Balanchine, should begin at age seven. Students are introduced to the five basic positions of the ballet lexicon. Once these are mastered, increasingly complex movements, each with a name, are introduced. The typical technique class mirrors this progression by beginning with simple movements done in place (at the *barre*), followed by more complex combinations done in the center of the room and across the floor. Although the exercises vary slightly each day, their sequence is strictly maintained. Training involves frequently correcting the positioning of the body; encouraging precision, dexterity, speed, and correct placement; and emphasizing the height of the extended leg, the height and duration of the leap, the length of a balance, and the number of turns accomplished with one preparation.

Training is competitive and hierarchical. With increased competence, the dancer enters more specialized realms of dancing prowess and an equally exclusive social milieu where skills are evaluated and ranked according to higher standards of achievement. The idealized career for the dancer takes him or her from ballet school to professional company, and then from the periphery of the staged action to the focal center of the choreography.

Technique, the mastery of a specific set of movement skills, is the backbone of Balanchine's artistic project. Only with the highly trained dancers ready in the rehearsal hall and the accompanist standing by can Balanchine begin to craft the elegant sequences of movements that make up the dance. Balanchine consults the score and demonstrates a phrase that visually comments on the musical structure. The dancers

George Balanchine rehearsing the
Stravinsky Violin Concerto, 1979.
Photo by Martha Swope. ©

imitate him and then perform for him. He watches, thinks, makes alterations, discards some material, embellishes some phrases, returns to the score; and so it continues through the afternoon. Rehearsals resound with vocables that elicit and emphasize perfect timing and shaping of the movement. "BAM." "POW." "The leg is THERE." "That's RIGHT." Throughout, an energetic, yet amiable and businesslike, atmosphere is maintained.

A typical day proceeds like the rehearsal, from one task or calculation to the next. The dancers take class, arrive for a costume fitting, attend company rehearsal, hold small group rehearsals, run out for something to eat, and return for another rehearsal or a performance. Balanchine himself consults the costumer, the orchestra conductor, and public relations personnel and presides over both the reconstruction of earlier dances and the rehearsals for new works.

Balanchine chooses his music and story line carefully because not all music can be choreographed. Some pieces are too long, too dramatic, or too dense. Music should offer an architectural framework for the dance, as Stravinsky suggests in this response to Balanchine's use of his music:

To see Balanchine's choreography of the *Movements* is to hear music with one's eyes; and this visual hearing has been a greater revelation to me, I think, than to anyone else. The choreography emphasizes relations of which I had hardly been aware—in the same way—and the performance was like a tour of a building for which I had drawn the plans but never explored the result.[19]

Mood and message are much less important than the capacity of the music to evidence structure and to support the replicate gestures of the dance. In his biography of Balanchine, Taper gives a humorous illustration of how Balanchine's visual explication of the music once resulted in the stunning effect of ballerinas being turned upside down to perform some intricate footwork. Asked about this, Balanchine reportedly replied, "Oh, I have to do that. That's where Webern inverts the theme. See, it's right here in the score."[20]

Criteria similar to those for music govern the selection of plot structures for the dance. Stories must be simple and, if not well known, at least predictable in their narrative sequence. For Balanchine, plot lends consistency to the dance, but it does not determine the realistic portrayal of characters and their circumstances, nor does it imply any profound statement about humanity. Balanchine is interested in beauty, not meaning. "When you have a garden of pretty flowers, you don't demand of them, 'What do you mean? What is your significance?' You just enjoy them. . . . So why not just enjoy ballet in the same way?"[21] The performance, rather than attuning viewers to their surroundings or to their own feelings, should inspire a sense of admiration and awe. Balanchine wants dances to be overwhelmingly beautiful, and when he succeeds the dance offers far more than entertainment and enjoy-

The American Ballet Theatre in George Balanchine's *Theme and Variations* (1947). Photo 1967 by Martha Swope. ©

ment, as this description of Balanchine's *Apollo* by critic Edwin Denby makes clear:

Extraordinary is the richness with which he can, with only four dancers, create a sustained and more and more satisfying impression of the grandness of man's creative genius, depicting it concretely in its grace, its sweet wit, its force and boldness, and with the constant warmth of its sensuous complicity with physical beauty. *Apollo* is an homage to the academic ballet tradition—and the first work in the contemporary classic style, but it is an homage to classicism's sensuous loveliness as well as to its brilliant exactitude and its science of dance effect. . . . And it leaves at the end, despite its innumerable incidental inventions, a sense of bold, open, effortless and limpid grandeur.[22]

Just as Balanchine's choreography pursues a classical conception of beauty, so his dancers dedicate themselves to the portrayal of ideal form. Dancers are asked not to feel something for or about the dance but to show the choreography. As one writer has observed from the wings of the stage: "The smiles press up so hard their cheeks quiver. Most of the eyes are set and dead. Hands are tense. Nobody seems to be breathing. Nevertheless, they smile. Sometimes, when the girls turn around, their mouths relax for a moment, but as soon as they face front again, especially if they are standing still, on goes the smile."[23] But far from being a hypocritical gesture, the smile is part of the dance movement. Like all facial expressions, it is part of the technical repertoire required of the dancer in performance. The earnestness involved in smiling or in any physical endeavor derives from the dancer's devotion to craft and skill, to performing each movement beautifully.

Balanchine and his dancers see themselves as part of a tradition, centuries old, in which procedures for transmitting knowledge about dance are defined as rigorously as the scope and content of the knowledge itself. Their dedication to the art of dance absorbs their lives and defines their sense of who they are. Balanchine's dancers respect and obey him as the unquestioned artistic authority; he reciprocates by treating them with care and concern. In turn, a society that assumes the importance of beauty to a cultured, civilized way of life supports and esteems both choreographer and dancers.

As his contribution to this tradition, Balanchine makes exhilarating and elegant dances to entrance enthusiastic yet discriminating viewers with images of human perfection. The dancers' confident appeal as they synthesize visual design, musical phrasing, and kinesthetic prowess captivates the audience and sustains their enjoyment. At the same time, viewers who recognize technical competence and apprehend musical and choreographic structure can intensify their understanding of the ideal as the performance embodies it.

Martha Graham expresses the essential dynamics of the human condition through her dances.[24] Her choreography explores a full range of human emotions and relationships between people, often by depict-

Martha Graham

Martha Graham in *Cave of the
Heart* (1946). Courtesy of the Dance
Collection, New York Public Library
of Lincoln Center.

ing a familiar group of mythical or cultural heroes whose circumstances and adventures suggest basic themes of human existence. Like Balanchine, Graham avoids any realistic portrayal of the story. But unlike him, she is concerned with the characters' inner experiences, their feelings toward one another, and their emotional responses to their situations. Her dances are designed to reveal an inner landscape, to illumine the "cave of the heart." [25]

The dance movement Graham creates to manifest this interior experience originates in the interior of the body. Typically, the movement follows a cyclic pattern that begins as the center of the body hollows out and then twists and spirals, opposing itself. The tension established by this relationship between parts of the body then radiates from the center out to the periphery and even beyond, establishing a bond between dancer and surrounding space. The body momentarily regains its volume but never its equilibrium, for the cycle of ebb and flow inevitably recommences, perhaps at a faster or slower pace, often as a response to another dancer's movement.

The movement alludes to a variety of internal feelings and at the same time documents the difficulties inherent in revealing and expressing those feelings: it is sinewy and restrained, percussive and elastic. Alternately succumbing to and then escaping from the body's boundaries and weight, it seems to erupt out of the tension between inner self and outer body. A moment of suspended balance is not a moment of accomplishment but rather a moment of transition in the dynamic tension between mental and physical efforts. Specific bodily shapes and qualities of movement may recur throughout the dance, but they always appear to be motivated by an evolving psychological state that lends them new shades of meaning. Movements in synchrony with the musical accompaniment replicate its melody, rhythm, phrasing, and orchestration. Yet these formal patterns of music and movement are not the focus of the dance. Instead, music and choreography together generate a dynamic, psychologically charged atmosphere so that the dance unfolds as an organic progression of emotional states.

Martha Graham and Company in *Dark Meadow* (1946). Courtesy of the Dance Collection, New York Public Library at Lincoln Center.

Dancers in the boxlike structure of the stage appear to be immersed in the atmosphere of the dance. Seemingly unaware of the audience and unconcerned with the presentation of the movement, they dance out the lives of the characters they portray. Although they sometimes look toward the audience, their gaze fails to acknowledge actual onlookers, searching instead for some supernatural validation or intervention in the dance. It is almost as though the audience were able to observe secretly the private world of the characters. In this sense the stage itself serves as an emblem for Graham's choreographic portrayal of internal experience—the stage, like the dancers' bodies, houses and reveals the characters' thoughts and feelings.[26]

According to Graham, dances should express "deep matters of the heart."[27] In them the dancer projects archetypal psychological events and relationships onto the stage.

The themes for the dance works come from many sources, as for all dancers. The necessity to express in dance terms some fundamental instant of life may send a dancer into the realm of sheer movement for a theme—again, it may occasion a design of mood—jealousy, as in *Cave of the Heart*—it may seek the half-forgotten world of memory as in *Dark Meadow*—it may dramatize an inner victory, let us say, over fear, as in *Errand into the Maze*—it may arrest the instant of destiny, as in *Night Journey*—it may seek to twist its own world into a bitter satirical comment, as in *Every Soul Is a Circus*—it may trace the poet's life, as in *Letter to the World*—it may seek an instant of celebration of spring, or marriage, or—exaltation, as in *Appalachian Spring*.[28]

Graham carefully chooses the themes for her dances, evaluating their personal relevance but also their universal significance. Unlike Balanchine, who begins a new dance by selecting music and then working directly with the dancers three or four weeks before the concert date, Graham often allows her idea for a dance to incubate a year or more. During this time she collects images from art and literature that enhance the development of the theme. She also searches in her own life for the roots of the dance's theme. She ponders, she broods, until eventually theme turns into drama and she can produce a script, an impressionistic account of a sequence of events for the stage.

Graham then commissions, or occasionally finds, a musical score congruent with her script in flavor and intensity. Once she knows the music thoroughly, she begins to choreograph, shaping the movement to fit musical structure and relying on music for insights into her theme. After working alone for some time, Graham begins to work with the dancers in her company, who often suggest movement she might fashion or edit to fit her vision. In her struggle to intuit the appropriate development of her ideas, Graham becomes secretive, temperamental, and filled with doubt. During rehearsals she rages at the dancers and at herself. While making a dance, she claims to be possessed: seized by the idea inside her, victim to cycles of destruction and creation entailed by her creative act, she suffers through the birth of her dance.

"Movement never lies," Graham is fond of saying.[29] It signals a person's true identity and feelings. Thus preparation for becoming a dancer or choreographer involves attending to the relationship between movement and the psyche. Whereas Hay's choreography grows out of the similarities between her own movement and the movement of other people and things, Graham's choreography focuses on the connection between a person's interior and exterior. Her dances present an enlarged, clarified version of psychologically motivated movement. In the same way that she abstracts from her own experience certain archetypal themes for the stage, she has objectified personal movement by finding in it a set of fundamental principles: the contraction and release, the spiral, the primacy of the central body in initiating movement, and the sequential growth of movement from the center of the body to the periphery.

Over the years, Graham has developed an extensive technical repertoire based on these principles from which the movements of her dances are taken. Graham's dancers practice this vocabulary daily, and her technique class, like Balanchine's, consists of a progression of well-defined exercises varied slightly from day to day. Few individual movements, however, have names. The terms *contraction*, *release*, and *spiral* heard frequently during the class name processes that occur in a variety of movements rather than specific movements themselves. Dur-

Martha Graham in rehearsal, 1965.
Photo by Martha Swope. ©

ing class, Graham or her company members who also teach emphasize correct positioning of the body and the dynamic qualities—the energy—with which the movement is performed. They say little about the personal motivation for the movement in class, although Graham's own pungent observations create an atmosphere of self-examination and psychological questioning. For example, she forbids students to slouch with their arms folded in front of them as they await their turn to perform. "This," she admonishes as she demonstrates the arms-crossed position, "is the first barrier that mankind ever erected." [30]

For Graham, the mastery of movement in technique class is part of a two-pronged training program. Certainly dancers must cultivate the body as a powerful, responsive instrument, but they must also prepare that part of the "being from which whatever there is to say comes." [31] Technique, then, integrates the rigorously trained body with the fully mature psyche through a discipline that entails acts of submission and liberation. Dancers submit themselves both to the demands of the craft, learning flexibility, strength, and control, and to the choreographer, whose vehicle they are for realizing a given dance. Dancers also develop an image of the idealized dancer they strive to become. By submitting to this image, they compete not with other dancers but with their own image of what they might become. All these acts of submission promise freedom—to express, to dance, and to be "born to the instant." [32] This experience of liberation justifies the years of rigorous preparation and struggle that precede it.

My technique is an attempt to prepare the body by formal and impersonal means to become a dancer's instrument, strong, subtle, fully conscious, free as only discipline can make it.

As it is an instrument with which to express great truths of life, it must be prepared for the ordeal of expressiveness. [33]

The "ordeal of expressiveness" begins when the choreographer must objectify internal experience in crafted movement, but the dancer then replicates this process in transforming the self into danced character. To perform the role of a character in Graham's dances, the dancer must find the experience of that character in his or her own psychological life, grow into that experience, and become completely identified with the character. [34]

The theatre dressing room is a very special place. It is where the act of theatre begins—and make-up is a kind of magic—the means by which you transform yourself into the character you hope to play. You make up your face as you think she might have looked; you dress your hair as you think she might have dressed hers. And then, there comes a moment when she looks at you in the mirror and you realize that she is looking at you and recognizing you as herself. It is through you, her love, her hope, her fear, her terror, is to be expressed. [35]

The final challenge for Graham's dancers comes in recreating the vitality and authenticity of the character and the character's choreographed movement for each performance of the dance. The character's expression must appear spontaneous despite the careful crafting of the choreography and the numerous repetitions of the dance. When the dancer is able to connect psyche to character and character to movement in the moment of performance, the creative cycle begun by the choreographer is momentarily completed. As satisfying as this moment is, however, the ordeal of expression does not end there. The creative cycle must begin anew as part of the inherent human need to understand and express human existence.

Graham thus envisions the choreographic process as integrating by the act of dancing several dualities—the spontaneous and the crafted, the psychological and the physical, the personal and the universal, the rational and the passionate, and the unconscious and the conscious—into a fragile but supreme moment. This moment holds out to both dancers and audience the promise of transcending the turbulence and fragmentation experienced in everyday life. This transcendence, however, differs from the one that occurs for Hay and her dancers. Whereas

Martha Graham Dance Company in *The Rite of Spring* (1984). Photo by Martha Swope. ©

Hay establishes an affinity with the world by tuning her subjectivity to worldly movement, Graham recomposes the person as an individuated, yet integrated, microcosm of the world.

As part of this transformative process, Graham hopes to convert the audience from objective onlookers to concerned witnesses. Like the dancers on the stage, they are asked to identify and empathize with the archetypal characters of the dance and thereby confirm a fundamental resonance between the dramatic rendition of life and their own lives. If the dance moves them deeply, it does so not because of its beauty or its grace but because of its passionate rendering of the human condition. Viewers following the emotional development of the dance come away feeling they have made contact with some primordial, essential truth, each in his or her own way.

Merce Cunningham

Merce Cunningham arranges opportunities to view the human body in motion by juxtaposing articulate human movements.[36] He claims that his dances express nothing but themselves, that instead of telling a story they focus on the physical facts of the body—what arms and legs, torso, and head can do in relation to gravity, time, and space. Although many movement sequences require great skill and dexterity, the dances do not emphasize virtuoso accomplishment, nor do they allude to ideal forms of movement. Instead, they emphasize the individuality of each human body: each dancer's body shape, style or quality of moving, and "appetite for motion."[37]

Movements in Cunningham's dances emphasize the body's jointedness, combining and recombining body parts in a variety of ways. Limbs often seem askew, unpredictably altering either their direction in space or the speed with which they move. Movements follow one another with no sense of development, causality, or flow. Occasionally dancers move in unison or pause to form an asymmetrical tableau. Often they walk on or off stage or to some new location in the space to begin a new sequence. Frequently more goes on in the space than can

Merce Cunningham and John Cage
in *Dialogue* (1972). Photos by James
Klosty. ©

be perceived at any given moment, and one's attention often shifts abruptly from one dancer or grouping to another. Order is apparent only in the discrete, purposeful actions of individuals; the overall sequence of events appears completely arbitrary. Certainly the music contributes no structure to the dance, as its own ordering principles, equally elusive, negate any relation between music and dance. More often than random coincidences in the rhythm or texture of the two arts, one finds violent contrast in their dynamics and intensity.

The result is not chaotic but matter-of-fact. The movement is straightforward, fully articulated, but seldom graceful or dazzling. The dancers' faces express keen involvement in their activity. Their gaze both diffuse and alert, they focus on the kinesthetic sensations of performing the movement and on the space around them, equally aware of audience, other dancers, and their own activity. The effect of this straightforward style is to present the dancers as pedestrian rather than fictional or symbolic subjects. Because movement represents nothing other than itself, the dance points up an expressiveness in movement itself and seems to empower it with a compelling and passionate logic all its own. Cunningham would argue that his dances, if they do express anything about the world, offer an "opening out to the complexity we live in." [38] These diverse enunciations, simultaneously physical and acoustic, impinge on our senses like life itself.

Cunningham begins to elaborate this sensual complexity alone in his studio. Dance making for him is private, not social, and he is described as reclusive and silent while in the process of choreographing. His silence, however, seems to result not from the intense soul-searching Graham undergoes but rather from a serious involvement in bricolage: he brings together what is at hand. Cunningham works at his dances by trying out new movements and noting "slips of the feet." [39] He makes charts and diagrams that help determine sequencing and group organization. He putters, thinking concretely about abstract space, time, and human motion. The combined activities produce dances. Like Balanchine, Cunningham sees himself as master craftsman rather than creator; Cunningham, however, does not try to make the perfect dance so much as to arrange for the unanticipated dance.

When he talks about dance technique, Cunningham, like Graham, refers to the body as an instrument and to the technically equipped body of the dancer as a means to express. But what does the body express for Cunningham? Unlike Graham's body, which expresses the inmost realities of the psyche, Cunningham's body expresses only "a way of moving."[40] More like Balanchine than Graham, Cunningham believes "it is upon the length and breadth and span of a body sustained in muscular action that dance invokes its image."[41] For both men, the dance's meaning comes from the movement itself rather than from the relationship between movement and psyche. Yet Cunningham differs radically from Balanchine in terms of the image the dance invokes. Where Balanchine develops the spectacular, virtuoso display of the perfected body, Cunningham presents the diverse activities of the articulate body.

Cunningham's technique supports his vision of dance through its investigation of the body's possible movement. Each body part can move in specific ways, and areas of the body participate in organized patterns of movement with other areas. For example:

The legs and arms can be a revelation of the back, the spine's extensions. Sitting, standing, extending a leg or arm or leaping through the air, one is conscious that it is to and from the spine that the appendages relate and that they manifest themselves only so far as the spine manifests itself. The spine, moreover, acts not just as a source for the arms and legs, but can itself grow taut or loose, can turn on its own axis or project into space directions.[42]

Because all movements of all parts of the body are equally interesting, each movement should be performed with concentration, fullness, and an awareness of its directionality in space.

Body and mind together master these movements. The mind tells the body what to do and then watches attentively during the execution of the movement. Body and mind diligently working to acquire technique establish between them a harmony, even an identity. In part through this devotion to mindful movement, the dancer achieves a

Merce Cunningham Dance Company in *Objects* (1970). Photo by James Klosty. ©

technical competence that manifests itself in flexible responses to novel situations.

A technique class with Cunningham works to develop flexibility in several ways. Classes begin with exercises that thoroughly explore the range of motion of each joint and establish basic patterns of movement for spine and arms, hips and legs, head and torso, and so forth. Quickly, however, combinations of movements are introduced, new for each class, that call for unusual timing and orientation in space. These movement sequences have no predictable flow. The body's weight shifts suddenly in combination with changes of direction. Idiosyncratic details are enmeshed in large movements of the whole body. Sequences are broken up, added to, recombined, and varied. The corrections in class that pertain to the placement of the body and the timing of the movement are also designed to encourage students to learn the new material quickly, retain it for possible further use, and adapt it to different spatial paths or durations.

Cunningham's choreography is also full of novel situations. His interest in movement for its own sake has resulted in eclectic approaches to dance composition ranging from intuition and game structures to bricolage and chance. A given dance might use aleatory methods to determine any or all of the following: the movements themselves, their order, their spatial path or direction, their duration; the number of dancers, entrances, and exits; the length and the order of sections of a dance. Through his use of chance procedures, Cunningham removes himself from direct decision making about the dance and thus allows for unanticipated discoveries about movement and its organization. He claims that the incidence of personal habits and preferences is reduced when the choreographer decides not exactly what will happen next but how decisions will be made. In many of his pieces, for example, Cunningham invents individual movements and then arranges chance operations to determine their sequence as well as the spatial path or duration of that sequence. Cunningham sets the boundaries by deciding whether movements can be repeated, or what spatial paths— circles, arcs, diagonal lines, zigzags—will occur, or what the outside limits on timing will be. Yet he is dissociated from direct authorship of the dance.[43] The outcome is a heterogeneous grouping of unprecedented movement patterns.

Cunningham also eschews decisions about music, costumes, scenery, and lighting, leaving entirely to specialists the realization of these aspects of the performance. He conceives of the set design, lighting, and especially the music as independent events that happen to occur in the same time and place as the dancing. Although he assumes that music and dance both unfold in time, Cunningham denies any intrinsic rapport between them in either structure or mood. He prefers to celebrate the individuality of music and dance rather than reducing them, as he would say, to a common denominator. "Dancing has a continuity of its own that need not be dependent upon either the rise or fall of sound, or the pitch and cry of words. Its force of feeling lies in the physical image, fleeting or static. It can and does evoke all sorts of individual responses in the single spectator."[44] His approach to collaboration, often bringing together set, music, and dancing for the first time in the final dress rehearsal before a performance, challenges both performers and viewers with an open field of possible associations.

Cunningham's approach to composition effectively disengages movement from a specific meaning or emotional referent. Because it shatters any sense of plot or emotional development, the chance ordering of movement sustains neither story nor literal interpretation. Still, the dances are far from random, cold, or abstract. According to Cunningham, his choreographic tactics provide for both dancers and audience the opportunity to be truly passionate.

Our emotions are constantly being propelled by some new face in the sky, some new rocket to the moon, some new sound in the ear, but they are the same emotions. You do not separate the human being from the actions he does, or the actions which surround him, but you see what it is like to break these actions up in different ways, to allow passion, and it is passion, to appear for each person in his own way.[45]

The dance separated from any specific statement it must make and the dancer separated from any emotional experience that must be conveyed can be filled with affective significance.

Cunningham's dancers bring their own passion and their own interpretation of the dance to each performance. Cunningham does not direct their motivation for the movement or even their technical mastery of it. He presents the sequences, directions, and timing; the dancers refine the phrasing, comprehend the value of each movement and the logic of the sequence, accomplish the movement within a precise amount of time, and attend to the movement's expressivity. Carolyn Brown, principal dancer with Cunningham's company for twenty years, characterizes the responsibilities of the dancer:

Merce requires of his dancers that the rhythm come from within: from the nature of the step, from the nature of the phrase, and from the dancer's own

Merce Cunningham and Carolyn Brown in rehearsal for *Night Wandering* (1958). Photo 1971 by James Klosty. ©

musculature; not from without, from a music that imposes its own particular rhythms of phrases and structure, or from a narrative or "mood." For Merce, I believe, a "musical dancer" phrases from the muscles, the sinews, the gut, and the soul. Each movement is given its full value, its own unique meaning—the movement is expressive of itself.[46]

Dancers do not imitate or empathize with Cunningham. They do not search their past lives for experience resonant with the theme of the dance, as they would in preparation for a Graham dance. Nor do they attempt the virtuoso execution of movement, often specifically designed to display their skills, as they would for Balanchine. The typical Cunningham rehearsal, Brown says, involves

no talk about meaning or quality. No images given. No attempts made to nurture expressivity in any particular dancer. The dances are treated more as puzzles than works of art: the pieces are space and time, shape and rhythm.

Merce Cunningham Dance
Company in *Event #45* (1972),
Piazza San Marco, Venice, Italy.
Photo by James Klosty. ©

The rest is up to us. We put the puzzle together, making of it what we can, bringing to it what our imaginations allow. What we bring can enrich or detract from his work; Merce accepts that—it's part of the risk, part of the possibility for discovery.[47]

Like the dancers, members of the audience are free to bring a variety of interpretations to the dance. The overabundance of activity in the performance space, coupled with the suggestion in many of the dancers' entrances and exits that the dancing continues beyond the boundaries of the space, accentuates the lack of a single authorial message. The unpredictable sequencing of different parts of the body and the unusual changes in dynamics and interactions between dancers offer multiple, diverse references to the world, none of which occur in logical order. The viewer can choose from among these references, occasionally fabricating incidental narratives, and can weave together significant moments of the dance. Each viewer's experience is unique, not simply because each person has a different heritage of associations to the dance but because each viewer has literally made a different dance.

Still, the viewer's interpretation of the dance will be firmly grounded in the persistent impression that human movement is the subject matter. The dance consists of physical statements and expresses the physical energy of the moving body. Carolyn Brown has proposed that Cunningham's dances feature the body moving on a continuum of space-time where space, time, and movement define each other in the dance.[48] Along this continuum the human being is portrayed as a moving body—articulate, intelligent, passionate. This, it would seem, is what Cunningham has in mind when he refers to dance as "a moving image of life."[49]

At one point in their careers, Balanchine and Graham produced a concert together, and in preparation for the event Graham visited Balanchine at work. As the story is told, she was amazed at Balanchine's process of composition.[50] His method of assigning sequences of movement to the dancers and then revising, discarding, and interjecting

Four Bodies and Subjects

FOUR CHOREOGRAPHIC PROJECTS

	The Meaning of Art	The Choreographer's Mission	The Purpose of Dance Technique
Hay	Communion	Discovering and becoming the dance	To attain harmony by performing the dance
Balanchine	Celebration	Crafting and perfecting the dance	To attain control by acquiring prescribed skills
Graham	Communication	Testifying through the dance	To express the subject by training the body
Cunningham	Collaboration	Drafting the dance	To become articulate by doing the movement

new material—all with apparent calm—seemed incomprehensible. And Graham was further astonished that Balanchine allowed spectators at the rehearsal. How could the private process of choreography be conducted in front of so many people? Deeply impressed with Balanchine's knowledge of music and movement and the open, courteous atmosphere of the rehearsal, Graham nonetheless remained dubious about the authenticity of his creative impulse.

This anecdote highlights the difference I have described in Graham's and Balanchine's approach to choreography. Graham's astonishment at Balanchine's procedure is understandable, for his pragmatic style could only confound her beliefs about creativity and art. In the following discussion of the four choreographers, I will expand on the differences in their aesthetics by comparing their attitudes toward making dances and their organization of classes, rehearsals, and performances.

The Concept of Expression	The Dancer's Body	The Dancer's Subject	The Viewer's Response
Recapitulating the harmony of the movement	A fluid aggregate of cells	Metaphorical allusions to the world	Accord
Executing perfect gesture	A medium for displaying ideal forms	A dedicated artisan	Exhilaration
Revealing inner motivations	A unified vehicle for expressing the self	Internal feelings, thoughts, and desires	Empathy
Moving articulately	Bones, muscles, ligaments, nerves, etc.	The activity in which the body is engaged	Attentiveness

Reflected in the organization of the dances and the preparations for them are certain fundamental assumptions about the nature of the body and also the self, or subject, of the person dancing. Each of the four choreographic projects cultivates not only a different body but also a different sense of selfhood for the dancers involved. These different bodies and subjects, in turn, allow us to deduce the viewer's experience of each approach to dance.

For Graham, the creative process of choreography entails disquietude and struggle. She is renowned for her fits of temper during rehearsal, her reclusiveness, and the trauma she undergoes in making a new dance. Graham's belief that "movement never lies" means that she must scrutinize each choreographic impulse and determine, for each moment of the dance, whether the movement accurately expresses the internal motivation she associates with the dance's theme. Motivations for the movement may be obscure, hidden deep within the psyche. Often difficult to objectify and order coherently, these motivations may seem so ineffable and fleeting that no material manifestation, even movement itself, could capture them. Thus the search for movement that "tells the truth" is arduous, but for Graham the intensity of her own struggle marks the authenticity of the search and the outcome.

As if in response to Graham's romantic, expressionistic vision of art, Balanchine once remarked with typical matter-of-factness, "If I were feeling suicidal, I would never try to express this in a ballet. I would make as beautiful a variation as I could for a ballerina, and then—well, then I'd go and kill myself."[51] For Balanchine, making a dance has little to do with inner motivations. Choreography is not a process of intense self-inquiry but the straightforward task of listening to music and watching dancers to hear and see what movements they suggest. Although production schedules or dancers' injuries may trouble Balanchine, he does not struggle for the inspiration to produce appropriate movement. The choreographic process requires precise calculations based on keen observation, but however absorbing and demanding, it does not involve self-scrutiny.

The creative process for Balanchine is one of ornamenting and elaborating specific sets of skills that his dancers have mastered. Rather than integrating opposites in his choice of movement, Balanchine commemorates a hierarchy of skills based not on attributes of inner and outer life but on the observable complexity and excellence of the movement. The motivation for choosing movement derives from a sense of both form and proportion between movement and music and between the movements themselves.

Cunningham shares with Balanchine an artisan's vision of dance making. Both men approach their art pragmatically, attending to the appearance of the dance more than the motivation behind it. They explicitly detach themselves from expressionistic conceptions of art and artist so that they can work with things in the world—bodies moving in space and time—rather than intangible emotions. For both choreographers, making dances is like solving complex, lively puzzles that demand their care and devotion and sustain them if they simply do the best job possible. Balanchine's ideas for dances, however, come from music and from an aesthetics of ideal form, whereas Cunningham's dances originate in what he perceives to be the physical facts of the human body and in the procedures he has developed for sequencing movement.

Using chance procedures, Cunningham can both escape expressionistic authorship of the dance and invent dance based on the idea of articulate human movement. Instead of relying on a tradition of complex skills, Cunningham experiments in the dance studio with the capacities and inclinations of his own body, and he also devises new grids for chance sequences to discover a diverse range of dance movements. This invention results from attention and dedication but not special inspiration. Dancing and making dances are simply activities that one performs. Although they require more concentration and dedication than sweeping the floor or watering plants, they are for Cunningham no less routine.

If Cunningham sees a cosmic significance in pedestrian activities, Hay sees pedestrian actions as part of a universal pattern of change. Making dances, for her, is more an act of discovery than invention. Like Cunningham, Hay frequently relies on chance procedures to determine the sequencing of her dances so that she can participate in the dance rather than expressing herself through the dance. Unlike Cunningham, however, who proposes new movement based on the body's own organization, Hay "tunes" movement to harmonize with the flux around her.

The creative process for Hay entails preparing herself as a site at which dances are made and performed. She and her dancers invite the dance to visit them. The dance results more from this communal invocation than from her individual initiatives as an artist. Seeing herself as a moment in a changing pattern, Hay aims as an artist to be as graceful and harmonious a moment as possible. She derives artistic satisfaction from the attainment of this grace and from a communally felt sense of proportion and harmony within the self, group, and world.

For Hay and the other choreographers, dance classes and rehearsals as well as performances sustain the artistic project. At each stage of the dance's production, choreographers and dancers participate in an orchestrated set of events that imparts symbolic significance to the dance. And technical competence, which each choreographer defines differently—for none of them could agree on a standard repertoire of skills any dancer must acquire—reflects the aesthetic goals of each artistic project. [Thus in Hay's class one performs dances, while in Balanchine's class one enhances skills; in Graham's class one trains the body, and in Cunningham's class one does the movement.]

Hay, for example, sees each class as a rehearsal or even as a performance. Rather than offering exercises that prepare students for dancing, her classes, which she does not call technique classes, consist primarily of learning and performing the dances themselves. Classes are an opportunity to establish a community, to work on cellular consciousness, and to perform a dance as a group. Many of Hay's group performances evolve directly out of these classroom situations. Students develop rapport and the ability to concentrate, they master the sequences of images, and then, at the appropriate time, they perform the dance for others. Very little changes when the audience is present. Rather than presenting the dance to the audience, dancers maintain a steady commitment to the images. Hay's conviction that the performance is part of a larger dance that is always going on erodes firm boundaries between class, rehearsal, and performance and places these activities on a continuum with the dance of life itself.

Cunningham also sees technique class and rehearsals as opportunities to perform a dance; however, he distinguishes between them because a different activity occurs in each—articulating the body in class and learning a dance in rehearsals. Exercises in technique class augment students' understanding of the organization of the body and develop facility in learning new combinations of movements, while rehearsals involve mastering specific movement sequences, including their exact timing and phrasing. Both class and rehearsals, however, require a full performance of the movement.[52] The dance concert seamlessly coordinates with class and rehearsals insofar as it presents an uninterrupted, highly organized version of the same dancing that goes on in preparing for it.

In contrast to Cunningham, Graham makes important functional distinctions between class, rehearsal, and performance. By developing strength, flexibility, and coordination, the technique class prepares the body to accomplish whatever the dance may demand. Movement sequences in class are not moments of dancing but opportunities to exercise a self-motivated discipline. The rehearsal then explores dramatic motivation and the theme of the dance, allowing the dancers to work out the dynamics of the characters they will portray. As the rehearsals progress, a dancer achieves a more comprehensive understanding of both the character and the body's responsiveness to the character's psyche. A consummate understanding of body and character, however, occurs only in performance, where after months and years of discipline the dancer experiences a momentary liberation from all discipline.

If Graham sees the three occasions of class, rehearsal, and performance as an organic whole, Balanchine conceives of them as parts of a progressive hierarchy. In class the dancer masters the vocabulary from which the dance is made by executing the steps with utmost skill and precision. Relying on the competence developed in class, rehearsals impart new skills: sensitivity to musical phrasing, the ability to grasp complex arrangements of steps, and an awareness of the group staging of the movement. The performance differs from both class and rehearsal in displaying to the audience the accomplishments acquired in class and rehearsal but with a style and charisma specific to that moment. Unlike Graham's dancers, who view the performance as a transcendence of skill, Balanchine's dancers exercise in performance their mastery over yet another set of skills, which they have obtained by performing and watching others perform.

Just as Graham and Balanchine separate life from dance and separate class from performance, so they identify their dancers as highly select individuals embodying innate and encultured qualities that mark them off from all other specialists in movement, and even from other dancers. Technique classes provide the necessary skills, but a true artist emerges only where this training is combined with innate talent. In Balanchine's case, the study of technique produces a quick, agile body and nurtures a dedication to dancing. That dedication, however, must already be present in the individual dancer, along with inborn musicality and a bodily structure suited to the accomplishments of dance. In Graham's technique, the student trains the body as an instrument responsive to a controlling, self-disciplined mind, mastering the body in order to express the self. Yet the self must be acutely sensitive to psychological life and willing to persevere in promoting expression. As Graham herself has observed, "When any young student asks me, 'Do you think I should be a dancer?' I always say, 'If you can ask me that question, no! Only if there is just one way to make life vivid for yourself and for others should you embark upon such a career.'"[53]

The elite calling of the dance profession described by Graham and Balanchine differs markedly from the more democratic conceptions of art and artist espoused by Hay and Cunningham. Both Hay and Cunningham envision some continuity between class and performance and a similar connection between life and art. Thus Hay believes anyone can dance so long as he or she is prepared to commune with the dance, and Hay's technique of cellular consciousness can be practiced anywhere at any time. Her method promotes the graceful, supple body and alert meditative mind essential to the performance of her choreography but also useful in the mundane world. While Cunningham is far more concerned than Hay with the mastery of a specific repertoire of movements, his technique aims at articulateness—a concept that, like Hay's gracefulness, indicates an aesthetic concern with the body's daily movement through the physical world. For Cunningham, the world is composed not of one universal pattern but of various human activities, one of which is dancing. What makes a dancer is not innate talent so much as the continuous study of and participation in dancing throughout life.

Each choreographer's vision of art, then, generates a world peopled with dancers and nondancers in which the artistic and the commonplace are differently defined. Central to each world are attitudes about the nature of the body and the subject who dances. Dancers, by participating in classes, rehearsals, and performances, come to understand who they are when they dance. For example, Hay's use of the metaphor of cellular life promotes an experience of the body as a constellation of minute, semi-independent organisms. Each cell conceivably has a life of its own and can be open to the world or shut off from it. Further, each cell can independently become the image being danced. Each cell is animated with a life energy that plays across the body, transmuting it and reconstituting it so that it can commune with the world by dancing the image of a specific entity or event.

In contrast, Cunningham conceives of the body as muscles, bones, sinew, and nerves, physically organized to move with tension, liquidity, percussiveness, and lightness and with enormous variations in shape and timing at each jointed segment. It moves through space in time, and its motion delineates relationships between the two. To articulate the body in space and time, the dancer must exercise assiduously but must also recognize and become attuned to the body as a material entity with its own logic. The body's intrinsic interest, then, resides not in its ability to display or to make manifest but rather in its own consummate physicality.

Balanchine seldom refers to the body itself. Instead, he describes the shapes it makes and the gestural elocutions of which it is capable. These various movements are displayed on the body as painters' visions are displayed on canvas. The body is not so much the tool creating the designs as the medium in which the designs occur. Competence at working in the medium demands rigorous practice, even though cultivating the body's capabilities for brilliant exposition involves not its inherent physical organization but rather its ability to adapt to ideal forms.

If Balanchine approaches the body as a medium of expression, Graham sees it as an instrument—a material, unitary entity rather like a musical instrument one learns to use for expression. Unlike Hay's sense of a constantly changing, unbounded body, Graham's sense of body is concrete and stable. As a discrete, physical object, the body exhibits identifiable properties and consistent characteristics that can be trained. The physical competence gained by this training, together with responsiveness to subjective motivations, allows the body to be used by the subject as a vehicle for communicating its concerns.

Of the four choreographers only Graham speaks of using the body. The other three seem to prefer an existence alongside the body, although each assumes the existence of a subjectivity in some way distinct from the body. Who or what is it in Graham's world that uses the body and how does it differ from the other choreographers' conceptions of the subject? Among the most prominent of all dualities organizing Graham's world is that of the exterior body and the interior self. Residing inside the body, the self is composed of thinking and feeling functions, conscious and unconscious attitudes, and a spiritual aspect or soul. Influenced by the body's physical needs and affected by the outside world, the self nonetheless lives an autonomous existence as unitary and as bounded as the body it inhabits.

Although the body is a natural, physical entity that reflects and responds to the life of the self, it seems to maintain a closer connection to the unconscious, feeling portions of the self than to the rational, conscious self. In fact, the body is so clearly associated with the more turbulent psychological functions that it frequently merges with them. One of the paradoxes implicit in Graham's world is this dual identity of the body: the body serves the whole self, but it also assumes the identity of one part of the self. In its second identity, it expresses the passionate, ineffable, libidinal, and unconscious aspects of human experience in dialectical opposition to speech. Speech expresses the rational, intellectual realm, and the body in motion expresses the emotional and instinctual.

For Graham, speech can lie; movement, originating in the "gut" and revealing the person's "true identity," never lies. Yet this equation of movement with emotional expression presents another paradox for

Graham: is it not a lie for the choreographer to stage specific movements while treating movement as an authentic representation of the self? And is it not a lie for the dancer, after learning a movement invented by the choreographer, to dance it as though it were the spontaneous expression of the character? As a choreographer, Graham must reconcile the contrived, even rational aspects of dance composition with her aesthetic interest in the immediate and spontaneous expression of irrational forces. As a dancer, she must confront a related dilemma: she must tell her own body to perform authentically the movement of another self, that of the character represented in the dance.

Graham resolves this contradiction by asking the dancer to engage in a process of "self"-transformation. The dancer must reshape the psyche into the psyche of the character to be portrayed. The choreography danced by this character-self will then be experienced by both dancer and viewer as the authentic expression of the character-self. In prescribing this transformation of the self, Graham relies on her belief that all human beings experience the world similarly. Because certain fundamental themes are common to human life, the dancer, by searching through past experience, can find personal attitudes and feelings consonant with the character's situation. The dancer can then add details to make the character comprehensive and coherent and the movement danced by the character-self rich and full.

Although Graham's self is capable of transformation, any new character-self it assumes will maintain an autonomous integrity like that of the original self. Hay, in contrast, asks that when performing her choreography the subject of the dancer become as mutable as the cellularly composed body. Both body and subject assume an existence like that of "gnarled trees" or a "slow, well-paced run." The subject does not become these images prior to the body as it would in a Graham dance, because the subject does not provide causal motivation for the body's actions. Body and subject simply participate in a given image together as different facets of that image. Moreover, the instantaneous switching from one image to the next emphasizes the radical decomposition and recomposition of body and subject in this process. The dancer is denied any transition between images that would help explain how the self evolved from one thing to another. If such transitions were included in the choreography, the dancer could maintain a certain "self"-consistency. Hay's dances would then become the stories of a versatile dancer whose self was fluid enough to become different things. Instead, the complete discontinuity between images in Hay's dances presents the dancer as the sum total of all the contrasting images performed.

Balanchine, unlike Hay, asks his dancers to portray characters, but these characters are defined by the movement they perform. They are designated by their actions and behaviors rather than by their feelings. A character's internal life, self, and motivation are never issues for the dancer as they are in Graham's pieces, nor does the dance movement originate from within the character-self. As a result, the dancer's subjectivity becomes joined to the act of performing the character rather than to the self of the character. The dancers' selves, like those of the characters they portray, are fused with the act of self-presentation.

If Hay's dancers are asked to become the images they perform and Balanchine's dancers to become artisans who perform perfectly, Cunningham's dancers are asked to become the movement of the dance itself. Both subject and body are assimilated into the experience of physical articulation, an experience that is mindful and passionate. The dance movement offers intense tactile and kinesthetic sensations—sudden and sustained stretching, compressing, swinging, shifting, tensing—and it may also evoke various associations—memories, feelings, fantasies, and thoughts. Dancers are encouraged, however, to focus primarily on the physical events of the dance and to register these in no causal order and with no primary source for interpreting the dance other than the movement itself. The dancer's subject thus becomes immersed, along with the body, in the activity of moving.

Implicit in these four contrasting conceptions of the relationship between subject and body are four definitions of the expressive act. These distinct ideas about expression form the basis of each choreographer's artistic project, dictating the individual standards of technical competence, the dancer's responsibilities in concert, and also a specific role for the dance viewer. In the case of Graham, expression is the act of getting what is inside the self out into the world. Expression integrates the interior psyche with the material, physical instrument and, ultimately, with the viewer's individual apprehension of the dance's concerns. For Hay, expression occurs when an inherent rapport between dancer and world is affirmed. Connections already exist between all "cells" of the universe; the dance discovers these connections as it embroiders dancers and viewers into one harmonious pattern. Balanchine, in contrast, conceives of expression as the execution of perfect movement. Expression is an act of achieving and displaying what is beautiful for a viewer who is able to appreciate and enjoy such a performance. For Cunningham, expression occurs when the body-subject moves articulately, speaking its own physical language to a viewer who attends fully to it.

In order to express their concerns, each choreographer designs dances with a specific viewer in mind or, more precisely, with a sense of what the viewer's involvement in the dance should be. And in many ways this model viewer's experience is similar to that of the dancer in class and in rehearsal. Graham, for example, asks her dancers to locate within themselves the emotion that the character in the dance experiences and similarly encourages her audience to experience for themselves the feelings of the character. For Graham, viewing the dance, like making the dance, integrates antagonistic life forces. Each of these forces, once contextualized by the project of art, comes to have a purpose and a function indispensable to the whole. The function of art itself is to provide just this moment of organic wholeness—but one in which emotions and subconscious feelings are allowed to flourish. To illustrate this point, Graham tells the story of a woman who was able to cry over the loss of her son for the first time since his death several months earlier after seeing *Lamentation* (1930), Graham's solo about the act of grieving.[54] In describing the incident, Graham emphasizes a fundamental similarity in the emotional life of all people. Everyone seeing the dance, she asserts, identifies it as an abstract version of the experience of grief. Moreover, the dance encourages viewers to succumb to an experience of grieving and relive these feelings for themselves. By following the emotional development of the dance, viewers can gain new insights into the organization of their own emotional life, renewing an awareness of their feelings and affirming their connection to a human community.

A dance by Hay also imparts a sense of community, but one in which individual feelings and individuality are put aside. She does not ask viewers to build a connection between individual identity and universal human experience, as Graham does, but to redefine or submerge the individuality of experience in a universal pattern of change. For her, the universality of experience is not an accumulation of individual experiences but occurs prior to any individual enactment of it. Thus what dancers attempt to create in class and what viewers see in performance is the graceful reference to something much larger than the collective experience of the individual participants. The dance, neither testimonial nor display, creates the opportunity for viewers and dancers alike to weave themselves into a variegated and changing pattern. Whereas viewers leave Graham's dances with a sense of emotional validation and, perhaps, a momentary resolution to the ongoing tension between individual and social concerns, they come away from Hay's dances with a congenial sense of their placement in the social and physical landscape.

Viewers of a Balanchine dance are not transported by the dance so much as enraptured by it. Balanchine hopes to draw the audience into the dance by enhancing their ability to discern choreographic genius, virtuoso execution, the subtle rapport among dancers, and the felicitous reciprocity of music and dance. Viewers exercising their aesthetic sensibilities are rewarded with a presentation that satisfies and sometimes even surpasses their rigorous standards. From their ongoing involvement in the dance emerges a hierarchy of moments of aesthetic appreciation similar to the hierarchy of skills and of dancers that composes the tradition; this ordering of perfection affirms for the audience the place and function of beauty in the world.

Cunningham's dances solicit no evaluation of beauty but provide the opportunity to perceive eloquent human movement. Viewers focus on an array of activities, none of them more important than any other, that reflects the array of life's events. The dance acquires its significance by inviting concentration on the nonordered so that viewers discover something unforeseen about human movement and human affairs. Whatever identification with the dancers occurs centers on the dancer as a moving body rather than on a character's experience. The audience may find the movement compelling, dull, brilliant, deeply inspiring, or mundane. But the dance asks only that these reactions stem from full concentration on the movement itself. Viewers who fully attend to movement increase their awareness of the diverse capacities of the articulate human body and thereby sense how deeply moving movement itself can be.

Any viewer, however, can invoke one set of choreographic assumptions in order to view the dances made using another set. Such a choice produces interesting but often misguided critical commentary. For example, the viewer who approaches Hay's, Graham's, or Cunningham's dances expecting the virtuoso performance implicit in Balanchine's dances will undoubtedly be disappointed. These three choreographers have different notions of technical competence, none of which satisfy the standards set by Balanchine. On the other hand, the viewer operating exclusively with the aesthetic assumptions of Graham's dances will find Balanchine's choreography mechanical and barren, "all form and no content." Similarly, Cunningham's work will seem abstract and overly intellectual, lacking an identifiable emotional motivation. Cunningham's viewers, in turn, could accuse Graham of reducing the meaning of movement to a single emotional motivation, and they would find Hay's dances too spiritual. These viewers would indict Balanchine for producing a sterile, constricted view of movement and a tedious consonance between music and dance. Viewers familiar only with Hay's dances would condemn Balanchine for the use of sexual stereotypes; for a politically conservative, hierarchical organization evident in his dances; and for their lack of relevance to daily life. Her enthusiasts would find Graham's dances melodramatic and Cunningham's dances too alienated.

Such interpretations in the contemporary dance world demonstrate the autonomy of the viewer in actively creating the meaning of the dance and imply a similar autonomy for the dancer or for any of the arts—music, lighting, costuming—that support the dance. If this range of interpretations exists for the dancer, viewer, or critic, are there any criteria on which to base a correct or full interpretation of the dance? The approach taken here assumes that the meaning of any dance resides in a series of translations: from choreographer's intention to kinesthetic form, from dancer's sense of mission to performed event, and from the event itself to the viewer's apprehension of it. Underlying and supporting these translations is a tradition of choreographic conventions—a heritage of codes and techniques of representation and principles for organizing movement—that constitute the very fabric of the dance itself.

Although a given choreographer puts these conventions to use, they result in a structure of symbols quite separate from that choreographer's motivation or intention. The meaning of the dance can be traced (as I have traced it in this chapter) to the ideas of the choreographer, but it is equally a product of the dancer's and then the viewer's interaction with the choreography. The tradition thus accommodates the choreographer's and dancer's creative impulses and the viewer's equally creative response.[55]

A knowledge of this tradition is built up through making, dancing, and watching dances and through talking and reading about them. In the same way that one learns to read an essay, novel, or poem, one learns to note such choreographic conventions as the reiteration and variation of movements, rhythmic phrasing, the use of body parts, the location of dancers in the performance space, the focus of a dancer's gaze, and so on. Chapter 2 offers a systematic description of many of these conventions, thereby suggesting an approach to literacy in dance.[56] Literate dance viewers, like choreographers, "read" dances by consciously utilizing their knowledge of composition to interpret the performance, and in this sense they perform the choreography along with the dancers.

CHAPTER TWO

Reading Choreography:

Composing Dances

Literacy in dance begins with seeing, hearing, and feeling how the body moves. The reader of dances must learn to see and feel rhythm in movement, to comprehend the three-dimensionality of the body, to sense its anatomical capabilities and its relation to gravity, to identify the gestures and shapes made by the body, and even to reidentify them when they are performed by different dancers. This reader must also notice changes in the tensile qualities of movement—the dynamics and effort with which it is performed—and be able to trace the path of dancers from one part of the performance area to another. And in addition to perceiving these features of the dance, the dance reader must be able to remember them. Only the viewer who retains visual, aural, and kinesthetic impressions of the dance as it unfolds in time can compare succeeding moments of the dance, noticing similarities, variations, and contrasts and comprehending larger patterns—phrases of movement and sections of the dance—and finally the dance as a whole.

None of these skills is easily acquired. Perhaps the most direct access to them is provided by the dance class. Regardless of its aesthetic and technical allegiance, almost any dance class cultivates an awareness of the basic attributes of movement. But even the viewer untrained in dance can learn to observe movement. By attending to one's own movement and that of others, one can develop a knowledge of the body and its motion. This, in turn, will allow one to identify and retain patterns of rhythm, effort, and visual design in performance.

Once familiar with movement, the viewer can apprehend the choreographic codes and conventions that give the dance its significance. These conventions situate the dance in the world and among dances that have preceded it. They also give the dance internal coherence and integrity. By focusing on these conventions in a particular dance, the viewer comes to understand not only what that dance means but also how it creates its meaning.

The following discussion offers a blueprint for choreographic meaning,[1] assimilating many choreographic conventions into five broad categories: (1) the frame—the way the dance sets itself apart as a unique event; (2) the mode of representation—the way the dance refers to the world; (3) the style—the way the dance achieves an individual identity in the world and in its genre; (4) the vocabulary—the basic units or "moves" from which the dance is made; and (5) the syntax—the rules governing the selection and combination of moves. This sketching out of the strategies and techniques involved in dance composition is simply that—a rough draft of the art of choreography designed for a specific cultural and historical moment. That is to say, the analysis pertains only to the Western concert dance tradition, not to dances of other cultures, and, within that tradition (as chapter 3 will show), to a uniquely contemporary perspective. In the interplay among these conventions, a complex series of resonances establishes the symbolic field of the dance, thereby permitting the viewer to perceive as dance pieces in which there is talking, or pieces taking place in the midst of people unaware that a dance is happening, or even pieces in which there is very little movement.

The viewer's interpretation of a dance begins with the announcement of the upcoming event: in newspapers and magazines, on posters, in

Frames

invitations, or on radio and television. Descriptions of the event in these announcements help establish its distinctiveness through references to generic types—ballet, modern, or contemporary—as well as through adjectives ranging from "brilliant" and "breathtaking" to "deeply moving," "compelling," "fascinating," "provocative," and so on. Graphics in the advertisements also evoke a particular image of the event. Photographs may depict dancers seeming to leap off the paper with picture-perfect daring. Or they may blur the image of a dancer gesturing in anguish or exultation. An abstract, minimalist pen and ink sketch suggests one mood, while a collage of stop-action images implies another. The location and price of the event are also significant. Loft or studio concerts offered for a donation or a small fee signify the experimental, the marginal, or the familial. The five-thousand-seat auditorium with ticket prices ranging from twenty to forty dollars implies a more traditional, professional production. All these factors guide the viewer toward certain expectations about the event by indicating how it differs from daily life and how it defines itself within its tradition.

On entering the performance space, the viewer finds further evidence about the nature of the event. In addition to the sense of intimacy or extensiveness, the feelings of familiarity or majesty that a space may convey, the physical arrangement of seating and performing affects the meaning of the event. The typical proscenium stage creates a theater of illusion, whereas smaller, more informal spaces lend themselves to performances in which events are to be seen as happening in a quotidian time and place. Proscenium auditoriums tend to preserve the strong distinction between life and art important to choreographers like Balanchine and Graham. Theaters-in-the-round or other nonproscenium spaces communicate the proximity of life to art central to Hay's vision of dance.

The proscenium theater emphasizes the separation of audience and performance by situating the action on stage in a different realm from that of the viewers. The architecture delineates a functional role for viewers—as observers who sit facing in one direction toward the stage—and for performers—as residents of the framed, boxlike structure of the stage. Because seating is better at the center of the auditorium—close but not too close to the stage—the proscenium arrangement also implies a single perspective from which the dance is to be viewed and a hierarchy of optimum viewing locations in the auditorium.

Theaters-in-the-round imply the opposite: the fact that any viewer can see other viewers watching the dance from other perspectives suggests that all viewing locations are valid and desirable. Equally important, the action in theaters-in-the-round is framed by the audience itself, and this frame is ambiguous. Dancers exiting from the space merge with the audience, while at the same time viewers can watch each other as part of the performance. Furthermore, the action in a theater-in-the-round is usually more physically proximate, and viewers can see dancers sweating and breathing hard. Under such conditions it is difficult to preserve the illusion that dancers are other than physically active people.

Variations of proscenium and theater-in-the-round suggest still other relations between viewers and performance. Boxlike stages of great depth require an audience to look in on the action, whereas flatter, wider stages imply a more accessible display. The thrust stage, surrounded on three sides by the audience, blends the intimacy of theater-in-the-round with some of the formality of the proscenium. Loft or studio concerts frequently seat viewers at one end of the room, thereby preserving the uniperspectival arrangement of the proscenium while housing viewers and performers communally in the same space. In any of these situations, the performance space itself may appear bare, revealing lighting apparatus and other technical paraphernalia, as if to set the stage for nonillusionistic presentation; or else all technical equipment may be draped so as to enclose the space as a magical site. Yet another variation of the relation between audience and performance occurs when the audience is asked to move about during a dance, when they are required to change locations between dances, or when the performance itself cannot possibly be seen in its entirety from any one place.[2] Such framing comments directly on the role of the architecture in situating the dance and emphasizes the viewer's active participation in deciding what is dance and what is not.

Programs with titles and notes for pieces further indicate what to expect from the dance. The title *Cave of the Heart* suggests a psychological drama, whereas *Dance for Three People and Six Arms* predicts a dance about the movement of the body by three dancers. *Orpheus and Eurydice* recalls a familiar myth, while *Juice* suggests a variety of metaphorical associations: everything from fruit to domesticity to electricity.[3] Program notes frequently offer the choreographer's interpretation of the piece and help situate the dance within the tradition. They may also furnish information about the careers of choreographer, dancers, and collaborators; about sources of funding; and about the auspices under which the event is presented. The concert may be part of a series of concerts selected and sponsored by a single producer or organization, or it may result from the individual initiative of the choreographer. It may address itself to a particular social or political issue or simply occur as one of the cultural offerings of a given season.

The nature of the program—one evening-length work or several pieces—and of the choreography—one artist's works or several—orients the viewer's attention in a particular way. For example, viewers of a single artist's concert consisting of several pieces, each dated in the program, will tend to historicize the dances with respect both to the artist's own development and to larger aesthetic trends. Furthermore, concerts consisting of several pieces often begin with a lighter, festive work and end with a celebratory dance, leaving more solemn or serious pieces for the middle of the concert and alternating solos or small group pieces and larger group works. Such tacit itineraries—or any deviation from them—make a statement about the overall intent of the concert that undoubtedly influences the viewer's reception of each dance.

Beginnings and endings of dances are another important frame guiding the viewer into the dance. The dance can affirm its specialness in the world with a highly ceremonial beginning that includes a precise and formal dimming of the house lights to a blackout, the arrival of the orchestra conductor, and the raising of an enormous and decorous curtain to reveal the stage. If at this point dancers enter the space and begin to dance, they profess two identities: that of the person who is about to dance and that of the dancer. As the person who is about to dance, the dancer acknowledges the occasion and the audience as part of beginning the piece. If, on the other hand, the lights come up on the action, the viewer is introduced to the dancer in one of two situations. Either the lights illumine the beginning of the action, or they reveal action already in progress. The former says to the audience, "This is presented for you," while the latter implies, "You are now able to see events that have been going on for some time." Like the architectural context of the dance, the specific uses of curtains and lights in relation to the beginning of the movement communicate the status of the dance in life and suggest that the viewer approach the performance as some-one included in or as someone looking in on the action.

At the other extreme, the audience can arrive to see dancers already in the space performing the dance. In this situation the dance begins when the viewers decide to watch the action as a dance. In other variants of the indeterminate beginning, dancers enter from or through the audience or show themselves preparing for the dance before informally beginning. All these conventions minimize the distinction between art and life, giving the dance a more mundane and concrete identity.

Similar options exist for endings. Lights can dim on action that continues, or the dance can resolve conclusively before the blackout. Dancers can take a formal bow as the audience applauds, or they can invite the audience to participate in a continuation of the dancing, or they can end ambiguously by exiting through the audience or gradually returning to more commonplace activities.

One final framing device, part of the dance movement itself, is the gaze or focus of the dancers. From the moment the action begins, the dancers' recognition of the audience can direct the viewers' attention in several ways. For example, dancers can make personal contact with audience members, looking directly at individuals, even exchanging a smile. Deborah Hay's dancers sometimes use this gaze, and thereby emphasize the similarities between viewers and dancers, saying, in effect, "We are simply people like yourselves, dancing, aware that this is a dance concert, but one that does not transform us into extraordinary beings." Alternatively, dancers can greet the audience *en masse*, gazing out majestically without seeing anyone in particular. Balanchine's dancers reach out to the audience in this way, sometimes directing their appeal to individual sections of the audience rather than to individuals. Graham's dancers, however, often focus their gaze in the performing space, attentive to the other dancers and the action taking place, absorbed in the world of the dance to the exclusion of any other world. By declining to acknowledge the presence of the audience, they ask the audience to look in on the action. Cunningham's dancers sometimes choose another option, focusing inward, attentive to the changing milieu of the body. This inward gaze, which Cunningham's dancers may alternate with a focus on the entire action of the dance, encourages viewers to apprehend the kinesthetic sensations of the act of moving.

Each of these focal directives helps establish a different kind of communication between dance and audience, by telling them where and how to look at the dance. The dancers' gaze may change frequently throughout the dance, from contact with the audience to concentration on the movement and back again. Whether it changes or not, however, the gaze remains one of the primary sources for understanding the dance to which the viewer can refer. One has only to experience the discomfort of watching a breach of this convention—for example, a single dancer smiling ostentatiously at the audience while others are absorbed in the dance—to realize the impact of this rhetorical device.

The dancers' gaze is the last in a series of frames that progressively define the context of the dance. The announcement of the event, its location, its title, the placement of the dance within the overall program, its beginning, and the contact that it makes with the audience through the focus of the dancers—all arouse in the viewer a set of expectations about the event: that it will be formal or familiar; sacred or playful; virtuoso, athletic, or soul-searching; classical, modern, or postmodern. Framing conventions also help to define the viewer's role—as spectator, voyeur, or witness—in watching the event.

The frame of the dance situates it by telling the viewer how the dance is different from other worldly events. Once the action is underway, however, the viewer may begin to see how the dance refers to those events through its mode of representation.[4] Four such methods for representing the world will be considered here: *resemblance, imitation, replication,* and *reflection.*[5] Although all four might appear in any given dance, one usually predominates, and this mode, as it signals worldly experience, implies a stance toward the world that is crucial to the dance's meaning.

One way to distinguish among the four approaches to representation is to show how each could signify the same event in choreographic form. Let us assume that the choreographer intends to depict a scene from nature, say, a meandering river. The choreography can *resemble* the river if it focuses on a certain quality or attribute of the river, perhaps its winding path, and repeats that quality in the dance movement. Winding can appear in the circuitous path the dancer traces on the floor or in the curved motion of an arm. The movement does not look precisely like that of a meandering river. In fact, it embodies a quality shared by many events in the world—a vine creeping up the side of a building, a snake moving through the grass, or a person choosing between two enticing alternatives. Consequently, viewers can easily make mistakes in identifying what the movement *resembles,* but this seldom matters. Either the precise nature of what is represented becomes clear as the dance continues, or an apprehension of something meandering is all that interpretation of the dance requires.

If the choreography *imitates* the river, it produces a schematized version of the river's appearance.[6] Imitation depends on a spatial and temporal conformity between represented entity and danced step. Thus the curves, width, speed, color, and texture of the river are carefully appraised and reproduced in the movement. The movement, although altered to the scale of the human body and simplified in certain ways, clearly indicates the size and shape of its counterpart in the world. Thus the river might be represented by a continuously moving line of dancers in flowing blue costumes, with other nearby dancers waving to each other across the line. *Imitative* representation leaves little doubt about the referent of the movement, so the viewer is encouraged not only to identify the movement as riverlike but also to evaluate how well it renders the river.

Rather than approaching the river as a set of visual and aural characteristics, *replication* signifies the river as a dynamic system, an organic whole made up of functionally distinct parts. The movement replicates the relationship of these parts—for example, between the flowing water and the bounded channel or between the current and a small island. This relationship may be seen in the tension between the surging energy and the limits of the body or in the interaction between two dancers, one containing or deflecting the movement of the other. As in *resemblance*, the exact identity of the *replicated* event may be unclear. The movement of the two dancers could as easily represent a relationship between mother and child or between the seasons of winter and spring. But in *resemblance* a single quality of the river is selected and then depicted, whereas in *replication* a relationship between qualities is represented. The systemic nature of the river or of the family becomes the dominant theme.

Finally, by *reflecting* its own movement the dance can suggest the river as one of many possible associations evoked by the activity of moving. Unlike the other three modes, *reflective* representation makes exclusive reference to the performance of movement and only tangentially alludes to other events in the world. Here the meaning "river" is particularly ambiguous. In fact, the idea of river may not be intended or necessary in any way to the interpretation of the dance. A sustained run across the performance space can mean nothing but itself, or it may invite the association "river." Thus the dance can, through *resemblance*, evoke the river as if to say "I am river" or proclaim through *imitation*, "I am like the river." Through *replication* the dance states, "I am riverness," and through *reflection* it signifies movement, of the river or whatever else the viewer sees.

If the choreographer chooses to delineate not a river but a social event such as a simple greeting or a moment of encounter between two people, a similar analysis still pertains. For example, the dance can *resemble* the greeting by selecting some attribute of the experience of greeting, such as the sudden awareness of the presence of the other person, and repeating that attribute in the movement of the dance. The awareness could be made apparent by a sudden opening of the dancer's bodily demeanor, a more alert and open carriage, or it might appear simply as a momentary pause in the phrasing of a movement. *Imitation* of the greeting, in contrast, would reproduce the greeting by approximating the gestures of salutation as dictated by the two dancers' social class, gender, and attitudes toward one another. The choreography might include an idealized version of a wave or bow or a look of agitation or flirtation as dancers come toward one another. *Replication*, however, would involve less focus on the social identity and more emphasis on the systemic relationship between the two dancers, less portrayal of attitudes and behavior and more elaboration of the interconnected feelings. Each dancer's psychological and physical stance toward the other would be part of an organic connection between them, and because of this connection the choreography would emphasize the responses of each dancer to the other and the transitions from one feeling to the next. Finally, *reflection* would show the greeting only as an inevitable part of moving in a given space with others. Dancers would manifest no special attention to one another beyond their typical alert gaze and attention to activities in the space.

Whatever the subject matter of the dance—a landscape, a social gathering, or an individual character's feelings—the formulas for signifying these events remain largely the same. But when and how does it become evident to the viewer that the dance is operating in one of these four modes? An indication of the representational mode can often be found, with the help of program notes and dancers' focus, in the first movement of the dance. However, as the dance unfolds, larger patterns and groupings of movements emerge, forming a hierarchy of levels in the dance in which different modes of representation occur simultaneously. The following examples taken from the works of Balanchine, Hay, Graham, and Cunningham and from earlier dances by Isadora Duncan and others illustrate several combinations of representational modes. Beginning with the individual movements and phrases of movements and continuing to the larger sections of the dance and finally the dance as a whole, these examples demonstrate the extent to which the mode of representation determines the subject matter of the dance.

In Balanchine's *Apollo* (1928), the viewer, prior to the beginning of the dance, has been informed of the plot by reading the program.[7] The lights come up on the character of Apollo, whose first gestures reinforce the written description: he *imitatively* represents playing the lyre while also restlessly or curiously searching the space, looking for someone to play for or with. Alternating with these gestures that clearly depict Apollo mastering the lyre are movements with no obvious referent in the world; they seem only to *reflect* themselves. These movements, taken directly from the repertoire of traditional ballet, demonstrate the dancer's agile mastery of movement but make no direct contribution to the story. After some time Apollo rests, and the three Muses enter. Once the Muses begin to dance with Apollo, Apollo's solo can be seen as a section of the dance. In the section as a whole, the mode of representation is *imitative*: the dance *imitates* the god Apollo exercising his musical and dancerly abilities. In the individual movements of the dance, however, two kinds of representation are evident: *imitation* and *reflection*. The dance oscillates between these two representational modes until the *imitative* narrative structure of the solo in its entirety is established.

The nineteenth-century story ballets frequently combine the modes of *imitation* and *reflection* in just this way. *Swan Lake* (1894–95) is a typical example. In act 2, Odette, the Swan Queen, implores the prince, "Please do not shoot my swans," in sign language, a schematized version of everyday gestures that might accompany this plea: "Please"—the hands are pressed together and extended forward; "do not"—they are waved back and forth in the vertical plane; "shoot"—they draw an imaginary bow; "my"—they cover the heart; "swans"—they extend out and back, covering the other swan dancers hovering behind. The phrases of the dance following this narrative sequence, however, consist largely of abstract forms and shapes. Taken as a whole, the dance operates in the mode of *imitation*. Odette's costume includes a crown and swanlike feathers; the prince is dressed like a prince. Undulating arm movements throughout the dance are schematized versions of the movements of swans' wings. And the scenery of the forest, lake. and court corresponds to a "real" environment where enchanted swans might live and princes hunt. But the ballet is also full of individual moments of dancing for the sake of sheer formal accomplishment and beauty. The narrative serves as a framework for these formal displays of movement even as it offers a realistic portrayal of an enchanted world.

Ballets from *La Sylphide* (1832) and *Giselle* (1841) to *The Sleeping Beauty* (1890) and *The Nutcracker* (1892) similarly combine formal display with more or less realistic plots. They portray diverse populations—dolls, exotic Oriental dancers, enchanted maidens, princes, or soldiers—by showing movements associated with the social behavior of these character types. *Imitative* representation, sometimes in the form of pantomime, often punctuates longer sequences of *reflective* representation. *Imitation* furthers the plot and provides a rationale for the sequences that *reflectively* represent the act of moving beautifully.

In the classical ballets and in many of Balanchine's dances, the overall *imitative* organization subsumes *reflective* representation. In Deborah Hay's dances, *resemblance*—the portrayal of a single quality or characteristic of an event in the world—subsumes *reflection* and *imitation*. A given movement described in her program as "hair wash" imitatively represents the act of washing hair: the dancer lowers herself to her knees, appears to immerse her hair in a pool or stream, and swirls the hair back and forth through the water. A subsequent image, "slow, well-paced run," *reflects* precisely that movement and nothing more. The dancer runs in a circle around the space with smooth, measured steps. Although this movement looks exactly like a slow, well-paced run, it does not *imitate* the run. In order to *imitate* running, the movement would necessarily streamline and enlarge the action to include slower, grander steps, with a special emphasis on placing the foot to indicate the "well-paced" aspect of the run. Whereas in *imitation* the dancer depicts the activity of running, Hay's dancer simply runs, gracefully but also literally.

These instances of *reflection* and *imitation*, however, occur relatively infrequently in Hay's dances in comparison with the number of individual movements that *resemble* the world by portraying a single quality or characteristic of a given event. "Turbulent river" and "love walk," for example, are represented respectively by tempestuous movements of the limbs and by a slow, serene walk with one arm raised, palm of the hand spread open. The viewer would need the program notes to know that the turbulent movement is that of a river or that the open walk represents a "love walk," even though the attributes of turbulence and lovingness are clearly evident. The narrative development of Hay's dances as a whole also operates within the mode of *resemblance*. The dances do not tell a story or present a place, such as the enchanted forest of *Swan Lake*, nor does the choreography *replicate* the world by delineating relationships between movement images. As the dancers shift abruptly from one image to the next, the dance comes to *resemble* Hay's Taoist vision of change itself, in which unpredictable diverse events occur one after another, held together not by the person who experiences them but by the grace and proportion of the universe as a whole.

The dances of Isadora Duncan provide a telling contrast to Hay's work because they also feature *resemblance* and occasional *imitation*. In Duncan's dances, however, these two modes occur within a larger narrative framework based on *replication*. Duncan's dances seem always to refer, ultimately, to a relationship between spirit and body, a relationship that she *replicates* in the dance movement. Thus in her *Waltzes* (ca. 1913), a series of short dances to music by Brahms that Duncan described as the "many faces of love,"[8] the dancer *resembles* innocent adoration, sensuous pleasure, playful flirtation, and other aspects of love during individual phrases of the dance by moving with the sustained weight of reverence, the quick lightness of play, or the shimmering undulations of sensuality. Transitional phrases between these individual sections, however, show the dancer as a person experiencing love in its various manifestations. During these transitions the movement flows from the center of the body out to the periphery, suggesting a progressive development from "inner" feeling to "outward" form and an organic relationship between one emotional experience and the next. The viewer sees individual movements that *resemble* each of the "faces of love" but, at the level of the whole piece, sees the dancer *replicating* a person who evolves, or rather shows her ability to change, from one state to the next.

In the same way, a dance like Duncan's *Revolutionary Etude* (1928) integrates through *replication* various aspects of struggle and revolt. The opening movements of the piece show the dancer rising in anguished rage toward the heavens and then plunging fisted arms toward the earth, only to rise again. A large, enveloping shape, precariously balanced—leg raised, head thrown back, arms overhead, fingers curled in clawlike terror—rapidly transforms into the strong direct downward action of the arms by drawing the periphery of the body toward the center and feeding the expansive energy of the shape into the plunging arms. The first shape *resembles* the unreleased energy of anguish, and the downward thrusting arms *resemble* the outrage of an angry outburst. But at the level of the phrase, these two moments of *resemblance* are placed within a cycle of movement that summons energy from the surrounding space and channels it into the earthbound thrust, after which the dancer rises to begin the cycle again. The transformation from expansive tension into directed thrust *replicates* the relationship between anguish and anger and the progression from feeling to the expression of feeling.

With each repetition of the phrase, the intensity of the performance increases, and consequently the power of the dancer's message grows. At the same time, the repetitions signal that the dancer is entrapped in a cycle of expression, its futility conveyed by the arms that can be directed only downward to the earth, not outward against the oppressor. The phrase of movement, rising and falling in the vertical plane, also *replicates* a relationship between a desire for change and the inability to effect change.

The dance then goes on to *imitate* a moment of weariness and depression—resting on one knee, the dancer dejectedly surveys her surroundings. But even during this pause feelings of rage collect, eventually building into a horrifying scream and a return to the rising and plunging phrase of the opening. This time, however, the phrase culminates in a series of punching movements that finally bring one fisted arm into the horizontal plane. The full force of the dancer's wrath is now directed out into the world. The arm, slightly bent, has not expended its full force on the world but remains tense and full, a symbol of immense power and strength. The final horizontal pose transcends the cycle of rising and falling and concludes the dance's *replicative* narrative structure. At the same time, the pose functions *imitatively* as an iconographic image of a worker gesturing in defiance and solidarity. Until now the dance has been situated in a timeless universe, with the dancer as a universal symbol of struggle and despair. The final *imitative* pose lends a historical and social specificity to the dance by closely approximating images, familiar to us today and certainly to Duncan's audience in the 1930s, of workers uniting under the banner of socialism. The pose thus allows the viewer to re-view the dance as interpreting the universal aspects of a specific situation—the condition of workers—and to see the dancer's final pose optimistically: the plight of human workers can be resolved through participation in the socialist party.

Martha Graham's dances function similarly, interjecting occasional moments of *imitation* into a larger *replicative* framework. For example, in *Embattled Garden* (1958) the curtain opens on a stage set consisting of two low curving platforms with metal rods projecting out of them and a taller post with more rods attached horizontally at its top. The two structures neither *resemble* nor *imitate* a garden and a tree, but they clearly represent these entities. Isamu Noguchi, in his set for the dance, organized certain features of gardens—their lush, embedded quality—and trees—their symmetry, their vertical growth, their network of trunk and branches—into sculptural wholes designed to emphasize the relationships among these features.

The movement itself relies on this same *replicative* mode to enact the mythic story of Adam and Eve. A man and a woman begin by dancing in sustained rapport in the garden area. Although the movement is reminiscent of gestures of emotional and sexual expression, it could not be said to *resemble* those gestures. Graham's use of bodily contraction, for example, suggests sexuality but also anguish, tension, and a general intensity of emotional experience. The contraction *replicates* the interconnections of these emotions by delineating a relationship between the body's center and its periphery and between the pelvis and the rest of the torso. As the duet draws to a close, a third figure is suddenly revealed high in the tree. This male dancer slithers down the trunk and by *imitating* the movement of a snake identifies himself as the serpent, thus orienting the viewer securely in the myth of Adam and Eve. The dancer does not continue to act like a serpent, however. In fact, the presence of a fourth, female, dancer and the subsequent interactions of the four dancers soon make clear that the role of the serpent is shared by two dancers, who together embody the sexual temptation confronting Adam and Eve. As the four dance in the garden, they take on abstract characteristics of male and female principles and good and evil forces. They portray desire, jealousy, anger, and temptation as parts of one organic system.

Graham thus interprets the myth by exploring the psychology of each character and the psychological relations between Adam and Eve. The dancers dress not in fig leaves or scales but in timeless flowing dresses and simple pants; they are neither "real" people involved in a tense interaction nor fictional people whose situation is specified

Martha Graham Dance Company in
Embattled Garden (1958). Photo by
Martha Swope. ©

historically or culturally. The plot of the dance lacks even the myth's usual narrative sequence. The dance ends as it begins, thereby affirming the cyclic or eternal ordering and reordering of interconnected symbolic forces.

Most of the dances in the twentieth-century modern dance tradition combine *imitative* and *replicative* representation in similar ways. The works of Doris Humphrey, Charles Weidman, Mary Wigman, José Limón, Hanya Holm, and Martha Graham typically use brief episodes of *imitative* representation within a *replicative* narrative structure. The *imitation*, in costume or in movement, creates historical or mythical backgrounds for psychological or psychosocial commentary. Limón's *The Moor's Pavane* (1949) dresses dancers *imitatively* in the costumes of the Venetian Renaissance, yet the plot of the dance, like that of *Embattled Garden*, outlines only minimally the narrative account, concentrating instead on the internal desires and motivations of characters. Wigman dresses like a witch for her *Witch Dance* (1914) but performs movements that *replicate* "witchness." That is, she does not *imitate* stirring toads into a kettle but rather assembles enigmatic menacing shapes of unpredictable duration into one foreboding figure. Humphrey's *The Life of the Bee* (1929) relies on *imitative* movement in depicting the social organization of bees. But because the dancers are not dressed exactly like bees and because the two queens meet with such restrained intensity of movement, the dancers all come to represent elements in an abstract model of social organization applicable to the lives of human beings as well as bees.

Imitation may also occur within the narrative structure of *reflection*. In Merce Cunningham's dances, for example, a dancer sometimes offers a hand to another dancer, as if to say, "Come, let us dance together," or dancers may bow to each other, saying, "Thank you for this duet." The viewer may even notice a fleeting moment of struggle between dancers or a brief flirtation within the larger agenda of the performance. Here, however, the use of *imitation* tends to emphasize the lack of overall narrative sequence. *Imitative* gestures occur so infrequently and unpredictably that they only remind the viewer that the dance, if it is about something in the world, is about the human body's repertoire of articulate movement.

The viewer unfamiliar with Cunningham's use of *reflective* representation may initially search the dance for a consistent framework of references to the world. However, the dancers' focus on the events occurring in the performance space and the composition of the movement itself direct the viewer back to the body moving in space and time. Dancers' interactions usually emphasize the activity of moving. Men and women lift each other and touch each other as moving bodies. They do not approach one another as concrete objects, nor do they show a need to communicate some thought or emotion to one another. They are simply awake, alert, sensitive people moving. Unlike the *reflective* representation that occurs in the classical ballets, however, *reflective* representation here involves no virtuoso execution of the shape and line of the movement. Although they may brilliantly perform complex sequences of movement, the dancers do not depict form so much as they elaborate on the body's physical organization. And their gaze, rather than appealing to the audience for an affirmative response, merely asks them to consider the physical facts before them.

Beyond this emphasis on the physicality of movement, there is little to be said about the mode of *reflective* representation. Dances operating in this mode elaborate their own world of references by focusing on their own movement. Just as they *reflect* themselves, however, they also inevitably *reflect* the viewers in the process of searching for and producing meaning for the dances. As part of that search, viewers may begin to examine more closely the dance's frame—its architectural context and the dancers' focus—and also conventions that have yet to be considered: the style of the dance, its vocabulary, and its syntax.

Styles   Any stylistic choice in dance implies a background of alternatives rejected in favor of some feature of movement that lends distinctiveness to, by signifying an identity for, its bearer.[9] Thus the term *style* has been applied to several aspects of the dance: individual dancers exhibit a personal style, dance movement may occur in a given style, choreographers can be identified by their style, and even dance traditions may be said to embody a certain style. Where the representational mode of the dance alerts the viewer to a broad framework for signifying the world, style in dance clarifies this framework by adding references to cultural identity. Thus conceived, style results from three related sets of choreographic conventions: the quality with which the movement is performed, the characteristic use of parts of the body, and the dancer's orientation in the performance space.

Quality in movement, defined as the texture or effort found in movement as it is performed, is most easily observable in a comparison of two dancers' executions of the same choreography. For example, one dancer performs the Swan Queen's speech to the prince, "Please, don't shoot my swans," with a light, tentative quality, thereby indicating her delicate, ethereal identity. The other dancer performs the same sequence with more force, directness, and quickness, indicating her regal authority and conviction. In either case the quality helps form Odette's character in performance and so gives Odette a more specific identity. Such interpretations, an important part of choreographers' and dancers' responsibilities, give characters a believable vitality and immediacy. If, on the other hand, the dancer, regardless of the role, consistently uses specific movement qualities, then these qualities help shape the dancer's own performance persona—a theatrical version of the dancer's personality. Thus Rudolf Nureyev's passionate, organic, leonine persona has frequently been contrasted with Mikhail Baryshnikov's more buoyant precision.

The work of the early twentieth-century movement theorist and choreographer Rudolf von Laban offers a comprehensive systematization of quality in movement.[10] Laban analyzes quality or, in his words, effort in movement by dividing it into four basic components: space, time, weight, and flow. Each of these four, in turn, consists of two opposite dimensions—indirect and direct for space, sustained and quick for time, strong and light for weight, and free and bound for flow. All human movement, according to Laban, exhibits constellations of these factors that form identifiable efforts or textures of movement. Nureyev's style, although diverse and complex, might be characterized in Laban's terms as involving a direct use of space, sustained time, a strong weight, and free flow, whereas Baryshnikov, especially in his performance of the classical ballets, exhibits a direct space, a quick time, light weight, and bound flow.

Laban further postulates that specific combinations of the four factors correspond to psychological states or drives. For example, certain combinations of weight and flow are associated with dreamlike, subconscious states of mind, whereas combinations of space and time may show that the person is engaged in conscious and practical thinking. Thus strength and bound flow together indicate cramped concentration or even gloominess, whereas lightness and bound flow enjoin to signify a tentativeness of feelings. And directness in space when added to quickness in time reveals a pointed and exacting thinking process, while a use of indirect space and sustained time signals a slow evaluation of all possibilities.[11]

As stereotypic as these correspondences are, they exemplify the prevalent cultural experience of matching observable qualities of movement with attributes of personality. This process certainly occurs when one views dance and describes dancers as moving with particular coolness, abandon, serenity, sexiness, or irony, based, in part, on the texture of their movement in performance.

Less systematic than Laban's analysis, but perhaps more wide-ranging and evocative, are the many adjectives and metaphors typically found in descriptions of dancing. Metaphors like Deborah Hay's— "a silver, helium-filled balloon is resting on the dancer's finger tip," or "the dancer's body is arched like a supple bow"—recall how quality brings richness and excitement to movement. These metaphors also permit fine distinctions between such qualities as flamboyance and panache, or the elegant and the graceful, or the serene and the contemplative.

In addition to quality in movement, style in dance results from a characteristic use of parts of the body with their various symbolic associations. Duncan's style, for example, revolutionized the dance world partly because she featured the solar plexus as an independent and motivating source of movement. Graham continued this radical departure from the fixed torso of the nineteenth-century ballet by introducing the lower abdomen and pelvis as an isolable area. At the time these women began to choreograph, movement of the pelvis was associated, as it still is, with sexual, primitive instincts and desires; the chest indicated emotions and feelings; and the head was thought to symbolize intellect, rationality, and the process of thinking. Similarly, the periphery of the body was seen as more articulate and intelligent than the intuitive central body, and the forthright, active, and social right side of the body contrasted with the obscure, unconscious left side. Duncan and Graham, like other choreographers and dancers throughout the century, relied on these and many more detailed cultural codes of the body to convey their artistic mission.

Duncan, for example, envisioning a new subject matter and motivation for dancing, spoke repeatedly about the need to bring a new feeling and spirituality to the dance. In one of the most frequent and striking poses in her choreography, pictured below, the use of parts of the body confirms her intention. Feet are firmly planted in the earth, legs heavily weighted, the chest uplifted and prominent, and arms opened up and out toward the sky. The body thus presents itself as a conduit from earth to sky. The lower body, site of the instinctual, provides a solid base of support for the emotional and spiritual center of the person that is yearning heavenward. The intellect, located in the head, focuses on and surrenders itself to the divine, a mute observer of the energy connecting the torso to the heavens.

Several dynamic lines of tension coexist in this stance, recalling Duncan's frequent use of *replication* as a mode of representation. The lower body roots itself in the earth while the upper body reaches upward; the center of the body presides over the periphery as the motivating source of the movement; and the surface body wraps itself securely around the interior body so that the chest is not splayed open, and emotion, rather than pouring from the chest into the surrounding

Isadora Duncan, 1916. Photo by
Arnold Genthe. Courtesy of the
Dance Collection, New York Public
Library at Lincoln Center.

space, is contained in its upward journey by the skin and supported by the spine. Where the tense relationships between areas of the body establish the mode of representation as one of *replication*, the stylistic treatment of the particular areas specifies the content of these relationships.

Whereas Duncan's style situated the individual in relation to the divine, Graham's combines a tense, restrained movement quality with the frequent use of the pelvis to depict the individual in relation to his or her own unconscious. In the Graham contraction shown by Yuriko, the action begins in the abdomen, codified as the site of libidinal and primitive desires. The symbolic contents of the abdomen radiate through the body, twisting and overpowering the body with their message. The intellectual and social right arm points to the origin of the message, while the left arm and hand, with fingers spread wide, testifies to its potency. The head, as in Duncan's pose, is overwhelmed and thrown back. But unlike Duncan's head, this dancer's head is wrenched sideways as though cast aside by the pelvic energy, and the mouth opens in vain, unable to speak intellectual commentary.

In Graham's choreography the quality of transitions into and out of a pose like this is restrained and developmental. The action begins in the pelvis, and the rest of the body follows segmentally and almost unwillingly. This tense texture, pervading most of Graham's choreography, documents both the trauma of her characters' situations and their resistance to acknowledging and expressing these situations. Graham's characters seem to be subject to the psychoanalytic mechanism of repression. The powerful message from the unconscious makes its way only with great difficulty through the emotional and intellectual centers of the person and into the world. Graham's style identifies both the individual and the artistic endeavor as full of internal contradictions. Where Duncan integrates the parts of the body as they yearn for the divine, Graham depicts the tense conflict between corporeal and psychological elements.

In Graham's style the pelvis and the hollowing of the abdomen suggest a sublimated sexuality. As the movement radiates toward the

Yuriko, member of Martha Graham
Dance Company, in *Embattled
Garden* (1958). Photo by
Martha Swope. ©

periphery, the sexual pelvic energy flows first through the upper torso, as though it intensified the emotional concerns of the character. Then the chest area directs the movement out to the rest of the body. In Balanchine's style the groin area of the dancers, especially the female pelvis, often highlighted by the ruffled tutu, is frequently displayed. Splits of the legs and the lifting and carrying of the female dancers bring the pelvis constantly into view. Intimations of sexuality, however, are consistently subsumed by the quest for geometrized form. Unlike Graham, Balanchine and other twentieth-century ballet choreographers often highlight areas of the body with sexual associations but then ask the viewer to substitute for these references the schema of abstract shapes that the body makes.

Contemporary ballet constructs this message for the viewer through the use of body parts in combination with specific movement qualities. Movement never initiates in the pelvis, for example, which remains attached to the spine while the legs move independently beneath it or forms part of the standing leg's support while the upper body curves forward or sideways. Both situations emphasize the placement of the pelvis with respect to the lines and shapes of torso and limbs. Moreover, in contemporary ballet, movement quality is crisp and precise. Positions are often attacked with a direct, concentrated, almost athletic intent. The arms, although occasionally following the body as it moves from pose to pose, do not create a sequential flow of movement from center to periphery, and the pelvis is not slowly revealed but instantly displayed. The chest projects out over the pelvis, its placement, like that of the pelvis, fixed by the spine's linear carriage of the body. The chest, adjacent to the pelvis but not influenced by its movement as in Graham's choreography, suggests pride, authority, and the importance of feeling, usually without indicating the presence of any specific feeling.

The head, insofar as it represents the intellect, is involved in several diverse activities. Whereas for Duncan and Graham the head is defined as a body part that responds to the actions of the torso, the head in ballet often watches the rest of the body moving, as though the dancer, by inspecting his or her own movement, could adjust for or be reassured by the correctness of the execution. The face participates in the dramatic action by indicating the feelings of the character being danced, or it makes contact with the audience and, in so doing, characterizes the dancer as someone whose awareness of the performance occasion is part of the staged action. Thus as a convention for framing the dance, the dancer's head and face identify the audience and tell them where to look; as a stylistic convention, the use of the head identifies the dancer as a person who considers and evaluates his or her own performance.

Both Graham and Balanchine discriminate stylistically between male and female roles, but they do so in distinctive ways. In Graham's dances, for example, men characteristically perform simple, angular patterns with strength and directness, and they lift and carry women. Women, typically more restrained in their movement, perform a complex and wide-ranging vocabulary of movements that emphasizes twists and turns of the torso. Although both sexes engage in a similar successional patterning of all body parts, men tend to provide a stable grounding for women's overtly emotional dilemmas. In contrast, women in Balanchine's dances perform delicate, intricate articulations of legs and feet, turns, and balances—suggesting how they excel in matters requiring delicacy and finesse—while men concentrate on leaps and larger or lengthier turns, indicating their competence at activities requiring strength and dexterity. When man and woman dance together, the man both assists and displays the woman as she executes a variety of designed figures. He generally remains in the background, solicitous and protective but in control of her ethereal, pliable beauty. For both sexes, however, complex actions occur at the periphery of the body, with the feet, almost as articulate as the head, performing small ornamental gestures and the hands expressing thoughts through mimed gestures.

Unlike Graham, who arranges the movement of body parts in an organic sequence, and Balanchine, who fits body parts to geometric designs, Cunningham and Hay use most body parts randomly, and they feature dancers in the same way. Hay's dances, although they occasionally refer to activities that are sexually stereotyped, such as washing hair or tying an apron, allow dancers of both sexes to perform these movements androgynously, usually as a group in loose unison. Cunningham's dancers likewise share a vocabulary, although men do more lifting and carrying than women. Both choreographers avoid any hierarchy of performers by arranging for dancers to do the same kinds of things for the same amount of time. Unlike Graham, Cunningham and Hay usually do not perform as main characters in their own dances, nor do they perform actions more complex than those of the other dancers, as Balanchine's principals do. For Cunningham, a quality of matter-of-factness, a pragmatic economy, permeates the performance of all movement and reinforces the pedestrian personas of the performers. Hay's dancers, by assimilating the diverse qualities of different images, portray a more mutable body and an equally protean persona. In Cunningham's dances the unpredictable and isolated use of body parts predominates, giving his pieces an abstract or even intellectual surface. Hay's more balanced use of peripheral and central body gives her dances a wholesomeness or an integrity not unlike Duncan's.

The choreographic style, then, depends on the use of the body in conjunction with specific movement qualities. It also results from a characteristic use of the performance space itself. Typically, meanings attach to parts of the space as to parts of the body, so that for every type of theater, from proscenium to theater-in-the-round, a three-dimensional spatial grid symbolically defines the space. Within this symbolic network, movement that occurs in the air, such as a jump or lift, or that gestures toward upper space is usually associated with the abstract, the pure, the heavenly, or the ideal, whereas movement occurring on the floor or oriented toward the ground evokes a more primeval or earthly existence. In addition, movement at the center of the space is more important than movement at the periphery.

On a proscenium stage, forward movement implies progress and increasing significance; recessive movement signifies receding time or regression. Doris Humphrey's account of a dancer traveling from one corner of the proscenium stage to the opposite corner aptly, if somewhat dramatically, describes these distinctions:

Stand a dancer in any of the four corners and note what happens. The upper two make the figure seem important with a remoteness, which suggests, if there is no other specific mood, a heroic beginning. The powerful verticals energize the body; it seems to be upheld by walls of both physical and spiritual strength. . . . The two upper corners, far more than the downstage two, convey a strong impression of significant beginnings because they have not only the two verticals, but lines racing to them from various parts of the stage to form right angles—always makers of conflict and power. There are two of these from the top and two at the stage level, which, with the two verticals, make six strong supports in the upper two corners. Add to these one more factor: the invisible diagonals which stream from the upper corners to the lower. These are certainly there, in spite of the fact that you cannot see them. Put the dancer to walking on one of these diagonals from up right to down left, and he is moving on the most powerful path on the stage. . . .

Two steps away from the corner, the six supporting lines no longer operate and the figure is alone on an adventure in which he leaves his stronghold. . . . There is a precarious weak spot on the way—the corner is far behind, the fortress of the center not yet gained. . . . Now the power of the center begins to fortify him—the center, where there is no precarious conflict, which balances him and upholds him. . . . I should say that there are at least eleven lines converging on it, plus the psychological security of the symmetrical design. . . .

Our dancer has now gained the center, and he is at his fullest strength . . . but he does not stop or linger. We see him moving toward the downstage corner and oblivion. We know he must traverse another dangerous place, the weak spot between the center and the corner, but we do not fear the menace because the end is so near. He reaches the proscenium. . . . The figure vanishes, cut off like a knife thrust by the final engulfing vertical. Just a simple walk, but how dramatic and pulsating in all its implications.[12]

Paths cutting across a theater-in-the-round performance space can be equally decisive. As the dancer travels toward and past the center, the importance of the activity waxes and wanes. Activity occurring at the edge of the space, while more immediate for viewers sitting near the dancers, is still construed as peripheral when compared with movement at or near the center.

The effectiveness of this spatial grid depends on the kind of movement that occurs within it, and its use differs widely from choreographer to choreographer. Humphrey, with her sweeping falls and rebounding rises, portrays the human body in a cyclic but lyric tension between heaven and earth, whereas Graham's dancers, more enmeshed in earthly concerns, do not spring back from the floor so much as rise from it with a restrained yet determined effort. Balanchine's choreography, like the ballet tradition of which it is a part, frequently gestures upward as if in search of abstract ideals. At the same time, Balanchine confirms the importance of his principal dancers by locating them in the center of the space, surrounded by the *corps de ballet*. Hay also begins and often ends her dances in the center, as if to receive and transmit its power. The majority of her movements, however, are around the center and thereby give no image precedence over another. Cunningham also avoids the center; more precisely, he equalizes both horizontal and vertical spatial grids by arranging movement randomly throughout the space. Because especially intricate or powerful movement in Cunningham's dances can occur anywhere, the center is redefined as part of a uniform field. In the same way, dancers neutralize the use of vertical space by leaping through the air with the same unbiased practicality evident in their falls to the ground. When performed on a proscenium stage, Cunningham's dances scatter meaning still further because the dancers frequently face away from the audience and often perform movement in the wings where it is, at best, partially visible.

As these brief illustrations indicate, choreographers define their individual styles by their characteristic use of space, quality, and parts of the body, but each also participates in a dance tradition that has its own style. For example, Duncan, Graham, and Humphrey are part of the modern dance tradition that distinguishes itself from ballet, jazz, tap, or show dancing through its articulation of the central body, its sequential movement, and its weighty connection to the ground. The earthly emotional vitality of the modern dance contrasts sharply with the ballet's precise, simultaneous movement of body parts, the ornamentation effected by the peripheral body, and the light, aerial quality.

Within these broad boundaries, however, choreographers frequently incorporate stylistic features from other traditions to signify ethnic or historical identity. Thus Jerome Robbins's ballets consistently integrate the swinging, syncopated weight changes of jazz; Maurice Bejart and John Cranko have included the modern dance's use of the torso in their ballet choreography. Duncan approximated the style of Greek dance in her pieces by using images from Greek art. The explosive verticality of Doris Humphrey's *The Shakers* (1931) evoked the ethnic characteristics of the austere nineteenth-century religious community. Graham's *Frontier* (1935) and *Appalachian Spring* (1947) were choreographed in the expansive, adventurous style that recalls the American pioneer spirit. Alvin Ailey brings elements from African and Afro-American dance styles into his modern dance choreography. Twyla Tharp combines jazz, tap, ballet, and modern dance elements in her work. These choreographers' references to other traditions involve more than interpolating specific gestures or costumes that *imitatively* represent the tradition. Choreographers achieve a particular style only when they weave gestures into larger configurations of movement using characteristic body parts and movement qualities.

Dancers, characters in a dance, choreographers, and dance traditions all exhibit specific styles. Style tells the viewer about the dancer's and choreographer's concerns and about the dance's place in the world. Growing out of the most fundamental cultural assumptions about the subject and the body, style infuses a dance with its particular identity, so that styles, even when described as "mechanical," "kinetic," or "cool," seem to the viewer both personal and familiar.

Vocabularies   Once the framing conventions have guided viewers into the dance and viewers sense how the dance refers to the world, they can begin to focus on the structural organization of the dance, first by deducing its basic moves and then by learning how these moves are put together. Although dance movement often unfolds seamlessly in time, isolating

Doris Humphrey and Dancers in
The Shakers (1931). Photo 1938 by
Barbara Morgan. ©

Martha Graham in *Frontier* (1935).
Photo by Barbara Morgan. ©

individual moves of the dance can help viewers determine its vocabulary.[13] Any movement that articulates a strong visual design, a clear, simple rhythm, or a recognizable dramatic gesture can easily be perceived as a distinctive moment in the dance. Many pedestrian activities, such as gesturing in greeting or conversation or performing tasks that involve pulling, kicking, walking, or crouching, have a finite duration and utility in their everyday performance that may give similar movements in the dance a sense of discreteness. The dancer's breathing and most certainly the dancer's focus may likewise bracket a specific movement and thus identify it as a basic building block of the dance.

The ballet and many types of folk dance, including square dancing, each have a lexicon of moves from which the vocabulary of a given dance is drawn. The ballet's lexicon, consisting of approximately two hundred steps and their accompanying verbal referents—for example, *arabesque, pirouette, sauter*—are taught in most ballet technique classes and documented in several dictionaries of ballet.[14] Although variations can be found from school to school, students of the ballet largely agree about the execution of these moves. This consistency, along with the names for the steps, demarcates them as the minimal units of any choreographed sequence. Since many steps in a given ballet are taken from the lexicon, the viewer well versed in it can appreciate a particular choreographer's selection of movement from and innovations in the lexicon.

In contrast to the ballet, whose existence depends on a well-defined catalogue of all permissible movement, the major modern dance traditions—those of Duncan, Graham, Humphrey, and Wigman—have developed certain principles for generating the steps of their dances. Duncan based her vocabulary on the idea of an elemental human motion evident in such simple activities as walks, skips, runs, swaying waltzes, turns, and falls. Graham's principles include the contraction and release, spiraling movements of the spine, and the organic sequence of movement through the body. Humphrey generated her vocabulary from the principles of the fall and rebound and from the sequential use of rib cage, shoulder, and arm and of hip, knee, and foot. Wigman adapted concepts of space, time, and force from Laban's analysis of movement. Although the vocabulary of movements takes many forms in each choreographer's work, a viewer familiar with the underlying principles can disentangle one move from the next. The fall, for example, in whatever form it occurs, is distinct from the release, and the spiral, regardless of its duration, usually defines a single move.

Stylistic features, such as Graham's restrained tension or Humphrey's lyricism, permeate the basic moves of a dance or the lexicon of a dance tradition, but they should not be confused with the vocabulary itself. The style washes over the entire vocabulary of a dance, giving it a cultural and individual identity, whereas the vocabulary sets structural limits on the number and kinds of moves in a given dance and determines their discreteness. Thus Erick Hawkins's relaxed and sustained approach to Graham's principles and Paul Taylor's more exuberant and athletic rendition of them exemplify different stylistic treatments of similar material, just as José Limón brought a certain regal carriage and dynamic intensity that he associated with his Mexican background to Humphrey's repertoire. In the same way, Balanchine's emphasis on speed and on the design capabilities of the long lean body gives the ballet lexicon a certain look in his dances. The new moves he introduces—the occasional inward rotation of the leg, angular arm positions, unusual lifts and carries—inspired by the abilities of his chosen dancers and by the nuances of the music, complement his stylistic treatment of the lexicon. Still, Balanchine's innovations, like the moves he borrows directly from the lexicon, have a perceptible structural distinctness. They can be separated from one another on the basis of their similarity or dissimilarity to moves in the traditional lexicon and on the basis of their rhythmic structure.

The viewer who cannot identify the movement as belonging to a familiar lexicon or distinguish it in terms of its visual or rhythmic acuity, may still be able to determine the vocabulary if he or she knows how dancers learn sequences of dance movement. Most schools of dance teach movement by segmenting sequences into very short sections that are repeated and analyzed in detail. In addition, a temporal structure of counts often fixes the sequence, giving it a meter and rhythm that brackets the movement in much the same way as the names of ballet steps. Or sometimes teachers describe movements with images or detailed instructions about the placement and activities of body parts. The viewer with some exposure to dance training can refer to these pedagogical procedures to detach individual moves from their sequence. And having isolated the moves of the dance on the basis of specific lexicons, familiarity with dance teaching, or simply a long and systematic observation of everyday movement and dance movement, the viewer can begin to analyze the syntactic principles that connect them.

Syntaxes   The viewer determining why one move follows another in a given dance encounters a variety of principles that inform the selection and combination of individual moves. These syntactic principles give an internal coherence to the dance, one that complements and resonates against the dance's references to the world. Thus in Graham's *Embattled Garden*, the syntactic decision to repeat the opening phrase at the end of the dance reinforces the references to cyclic, universal forces in both the *replicative* representational mode and the style of the dance. As the opening moves of the dance are repeated with the lights dimming to blackout, the audience is left with the impression that the interaction among these archetypal characters will continue forever. And in *Swan Lake* many of the movements from Odette's solo in act 2 are repeated in a variant way by Odile, the evil princess, in her solo in act 3, thereby emphasizing the deception of the prince and contributing to a more complex portrayal of good and evil in the ballet as a whole. Syntactic choices such as repetition or variation have been loosely collected here under three major headings: *mimesis*, *pathos*, and *parataxis*. All three of these principles may be working in the same dance at different times, or, like the modes of representation, different ones may operate simultaneously at the levels of phrase, section, or the dance as a whole.

The first principle, *mimesis*, can operate in several ways. A move just executed can be repeated. This happens frequently in Deborah Hay's dances and also in the classical ballets where a short phrase of movement is often repeated twice or three times before the dancer goes on to the next phrase. A move or phrase can also recur later in the dance, as in the phrase described above from *Embattled Garden*. Recurrence is one of the most common and readily apparent structuring devices lending both coherence and complexity to the dance: moves previously associated with one dancer or seen in a specific context can recur in a new context that gives them added significance.

The principle of *mimesis* also functions whenever the choreography reproduces the structure of the music or even the narrative structure described in the program notes. Dances frequently exhibit some syntactic choices based on the structure of the accompanying music. Balanchine, for example, tends to design the individual moves and phrases, the spatial location of the dancers, and what could be called the orchestration—the solos, duets, and small and large group phrases—on the basis of equivalent structural features of the music. In his story ballets, he bases additional syntactic decisions on the narrative structure. Moves must occur in a certain dramatic order if the plot is to be developed.

Graham also reproduces structural features of the music in her dances, although another syntactic principle, *pathos*, usually governs many sections and the dance as a whole. Whereas Balanchine first chooses his music and then transforms it into dance, with or without plot, Graham both commissions music and devises movement for the dance based on her chosen theme. This difference in approach is clearly evident in the two choreographers' dances. In Balanchine's dances the viewer sees the structure of the music articulated, while in Graham's dances a progression of human feelings unfolds. Decisions informed by emotional life, dream life, or the realm of intuition, inspiration, and impulse guide the sequencing of Graham's pieces. It can simply "feel" right to place one move after another. Thus Graham's characters may journey from jealousy to anger to despair in a way that follows a comprehensible, if not predictable, logic.

The following scenario for a dance by Mary Wigman, another choreographer who made frequent use of *pathos*, vividly illustrates this syntactic approach as well as the stylistic conventions of spatial location and movement qualities:

There she stands, in the center of space, the eyes closed, feeling how the air presses down upon her limbs. One arm is raised, timidly groping, cutting through the invisible space, thrusting forward, with feet to follow: direction established. Then, as if the space wanted to reach for her, it pushes her backwards on a newly created path: counter-direction: a play of up and down, of backwards and forwards, a meeting with herself, battling for space within space: Dance. Soft and gentle, vehement and wild.

It is as if awareness would light up in her. The large invisible and yet translucent space opens up in front of her, shapeless, billowy—and the lifting of an arm, changing and shaping it. Ornaments emerge, weighty, huge, and they submerge, delicate arabesques capering by, then they disappear: a leap into the center: a fast turn: the walls seem to give way. She drops her arms. She stands still again and gazes at the empty space, the dancer's kingdom.[15]

An initial desire to explore space prompts the dancer's first timid gestures, which evolve toward celebratory ecstasy and finally calm certainty. The steps back and forth on a line, the alternation between "soft and gentle" and "vehement and wild" movements, the gradual increase in the amount of space taken up by the dance—all signal a steadily developing tension between dancer and surrounding space. This struggle progresses toward the whirling center turn, the climax of the entire dance. In a way that can be felt and understood if not explained, each syntactic choice builds the relationship between psychological and physical space in the dance toward an inevitable conclusion.

The third syntactic principle, *parataxis*, includes diverse procedures for sequencing movement that range from aleatory techniques to variations on spatial or temporal properties of movement. These procedures have in common a formulaic approach to the organization of movement. Like the principle of *mimesis*, *parataxis* involves easily identifiable properties of movement—its shape, its use of body parts, its rhythm—rather than the less tangible feelings or images associated with it.

For example, Cunningham's aleatory syntax, discussed in chapter 1, arranges predetermined moves randomly in the space and randomly sets their duration. Hay uses chance techniques along with *pathos* to determine the sequence of her images. Although sometimes confused with improvisation—the spontaneous choice in performance of a particular vocabulary and an ordering for that vocabulary—the aleatory syntax of Cunningham, Hay, and others differs from improvisation in several respects. Improvised dance emphasizes the choreographer's freedom to choose among vocabularies and to use any of the three syntactic principles discussed here during the performance. In contrast, choreographers using chance procedures give themselves over to the system of decision making that correlates the results of chance operations with specific movement options. Furthermore, these chance operations are usually conducted prior to the actual performance, thus fixing the choreography before it is performed.

In addition to aleatory procedures, contemporary choreographers have experimented widely with two related *paratactic* procedures in their dances: they convert mathematical equations and game structures into templates for dance sequence. Trisha Brown and Lucinda Childs, for example, have often used equations of accumulation and substitution to determine movement order. Phrases are repeated, each time with the insertion or substitution of new moves, or else they recur, each time with a different mathematically determined path through space. In some of her early pieces, Brown converted measurements of distances and objects in a room into directions for a dance, deriving floor patterns, vocabularies, and lengths of phrases from the geometry of a given environment. Similarly, Yvonne Rainer, David Gordon, Steve Paxton, and others have sometimes adapted the instructions for various games to determine movement order and the structure of the dance as a whole.

Perhaps the most prevalent *paratactic* technique for arranging movement, one found at some level in most choreographers' work, is variation. Variation is accomplished by focusing specifically on the spatial, temporal, or tensile properties of a move or phrase. For example, a circular move performed by the arm could be enlarged, or made smaller, or executed with the dancer facing a different direction or standing in a different plane or moving in the reverse direction. The circle could be taken up by different parts of the body—the legs, the pelvis, or the head—or the circle could become the basis for a floor pattern guiding the dancer through space. The temporal properties of the circle could be varied in speed, made faster or slower, or accelerated or decelerated; or the performance of the circle could be punctuated with stillnesses or accented to give it a rhythmic pattern. The circle could also be performed with various textures ranging from the tense and heavy to the liquid and light.

Any of the variations mentioned above can be combined to produce further changes in shape and dynamics: the rhythm of a phrase of movement can be varied as different body parts take it up; a phrase may be given a different spatial orientation or performed at a different level; or it can be reversed, or performed in retrograde (that is, as it would look in a film of the movement run backwards); or stillness can be added to a phrase progressing along a specific path through space. And all these variations are compounded still further when the number of dancers increases from one to many: several variations on a given theme can be performed simultaneously; the same shape can occur with different facings; rhythmic variations can conclude in unison; group sculptures can be broken down and reassembled.

Infinite variations of this sort can be created as long as they are perceptible as elaborations on some clearly defined theme. By allowing the viewer to perceive simultaneously the similarities and contrasts among movements, variations make a substantial contribution to the dance's internal consistency and integrity. In dances that display beautiful or ideal forms in movement, variations permit a systematic treatment of phrases ranging from simple to complex and from the unadorned to the ornamented. Where the dance tells a story or portrays psychological experience, variations develop the character and the character's situation. And where the dance elaborates a vision of the activity of moving, variations extend and amplify the possibilities for physical articulation.

Variation can serve as the overriding syntactic principle of a dance, or it can occur at the level of the move or phrase (in the form of a sequence based on dream life) or as a reproduction of the music. In the same way, a sequence of associations based on *pathos* can be varied or reiterated, a sequence based on chance arrangements can form part of a section organized by *pathos*, repetition can occur as part of a game structure, and so forth. Any syntactic principle can be subsumed by another operating at a higher level. The syntactic principle governing the dance as a whole, when considered along with the style and mode of representation of the dance, could be said to account for its narrative development.

Reading the Performance

The frame, mode of representation, style, vocabulary, and syntax of the dance, as they are presented here, provide a set of structural guidelines to the dance's meaning. The actual process of reading a dance, however, requires far more than a direct application of these structural features. For any given dance, the viewer must weave together the dance's references to the world and to other dances with its internal organization to establish the harmonies, tensions, and counterpoints that give the dance both its meaning and its energy.[16]

Initially, such framing devices as the scenery, the program notes, or the dancer's focus may lead the viewer to look for a particular representational mode or syntactic ordering. The program notes may indicate that a conventional *pas de deux*, consisting of a duet, male and female solos, and concluding duet, is about to take place or that a story of love and intrigue lies ahead. A dancer's focus on the audience may ask them to appreciate the execution of the movement, or it may tell them, "This is the length of a phrase." The style of the dance also helps the viewer identify the dancers or characters and the intent of the dance. Then the viewer can begin to assess the basic moves of the dance and their syntactic order—whether they are organized by *pathos* or by *parataxis*, where and how repetition occurs, whether and at what level of the dance variation is utilized.

This awareness of the ordering principles of the movement allows the viewer to return to representational and stylistic references and to appreciate how rhythmic and spatial patterns are "fleshed out" through the use of specific gestures, subtle refinements of style, and symbolic shapes signifying worldly events. During the course of the dance, the viewer repeatedly enacts, at ever-increasing levels of organization, the reciprocal process of interpreting how the dance represents the world in relation to how it is organized. The larger issues of the dance as a meaningful commentary on the world and its relation to other such commentaries begin to emerge as the various conventions in the dance inform and resonate against each other.

Undoubtedly, there are as many combinations of the five choreographic conventions described here, operating at every structural level, as there are dances, and the possible interpretations of a given dance are as numerous as the viewers watching it. Certainly, too, systems of choreographic signification exist that are quite different from the one presented here. Regardless of the specific form of the analysis, however, reading dancing enriches and enlivens our experience of it. The more familiar we become with the choreographic signification, the more retentive our memory for movement; the more we perceive the dance kinesthetically, visually, and aurally, the more we can move with and be "moved" by the dance.

CHAPTER THREE

Readings in Dance's History:

Historical Approaches to

Dance Composition

Because they offer such distinctive visions of the choreographic process and of the body and subject who dance, the works of Hay, Balanchine, Graham, and Cunningham encourage inquiry into how dances are made. The synchronic comparison of these four choreographers in chapter 1 brings into sharp relief their different approaches to dance composition and consequently focuses attention on dance as a system of codes and conventions. One can gain a critical perspective on choreographic conventions such as those presented in chapter 2, however, only if the conventions themselves are given some historical bearings. The following account of the development of American concert dance grounds the choreographic conventions in a historical situation in order to illuminate both their specific meaning and the interpretive process of "reading" that meaning.

A well-known body of materials documents the American concert dance tradition and its European antecedents: choreographers' essays and notes, scores for dances, illustrations and photographs, programs, films, and reviews. Reading through these with an eye to the organization of the dances, one can arrange an account that specifically addresses changes in the dance's frame, representational mode, style, vocabulary, and syntax. At four specific moments in that account, changes in the use of choreographic conventions seem to evidence a paradigmatic coherence similar to that of the four models for dance making outlined in chapter 1. For each historical moment, not only are the strategies for composing dances strongly reminiscent of the contemporary models, but the dance literature and related discourses on etiquette, rhetoric, and physical education also indicate a similar cultivation of the body and subject. I have chosen to focus on these four moments in the history of concert dance and their relation to contemporary forms in order to identify the historical specificity of meaning in dance.

The following descriptions of historical dances, like the portraits of the four choreographers, cover only general features. Although they include no account of the individual differences in dances or choreographers, they do offer a format for comparing historical forms with one another and with contemporary dance forms. As presented here, the relationship between dances of the past and present is one of reciprocal engagement. To the extent that historical dances show us the origins of and precedents for our contemporary situation and thereby illumine that situation, so the dances of the present, in this case those of Hay, Balanchine, Graham, and Cunningham, serve as lenses for viewing and interpreting the past.[1] As lenses juxtaposed, these four approaches bring into focus familiar choreographic terrain on which to build an understanding of different forms but also tacitly indicate a nonhierarchical and pluralistic procedure for organizing historical materials. Instead of advocating a single aesthetic project by showing its resilience over time or its development through various stages, the arrangement of historical dance forms side by side supports and encourages a diversity of choreographic pursuits.[2]

Allegorical Dance in the Late Renaissance

The tradition of presenting concerts of dance for entertainment and enlightenment can be traced to sixteenth-century European court spectacles—Italian *intermezzi*, French *ballets de cour*, and English masques. These first dance performances, produced under the auspices of reigning monarchs and the aristocracy, were arranged for social and political rather than religious occasions. Unlike the masquerades and social dances that frequently served as evening amusements in aristocratic households, these events emphasized both the importance of dancing and the need to conjoin all the arts. Despite their exotic scenic effects and their boisterous, high-spirited mood, these performances nonetheless aspired to certain aesthetic ideals that distinguish them from other types of divertissements and mark them as the first in a tradition that has continued to build on and refer to its own past.[3]

At first glance, these early dances, with their lavish costumes, ornate paraphernalia, and mythical content, seem radically different from the quiet, meditative work of Deborah Hay. But the documents describing Renaissance productions reveal both a concern with aesthetics and an approach to dance composition similar to Hay's. Like Hay, for example, the Renaissance choreographers situated their performances in an ambiguous area between participation and presentation; they advocated a style based on a conception of grace requiring that movement, whether grotesque or stately, be performed with fullness, conviction, and legerity; and, perhaps most significant, they relied largely on the mode of *resemblance* for representing the world in their dances and in doing so suggested a rationale for dancing similar to Hay's—to articulate a graceful rapport between dancer and society and between human movement and the movement of the universe.[4]

Admittedly, the social and historical forces surrounding the two sets of performances could not be more dissimilar. Hay's avant-garde dances are located at the margins of power, whereas the court dances were consummate achievements of the most powerful elite of Renaissance society. Nor do Renaissance conceptions of comportment and the role of movement in everyday social life bear any similarity to our own. These differences influence the specific meaning of choreographic conventions in the two sets of dances. Thus the theater-in-the-round as used by Hay fosters a sense of familial intimacy in a world dominated by spectacle and the spectacular, whereas a similar viewing arrangement in the Renaissance reinforced a sense of the world as an invulnerable microcosm in which the members of all social classes were inscribed and held in place. Still, if one is to comprehend what it might have been like to choreograph, perform, and watch Renaissance dances, then it may be helpful or even necessary to enter into them, using a contemporary example like Hay as a guide.

The Renaissance court spectacles were usually performed just once. Choreographed for a special occasion, they were commissioned and paid for by the royal families of Europe to display their royal power to the aristocracy, visiting dignitaries, and general population in attendance.[5] Viewers typically stood, surrounding the performance on three sides, and looked down on the action. A stage on which much of the activity occurred was sometimes constructed at one end of the room, but the dances themselves and all large group scenes spilled off the stage onto a large area of floor. Adjacent to this area, a special raised platform for the royal entourage was often constructed. Viewers witnessed the royal family either watching the production or dancing in it themselves. Because most participants in the entertainments were amateurs—nobles at court—the boundary between art and everyday performance at court must have been hazy at best. Often costumed dancers promenaded through the audience before the event and then danced with the viewers during the hours of social dancing that followed the presentations.[6] In addition, the dancers and those in the audience who knew them probably traded glances throughout the performance, even though the elaborate masks and costumes encouraged an absorption in the theatrical illusion of the production.

The frame of the Renaissance dances, much like that of Hay's dances, was made porous and ambiguous by the friendships among members of the audience and performers, the gradualness of beginnings and endings, and the proximity of members of the audience to the dance and to one another. Moreover, like the spaces in which Hay's dances are performed, the Renaissance theater-in-the-round created an intimate environment for the action. Because the audience looked

Le Ballet comique de la reine (1581).
Courtesy of the Bibliothèque
Nationale, Paris.

down on that action, however, viewers probably had the sense of a more firmly anchored viewing location than Hay's audiences enjoy. The Renaissance viewers were not placed on a par with the dancing but rather were asked to watch it from a carefully delineated and fixed position. This feature of the dance's spatial organization was considered desirable by the sponsors of the event because it reinforced an aura of restrained formality and because it commemorated the hierarchical organization of society. In contrast, the arrangement of Hay's audience promotes a casual and more democratic sociability.

Because of the viewers' position above the dancing, but also because of the sights and sounds of the performances themselves, Renaissance productions induced none of the quiet, meditative concentration required by Hay's work. The performances were usually composed of distinct segments—as many as thirty diverse vignettes—grouped into three to five major acts and held together by a minimal plot. Spoken and sung dialogue, delivered by the principal characters, intermingled with the dancing. A small orchestra seated at the edge of the performance space provided musical accompaniment throughout. Sudden changes in scenery, bizarre costumes, and the appearance of fanciful "machines" (large, movable sculptures) delighted viewers and kept them busy interpreting the dance's significance. They could find numerous allegorical references in a small stuffed animal perched on a hat, a contemporary detail embedded in a painted scene of ancient Rome, or the placement of dancers in relation to one another.

Audiences must have been spellbound, overwhelmed by the opulent magical world unfolding before them and enchanted by the imaginative renditions of mythical and contemporary life. Occasional mistakes by the dancers, mechanical disorders in scenery or machines, or the responses of royalty might remind the viewers of the artifice of the presentation. Still, they could only be charmed by the occasion, the dance itself, and the ambience of the entire hall. As they watched, a variety of possible references and meanings became apparent, not the least of which was the allegorical significance of their own placement in the hall: the audience observed as the royal family presided over a society in which everyone moved in accord. Knights, fools, witches, and hermits all coexisted in their rightful places. The spectators, able to identify their own position in this model society, were thus encouraged to apprehend as equally just their own social situation. At the same time, the audience affirmed the privileged place of humans in the greater order of things: they could understand their own existence and guide the course of events in accordance with the wishes of a God who, by watching the audience watch the dance, presided over all.

This pervasive vision of a divine viewer and choreographer distinguishes Renaissance productions from Deborah Hay's theater-in-the-round gatherings. Hay must create her own mystical sense of a universal dance. Hers is a special, idiosyncratic world view that exists, like the concerts she initiates and arranges, within the broad spectrum of contemporary attitudes and beliefs. For the Renaissance choreographers, however, the persuasive notion that all movement in the universe was a dance explained the order of things. Whereas Hay's mandate that we "bring [our] dances . . . to the . . . A&P" strikes us as novel or even transgressive, the description of the dance of the universe written in 1596 by the English poet Sir John Davies, although more eloquent than many, affirmed a common idea:

For what are Breath, Speech, Ecchos, Musick, Winds,
But Dauncings of the ayre in sundry kinds?[7]

In Davies's poem not only does the air dance but also water and fire, the flora and fauna of the earth, and the stars and planets overhead. Dance is everywhere, murmuring in the movement of leaves, in the play of emotions across a face, even in the flight of a bird. Dancing by people offered a special version of this universal dance because it was more organized and graceful than other forms and because it commented on people's lives, expressing "their most-secret thoughts."[8] But like the dance of the universe, concert dances derived their meaning from a similitude of movement, costumes, props, and music to events in the world based on the mode of *resemblance*.

Movement in the dances tended to *resemble* the world in one of

Le Ballet des polonais (1573).
Courtesy of the Bibliothèque
Nationale, Paris.

two ways: either it shared numerical or geometric features with the world, or it contained some common attribute of texture, color, or timbre. A group of thirteen dancers, for example, might refer to the king because his name consisted of thirteen letters.[9] A square pattern on the floor made by four dancers could signify a variety of things: the four cardinal directions, the four seasons, the four elements—earth, air, fire, and water. A circular pattern, with no beginning or ending, with no angles, and thus infinite, evoked the heavens. The seemingly alchemical transformation of square into circle could symbolize the fusion of heaven and earth.

Since the audience surrounded the performance and frequently looked on from above, the dances emphasized the number of dancers and the floor patterns they traced as much as the gestures and shapes of the body. The development of geometric correspondences between dance and world into an elaborate science is indicated in the floor patterns from *Le Ballet de Monsieur de Vendosme* (1610). These diagrams show how the circular, square, meandering, or diagonal paths along which the dancers moved shared structural features with moral virtues. The condition of being loved by all (*aime de tous*) was represented by a set of lines radiating from the central area. Ambitious desire (*desir ambitieux*) shows the relentless, driving force of desire, while supreme power (*pouvoir supresme*) consists of a large circle that encloses and is buttressed by a lattice of primary shapes.

Geometric designs found in the movement of the limbs or in the dancer's path through space could also refer to an ongoing celestial dance. In this excerpt from his "Trois dialogues de l'exercise de sauter et voltiger en l'air," master gymnast Archange Tuccaro describes some of the many correspondences between dancing and the movement of the stars and planets:

All these things [the retrograde motions and diverse conjunctions of the sun and moon], if one wanted to consider them completely, could be known in advance because they are exactly imitated and represented in the dance; inasmuch as the diverse dance movements are executed opposing one another by those who dance, they are nothing but an imitation of the diverse movements

Floor patterns from *Le Ballet de Monsieur de Vendosme* (1610). Courtesy of the Bibliothèque Nationale, Paris.

leur premiere figure, laquelle, suivant l'alphabet des anciens Druides (trouvé depuis quelques années dans un vieil monument), representoit un *caractere* d'iceluy alphabet poincté du nombre de douze, signifiant :

AMOUR PUISSANT

De ceste premiere figure, ils en formoient une seconde, representant aussi un autre *caractere* dudit alphabet, poincté de mesme nombre, lequel signifioit :

AMBITIEUX DESIR

Et après ceste seconde, ils en faisoient une troisiesme, d'un autre *caractere*, signifiant :

VERTUEUX DESSEIN

23

Et puis ceste quatriesme qui signifioit :

RENOM IMMORTEL

Les susdites figures se marquoient chacune d'une cadance entiere, tournant ou retournant en leur mesme place ; puis, après ces quatre, les viollons sonnoient la seconde partie du Ballet, et les Chevalliers, d'un autre pas plus gay et plus relevé, presque du tout à capriolles, ils rentroient d'un bel ordre en la cinquiesme figure, representant aussi un *caractere*, poincté du nombre susdit, signifiant :

GRANDEUR DE COURAGE

Et de la cinquiesme à ceste sixiesme, qui signifioit :

PEINE AGREABLE

Puis la septiesme signifiant :

CONSTANCE ESPROUVÉE

Et la huitiesme signifioit :

VERITÉ COGNEUE

Après ces huict figures bien formées et bien distinctement representées, les susdits viollons sonnoient d'un nouvel air la troisiesme et derniere partie dudit Ballet. Et les douze Chevalliers, changeans aussi d'un nouveau pas, venoient differemment à former la neufviesme figure, representant un *caractere* dudit alphabet, lequel signifioit :

HEUREUX DESTIN

Puis tomboient, tousjours dançans, en ceste dixiesme figure, dont le *caractere* signifioit :

AIMÉ DE TOUS

En après ils venoient marquer ceste onziesme, signifiant :

COURONNE DE GLOIRE

Et puis, avec une gravité superbe, ils formoient ceste derniere figure, marque du parfaict *caractère* qui fust audit alphabet, qui signifioit :

POUVOIR SUPRESME

A la fin de laquelle ils se trouvoient au plus proche du Theâtre, où ils se reposoient jusques of the heavens, and the return to one's place that is performed at the end of the dance is nothing other than the clear attempt to imitate the retrograde motion of the sun and moon. What is more, the passages in the dance where one foot is held still while the other moves: these are similar to the planets when they have, according to the astrologers, achieved the full extent of their retrograde movement. The changes of direction in dancing and the new configurations one makes are nothing other than the spirits located in the heavens; and the beautiful and diverse retreats, straight and oblique, that one executes with so much grace are the same as conjunctions and oppositions of three, four, and even six planets that occur almost every day among the heavenly bodies in their celestial sphere.[10]

In this passage, Tuccaro applies to dance the argument made frequently throughout the Renaissance that human events resemble celestial events. The Neo-Pythagorean conception of a universal harmony based on number and proportion permeated all the arts, providing a foundation for both choreographic representation and the collaboration of music, poetry, and dance.[11] Each art form, it was thought, could accord with another by *resembling* its metric properties.

In addition to the wealth of allusions in the numerical and geometric features of the dance, the production offered references to the world based on shared movement qualities and on what might be called bearing. The lowered head of a dancer, for example, could signify humility or shame because it reiterated the lowered status of a person experiencing either sentiment. Continual sighing might indicate a character's sadness. Coarser, rowdier movements depicted the peasant class, while small, refined gestures denoted the aristocracy. Women performed lighter, curving gestures and men bolder, more weighted movements. Simple sets of correspondences like these could also be collated to produce more complex references to humans, animals, and fantastic creatures alike. The cat, for instance, known as a hypocritical creature because of its soft, sweet exterior and its cunning, selfish behavior, was designated to accompany the Fairy of Games in the ballet *Les Fées des forests de S. Germain* (1625), to comment on the deception involved in the art of gambling.[12]

While the cat designated traits of character, another dancer's costume suggested profession or trade, usually by displaying an insignia or small sculpture of some item involved in the work. Thus musicians, rather than dressing like musicians, wore musical instruments and bakers sported loaves of bread. Especially through color, costume might also depict sentiments, like those of a Pilgrim of Love from *Le Masquerade du triomphe de Diane* (1576):

He had a large hat of grey velvet to show the torment that his spirit endured; and the hat, like those of all Pilgrims, had great wings, which, on one side, had been tucked up under a large gold cord, decorated with a medal and under which rested a large egret's plume, signifying the inconstancy and unsteadiness that one experiences in love. His orange, satin costume, that of an ancient cavalier, trimmed in gold, represented the despair that accompanied him; even his green robe which fell just to his knees showed that he nourished little hope.[13]

Many such *resemblances* in any dance waited to be discovered, yet despite the number of signs to be deciphered, the procedure for interpretation remained remarkably consistent: embedded in the movement, costumes, or props of the dance were certain properties or attributes that also belonged to events in the social and natural universe.[14]

Like the Renaissance choreographers, Hay develops images out of the perception of attributes—although usually of texture or bearing rather than number—shared by worldly event and danced movement. And just as she experiences the creation of her images as the discovery of inherent correspondences between things, Renaissance choreographers alluded to their own choreographic decisions as self-evident reflections of an existing state of affairs. Although Hay's choreographic process appears highly intuitive or even occult when compared with the pervasive, almost scientific logic of Renaissance symbolism, her dances, like the Renaissance court dances, encourage the audience to decipher their meaning. Despite these similarities, there exists an important difference in the impact of the two sets of dances, again because of the predominance of *resemblance* as an interpretive strategy in Renaissance society.

The Renaissance performances fabricated extensive fantastic or mythical landscapes featuring diverse populations that not only situated the dances in a highly structured universe, as Hay's work does, but also allegorized the contemporary social world. Even as they showed Apollo ruling over his kingdom, or the sorceress presiding over her enchanted realm, or the Crusaders laying siege to Jerusalem, these characters referred to other events. Dancers would dress like birds not to look like birds but rather to portray some contemporary social or political event, such as a vulnerable religious sect being stalked by a sagacious "fox." Both "bird" and "fox" would, in turn, occupy particular places in a larger moral order. Similarly, Hay's dancers, when they enact "bird dance," show neither the behavior of birds nor the degree to which humans can successfully portray birds, but rather some characteristic of bird movement that resonates with larger patterns of movement in the universe. However, because *resemblance* is no longer a dominant mode of interpretation in our society, Hay's audience tends not to attribute to the bird dance any social or political references. Her dances articulate linkages between individual and universal patterns, but seldom can they interject layers of social, political, or moral commentary.

For the levels of allegorical significance in Renaissance dances to manifest themselves clearly, an appropriate subject matter was crucial. Accordingly, aestheticians of the period insisted that topics for the dances be chosen with great care to meet several rigorous requirements.[15] First, topics should provide a pretext for diverse and plentiful action to occur. The precedent for individual acts, or entrées, each with its own costuming and dancing, had been set early in the sixteenth century, and the taste for variety could not be abandoned. Activities ranged from stately promenades by cavaliers and ladies to the chicanery of fools, mythical beasts, fairies, goblins, and witches. Court dance organizers determined that topics should embrace this diversity of characters and activities while offering some overarching rationale for their existence.

Second, the topic should support a particular ordering of the acts. Saint-Hubert, organizer of several concerts and author of the treatise "How to Compose a Successful Ballet," offered this advice concerning the dance's syntax: "If there is a mixture of the serious and the grotesque, two grotesque entrées should not appear in succession; if they can be harmoniously mixed in with the serious, they will be much more diverting, and the audience will be more inclined to admire the former, and laugh at the latter." [16] Saint-Hubert identifies two major concerns of dances of the period: they should contain surprising contrasts, abrupt changes in mood, and visual spectacle, and they should embody a sense of regulated harmony. If something fantastic and bizarre took place in one act, the following act had to reinstate order and propriety. Only certain topics allowed this symmetrical display of opposites.

And finally, topics should address the contemporary social and political situation. Because they were commissioned by heads of state, the performances often affirmed the existing organization of power, condoned a transfer of power, or heroized the ruler and praised the court. Since many people from every economic class witnessed the productions or heard about them, their effect in demonstrating kingly or queenly powers and virtues should not be underestimated. [17] Rulers frequently chose their own subject matter or rewarded the entrepreneur who proposed a particularly flattering or timely myth.

Topics fulfilling all these requirements were to be found in classical mythology, Romanesque literature, and the poems of Tasso and Ariosto. One popular plot involved a powerful jealous sorceress able to upset order in every aspect of life. The ruler eventually intervened to restore order and liberate the people from the chaos of their enchanted existence. Such a plot contained numerous possibilities for dancing by exotic characters—the sorceress's henchmen and the disturbed population. When it was used in *Le Ballet de Monsieur de Vendosme*, performed at the court of Henry IV, the king himself, seated on a dais at the edge of the performance space, acted the part of the ruler. [18] After a parade of various nymphs, naiads, and enchanted knights, the sorceress approached the king and, in a defiant recitative, proclaimed her superior power, citing the parade as evidence. The king's glance, however, was sufficient to restore order to the disoriented population, and when the sorceress returned at the end of the ballet, she could only acknowledge his absolute power. This allegorical allusion, though not particularly subtle, was undoubtedly persuasive.

A more elaborate version of the same plot, *La Deliverance de Renaud* (1571), entailed a complex set of allegorical references in which Louis XIII, then aged sixteen, took a leading role.[19] With his timely appearance in this ballet, Louis prophesied his own rise to power in a time of political uncertainty. He also reasserted the central authority of the Parisian kingship, favorably impressed Protestant groups, and gave warning to Catholic rebels and to enemy nations whose ambassadors were then visiting at court. In this ballet, Renaud, a soldier on his way to the Crusades, has fallen into the seductive hands of an evil sorceress (cast as a foreigner) who attempts to disrupt the entire Crusade by taking the elite as prisoners. Two ancient Roman soldiers (their non-Catholic origins would have been noticed) hold up to Renaud a mirror that forces him to behold his own decadence. As Renaud repents, the sorceress rages in vain. The royal army enters, headed by Godefroy, the leader of the campaign (danced by Louis); Peter the Hermit, accompanying him, lectures on the science of mirrors and reflections that has liberated Renaud. The ballet culminates in triumphal dancing as Godefroy presides over the new order.

The presence of Peter the Hermit in *La Deliverance de Renaud* indicated yet another level of allegorical reference: to a universal moral order. Both the actual plot and its political references were ultimately subsumed in the cosmic patterns of good and evil, knowledge and desire. Thus the hermit signified the rational thinking that triumphed over the sorceress's lustful desires, and even though the king himself reinstated order, his actions were the inevitable conclusion to a universal scenario in which good triumphs over evil. This moralistic interpretation was reinforced by the regular alternation between stately and grotesque acts; the mutual and balanced participation of music, dance, poetry, and the visual arts; and the presence of a symbol of divine knowledge, the hermit.[20]

Because they could only reproduce, even as they gestured toward, the isomorphic structures of court and cosmos, the Renaissance performances offered relatively little in the way of plot. Individual acts reflected the symmetrical union of opposites instead of developing a narrative. The extravagant act that usually concluded the performance, celebrating the balance of good and evil evident throughout the concert, followed from the accretion of ordered and chaotic moments, not from an organic development of character or theme. In this overall sequence of movements, principal characters appeared intermittently or inconsistently. Human beings were not responsible for the progression of events, nor were they involved in schema of cause and effect that required an individual will. In *Le Ballet de Monsieur de Vendosme*, no mounting anger led the king to take revenge on the sorceress. Rather, his action was as abrupt as it was inevitable. He simply stood up at the appropriate moment, signaling the foreordained movement from evil to good. Similarly, Renaud's repentance was precipitated not by some internal realization of the good but by emissaries from a social group regulated by divine canons of knowledge. Good simply happened next in the cosmic flux. With these instantaneous transitions and the simple and intermittent actions of the characters, the court dances could hardly be said to be about human beings, still less about performers representing human beings. Instead, they presented living, dancing ideas.

Here again the Renaissance performances are similar to Hay's. Her dances do not present the stories of individual, autonomous subjects but situate the individual in a seemingly timeless social and natural landscape. Nor do they progress toward a cathartic climax but derive their power from an accumulation of discrete actions. And even though her own ordering of images reflects none of the balanced opposition evident in many of the court dances, it does suggest some larger pattern of change.

By creating a protean subjectivity for the dancers, however, Hay's performances enhance or even affirm a commitment to both self-exploration and fluid self-definition. During the performance individual dancers are stripped of familiar signposts of identity and create new identities. The polymorphous subject in the Renaissance productions, fashioned out of the reticulation of familial, professional, economic, and religious obligations, suggests, instead, a complex interplay between individual will and social regulations.[21] As a product of these social forces, the individual subject does not explore alternative roles so much as play out a set of preordained roles.

In the Renaissance productions, the regulation and apportionment that governed the plot of the dances appeared in both the syntax of the individual choreographed steps and the style of their execution. Records of the choreography, though sparse and incomplete, indicate that choreographers borrowed extensively from the social dances of the period, which have been documented in some detail. Descriptions of specific social dances can be found in the published works of several Renaissance dancing masters, most notably Domenico da Piacenza, Antonio Cornazano, Michel Toulouze, Guglielmo Ebreo, Antonius de Arena, Fabritio Caroso, and Thoinot Arbeau, and in Sir Thomas Elyot's *The Book Named the Governor* (1531), which summarizes the proper education for a member of the English ruling class.[22] Because Renaissance society required poise and grace, Elyot recommended dancing lessons, as well as fencing and riding.

Indeed, Elyot argues forcefully that dance not only imparts grace but also inculcates moral virtues. Although far more detailed in its analysis of dance movement than similar works of the period, *The Book Named the Governor*, like them, assumes a *resemblance* between the dance and a moral order:

The first moving in every dance is called honor, which is a reverant inclination or curtsy, with a long deliberation or pause, and is but one motion comprehending the time of three other motions or setting forth of the foot. By that may be signified that at the beginning of all our acts we should do due honor to God which is the root of prudence; which honor is compact of these three things: fear, love, and reverence. . . .

The first movement of the simple social dance Elyot describes is a curtsy, or *honor* that, because of the number of counts it takes and the lowering of the body, *resembles* the honoring of God.

By the second motion, which is two in number, may be signified celerity and slowness; which two, albeit they seem to discord in their effects and natural properties . . . yet of them two springeth an excellent virtue, . . . *maturity*. Maturity is a mean between two extremities, wherein nothing lacketh or exceedeth; and is in such estate that it may neither increase nor diminish without losing the denomination of maturity.

The movement Elyot describes here is a *branle*, a swaying from side to side that produces harmonies between opposites.

The third motion, called singles, is of two unities separate in passing forward—by whom may be signified providence and industry—which after everything maturely achieved, as is written before, maketh the first pass forward in dancing.

Here he describes a step forward on one foot that, because it separates the two feet, resembles the two virtues of providence and industry, virtues that move one forward in life.

Commonly next after singles in dancing is a reprinse which is one moving only, putting back the right foot to his fellow. And that may be well called circumspection, which signifieth as much as beholding on every part what is well and sufficient, what lacketh, how and from whence it may be provided; . . . And because in it is contained a deliberation, in having regard to that that followeth, and is also of affinity with providence and industry, I make him in the form of a retreat.[23]

The circumspect and deliberate step back after the step forward unites providence and industry with the virtues of prudence indicated in the steps that follow. The entire sequence Elyot describes here, with its plentiful allusions to virtue, would have taken up only four measures of music. The dance, then, even at the level of individual steps, could be seen as commenting on moral order.

The gestures and attitudes of dancers, Elyot argued, were also symbolic. A man and woman joining hands in a dance could represent the golden mean, a resolution of the tensions inherent in the contrast between men and women. The man's hardiness, strength, and courage, as represented in the vehemence of his movement, combined with the mild, timorous nature of the woman, as reflected in the delicacy and petiteness of her movements. Dancing together, they produced magnanimity, constancy, continence, and a host of other virtues.[24] Where the individual moves, such as the step forward or the holding of hands, *resembled* various virtues, the syntactic ordering of the moves demonstrated the harmonious relationship among those virtues. Reiterated and recombined phrases formed larger patterns that braided individual moral attributes into a single orderly chain.

In general, social dances of the period concentrated on movements of the legs and feet. The arms flowed smoothly, gesturing to or touching other dancers as the torso subtly shifted and swayed to accommodate changes of weight. The spine was not rigidly held, and the limbs seemed to attach themselves loosely to the central body and to move easily through the space. By today's standards, the body did not move much. Yet during an evening when several contrasting dances were performed, a dancer would undoubtedly feel that the extremes of quickness and slowness, largeness and smallness had been experienced, within the limits of what was deemed appropriate, and that the assemblage of dances, taken together, celebrated a full and balanced discourse.

Choreographers composing dances for court productions might appropriate an existing social dance, determine a new spatial distribution for the dancers, and add a few movements *resembling* character type. Or they might arrange entirely new sequences of elaborate variations on familiar steps, sequences that reentered the social dance repertoire as new dances.[25] However they were adapted, the social dance forms familiar to the amateur dancers were an invaluable resource for choreographers fashioning movement in accord with plot and music.

This reciprocity in the Renaissance between social and concert forms differs markedly from Hay's contemporary situation. Even in her early pieces that draw heavily on the social dance lexicon and presume a certain adeptness at social dance on the part of her dancers, her invention of movement predominates. Where Renaissance choreographers distinguished themselves through their individual treatment of common forms, Hay establishes her identity as a choreographer partly by inventing altogether new movement. This movement involves all parts of the body, often sequenced unpredictably, and explores the body's capacity to move while lying, sitting, or turned upside down—orientations rarely seen in the Renaissance productions. In the contemporary dance world, however, Hay's performances nonetheless come closest to approximating the grace of the Renaissance concerts. Hay, through her ideas of cellular consciousness, shows a concern like that of the Renaissance choreographers, with their theories of concinnity in and among bodies, to establish a genial rapport among all parts of the body and between the body and its surroundings. As a result, she might be said, like the Renaissance choreographers, to produce movement—fluid and sustained, deft and full—that avoids any excess or restraint.[26] Performing such movement skillfully depends less on conforming the body to a particular shape at a given time than on accommodating one's own supple movement to that of others and to the features of the space itself. In this sense, dancers in Hay's concerts, like those who danced in the Renaissance performances, distinguish themselves not by displaying virtuoso skills but, instead, by exercising their sense of proportion and timeliness.

In the Renaissance, steps for both social and concert forms were fitted to the measure, meter, timbre, and harmonic mode of the music. The steps did not necessarily replicate the melodic line of the music, nor was a step taken on every beat, but they occurred in tempo, and their pattern corresponded to the periodicity of measures and phrases. Four-count patterns of steps, for example, were accompanied by four-count measures of music. Ten-measure phrases of steps concluded in synchrony with musical phrases of the same length. Furthermore, the steps took into consideration the mood of the music as indicated by its harmonic mode and the timbre of the instruments. Dancers did not jump around in a sprightly manner to music in a minor key, nor were manly dances performed to the delicate strains of the flute.[27]

In the social dances devised throughout the fifteenth and sixteenth centuries, music and dance accorded in just these ways. The *branle,*

galliard, allemande, gavotte, and courante, among others, each evoked
an atmosphere based on their rhythm and key, as Davies shows in his
description of the galliard:

But for more divers and more pleasing show,
A swift and wandring daunce he did invent,
With passages uncertaine to and fro,
To the quick musick of the Instrument.
  Five was the number of the Musicks feet,
  Which still the daunce did with five paces meete.

A gallant daunce, that lively doth bewray
A spirit and a vertue Masculine,
Impatient that her house on earth should stay
(Since she her selfe is fierie and divine)
Oft doth she make her body upward flyne,
  With loftie turnes and caprioles in the ayre,
  Which with the lustie tunes accordeth fayre.[28]

In adapting a social dance such as the galliard for concert presentation, the atmosphere created by rhythm, key, and steps would be of
prime concern. Thus the galliard, because of its gallant spirit, would be
used in a dance of knights on their way to battle; or, in an earthier style
with certain slapstick acrobatics, it could serve as the basis for a dance
of fools or clowns.

 Although Hay's dances do not consistently develop metric or tex-
tural correspondences with the music and, in fact, often diverge from
the music in rhythm and mood, they do work with the music to create
a single landscape. Sometimes music and dance clearly address the
same image; at other times they develop similar phrasing based on patterns of breath; and at still other times, they wander apart in tempo
and intensity, thereby indicating their integrity as independent compositions. Throughout the performance, however, the two arts seem to
resonate with and support each other.

 The collaborative method of putting together the Renaissance
dances reflected a similar harmony and balance among the arts. A
member of the nobility or the poet responsible for the dialogue might

conceive the idea for a production. Poet, composer, choreographer, machine maker, costumer, and scene designer working together would then determine the content and number of the acts and the general organization of action in the performance space. The music's meter would dictate the tempo of the steps, the arrangement of the dancers might call for the appearance of machines, the appearance of a given character would determine musical orchestration, and scenery and costume would conform to plot structure. Although each art could influence the others in a variety of ways, in theory no one art could dominate the others because of their equal participation in and subordination to the theme. Thus each art medium inscribed or provided a commentary on the same message—a message about the harmony of the universe.

The Renaissance court productions functioned as a lively meditation on the resemblances between the movements, sounds, and visual designs that composed them and other patterns in the social and natural world. Like Hay's dances, they encouraged active participation in this meditation by presenting viewers with an occasion for their enthusiastic observation and interpretation as well as an opportunity for their contemplation of their own placement within a larger design. In our contemporary society, the experience of this resonance between self and world might enhance one's self-awareness and provide a deeply felt, if transitory, sense of community. The Renaissance performances, in contrast, had a more didactic, even admonitory, effect. As much as they charmed their audiences with their gracefulness, they also reinforced the order they portrayed. Viewers and performers alike were, both literally and figuratively, put in their places.[29]

From their various stations within the dance, all participants could endlessly decipher the performance. They did not, however, evaluate the likeness of that performance to the world any more than the choreographers and organizers attempted to produce such a likeness. The choreographer who wanted to *imitate* the world would analyze and then reassemble its appearance in the dance. This interest in the appearance of things and in people's lives as worthy objects of study suddenly changed the conception of dance around 1650. With the relative political stability and increasing wealth of all the European courts during the last half of the seventeenth century, performances began to celebrate human aesthetic achievement rather than the allegorical significance of the human being's location in the universe.

The proscenium arch, established in Italy and England by 1610 and introduced throughout Europe by 1650, signals a radical shift in the concert dance tradition. Dances as intimate, palpable microcosms reflecting universal order were now cast into one end of a long room, elevated, and framed. This technological innovation allowed for more rapid scene changes and elaborate scenic detail in the multiple curtains hung at the sides and back of the stage. In addition, the proscenium framed the dance as a distinctive and exclusive environment—one without ambiguous gaps and spaces for potential contact with the audience—and thereby removed the participant-viewer to a new location, that of the observer. Dances no longer embodied a virtue-filled social and natural landscape but increasingly presented to a discriminating public perfected pictures of human society. The predominant mode of representation changed from *resemblance* to *imitation*.

Unlike Deborah Hay, whose work offers an unanticipated analogue to the Renaissance performances, George Balanchine seems an obvious inheritor of the neoclassical tradition that developed at the end of the seventeenth century. Not only does Balanchine retain the proscenium viewing arrangement, but he also makes use of the basic lexicon of bodily positions identified and codified just after the shift to the proscenium stage. And he depends on a concept that becomes firmly established only in that period: dancers as professionals dedicated to acquiring specific skills, salaried, and ranked according to their competence.[30] Even more important, Balanchine sustains the search for an ideal or set of ideal bodily forms, a search that begins as the allegorical aesthetic gives way to the pictorial.

Neoclassical Dance in the Eighteenth Century

Imitative representation, however, does not function in Balanchine's choreography as it did in the eighteenth century. Balanchine's dances often *imitate* fairy-tale or mythic realities that have little basis in the contemporary world. His plots serve as pretexts for presenting beautiful images danced with skill far exceeding that of most viewers. As aesthetic endeavors, his dances represent action far removed from any commonplace situation. Eighteenth-century dances were similarly devoted to virtuosity and concerned with beauty. Their treatment of subject matter, however, suggests that, unlike Balanchine's dances, they presented perfected visions of society to illuminate, or even provide a model for, social conduct in their own times. Although viewers could not attain the dancers' skill at performing movement, they could understand it as an example of optimal physical elocution. In the climate of Enlightenment Europe, the ballets probably stimulated the desire to understand accurately and then to perfect human conduct. This pedagogical as well as aesthetic function of the neoclassical ballets will be elaborated in the following comparison between Balanchine's dances and their eighteenth-century antecedents.

In the latter part of the seventeenth century, the royal family that sponsored the dances continued to occupy the best seats for viewing them. They sat at center front, with only the musicians separating them from the action. Eventually, as performances moved into public halls and were sponsored by state institutions such as the Paris Opéra, seating was determined by social connections and the price of the ticket. In the larger halls constructed throughout the eighteenth century, private boxes in tiered balconies that wrapped around the hall from one edge of the proscenium to the other offered optimal seating. The ground floor, or pit, was reserved for working class spectators, who stood throughout the performance.[31] The candlelight and oil lamps that could be dimmed but never darkened completely encouraged members of the audience to view each other as they had at the court dances.[32] Ultimately, however, everyone's gaze was directed toward the action on the stage. Dancers, now frequently without the

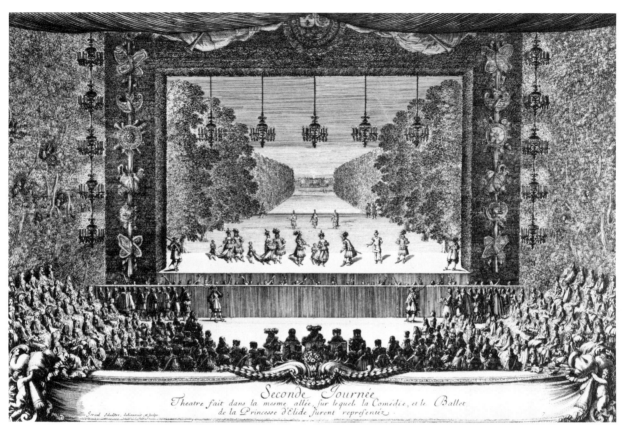

Seconde Journée
Theatre fait dans la mesme allée, sur lequel la Comédie, et le Ballet
de la Princesse d'Elide furent représentéz

Les Plaisirs de l'isle enchantée, La
Seconde Journée (1673). Courtesy of
the Dance Collection, New York
Public Library at Lincoln Center.

Le Chinois and La Chinoise,
costumes for *Les Indes galantes* by
Jean-Baptiste Martin (1750).
Courtesy of the Dance Collection,
New York Public Library at Lincoln
Center.

masks they had worn in the Renaissance dances, returned the gaze with cool formality, though they occasionally acknowledged some eminent patron.[33]

The scenic environment, no longer sculptural or transportable, became increasingly extravagant. Panoramic vistas or intimate boudoirs, idealized rather than realistic images of places, were depicted in sumptuous color and great detail. Costumes, rather than offering a plenitude of half-obscure clues to the character, tended to embellish or exaggerate the actual fashion of the period. Milkmaids were adorned with countless tiny bouquets of flowers; nobility wore all manner of gold ruffling and glittering jeweled diadems. Turkish, Indian, Chinese, or African characters displayed an odd mixture of indigenous and baroque costuming: dancers in slightly altered classical eighteenth-century dress wore turbans or Chinese coolie hats, as in the costumes designed by Jean-Baptiste Martin.

The audience presented with such brilliant images of human society in its various forms was appreciative and enthusiastic but also critical. Certain dancers, costumes, or scenery pleased them, while others did not fulfill expectations. Both the proscenium frame and the dancers' obvious attempts to excel promoted a climate of comparison—between one dancer and another and between choreographers, plots, or scenes in the dance. Applause, although generous, was followed by conversations among members of the audience about the ballet's relative success.[34] This blending of critical observation and unabashed admiration signaled a new identity for the viewer. Meaning in the Renaissance productions had circulated among all dancers and viewers, including God; now it was the members of the audience alone who had the power to interpret and judge the dance.

In a contemporary reflection of this new critical disposition, followers of Balanchine's performances at the New York City Ballet, well informed about a given dancer or a new collaboration, frequently contrast one performance with another. Like the rectangular enclosure of the proscenium itself, this knowledgeability frames successive images of the dance for retention and comparison. The eighteenth-century audience, however, compared both the images of successive dances with one another and images from the dance with those of life itself.

Jean Georges Noverre, a foremost choreographer and dance theoretician of the eighteenth century, set forth the representational intentions of the proscenium ballets in his *Letters on Dancing and Ballets* (1760):

The well-composed ballet is a living picture of the passions, manners, customs and ceremonies of all nations of the globe, consequently, it must be expressive in all its details and speak to the soul through the eyes; if it be devoid of expression, of striking pictures, of strong situations, it becomes a cold and dreary spectacle. This form of art will not admit of mediocrity; like the art of painting, it exacts a perfection the more difficult to acquire in that it is dependent on the faithful imitation of nature.[35]

Noverre, who considered his own perspective on choreography radical and unique, argued against what he saw as the alarming tendency in the choreography of his time to focus entirely on physical prowess. This tension between expressive and technical elements in choreographers' debates in the eighteenth century continues in discussions of aesthetic positions in contemporary ballet. Underlying, and perhaps even giving rise to, this debate, however, were common choreographic concerns evident in most productions of the period and clearly summarized in Noverre's definition of "the well-composed ballet." These concerns included the visual effectiveness of the dance, the necessity for lively and compelling scenes, the similarities between dance composition and painting, and the ability of dance to *imitate* the social and natural world.

How was the choreographer to *imitate* the world? Noverre advocated acute visual observation of the manners and customs of people, their expressions of sentiment, and the decorum of behavior. Based on these observations, the choreographer was to select certain key gestures and distill typical patterns so that the dance could present a precise and dignified formulation of life and thus speak strongly to its viewers. Even if most choreographers, including Noverre himself, did not follow precisely this prescription for choreographic competence, they did agree on the primacy of vivid depictions of people in action. As a result, a new vocabulary of gestures, schematized renditions of the movements of social intercourse, human sentiment, and ethnic identity, entered the choreographic domain. The "Chinese dancers" shown above illustrate this approach to representation, which involved isolating the most concise and telling gestures of a people, such as the pointed index finger "à la Chinoise" of the female dancer or the exotic wide stance of the male. In formulating such gestures, choreographers were able to draw on two related disciplines—rhetoric and pantomime.

The interest in rhetoric—public persuasion through speech and gesture—was well developed by the eighteenth century. Fifteenth-century treatises had emphasized the importance of bodily comportment in all public presentations; by the late 1600s, such manuals included detailed illustrations as well as verbal descriptions of the gestures of hands, face, and body that corresponded to mental states or intentions.[36] The astute rhetorician, the manuals claimed, could compel, extol, approve, condemn, forbid, employ irony, and, in general, argue any issue effectively with words and gestures. Not only at court, where a rigorous protocol of posture and gesture was enforced, but also throughout society, rhetorical dexterity was considered essential. The study of rhetoric supported not only the work of seventeenth-century choreographers but also that of painters and dramatists, who sponsored the publication of numerous manuals on representing passions and social intercourse through bodily action.[37]

The developing art of pantomime made use of similar rhetorical postures and gestures. The pantomime or dumbshow of the Italian commedia dell' arte troupes of the fourteenth and fifteenth centuries had matured by the seventeenth century into an elaborate and popular form of entertainment. Stereotypic characters such as the captain, the old doctor, Pulcinella, and Harlequin engaged in acrobatic cavorting, tumbling, and juggling. They mimed comic and often bawdy dialogue and also versions of everyday tasks. Even though such behavior was considered incompatible with the noble aesthetic aspirations of the ballets, choreographers were influenced by and made use of the schematized gestures of mime for real-life activities.

John Weaver, another of the important choreographers and theoreticians of the period, envisioned pantomime as central to the ballet. In *The History of the Mimes and Pantomimes*, he alludes to the concern with "just and artful imitation" common to dance and mime:

Dance is a science imitative and demonstrative, an interpreter of all things enigmatical and an explainer of ambiguities. That is to know what is fit and proper and to express it. I mean here by Expression a Justness of Performance, so that the whole Business of a Pantomime consists in Knowledge of Ancient History and Fable; the ready Remembrance of it; and the Expressing the Story he represents with Decency and such Artful Gestures, as by his motion alone to represent the whole to the Understanding and Pleasure of the Spectator.[38]

Weaver was one of the first choreographers to use extended sequences of pantomime in his ballets. His interest in mime stemmed from both his exposure to the low-life commedia dell' arte figures and his extensive research into Greek and Roman descriptions of the art. These texts by Lucian and others confirmed that movement could silently depict an entire story or scene with "Decency and Artful Gestures."[39]

Because he saw himself as resurrecting and reintroducing this lost art, Weaver instructed his audience in skillful movement observation and in the exact meaning of the imitations he had "discovered." His libretto for *The Loves of Mars and Venus* (1717), for example, explained a catalogue of passions:

This last Dance being altogether of the Pantomimic kind; it is necessary that the Spectator should know some of the most particular Gestures made use of therein; and what Passions, or Affections, they discover; represent; or express.

Admiration. Admiration is discover'd by the raising up of the right Hand, the Palm turn'd upwards, the Fingers clos'd; and in one Motion the Wrist turn'd round and Fingers spread; the Body reclining, and Eyes fix'd on the Object; but when it rises to

Astonishment. Both hands are thrown up towards the Skies; the Eyes also lifted up, and the Body cast backwards.

Jealousy. Jealousy will appear by the Arms suspended, or a particular pointing the middle Finger to the Eye; by an irresolute movement throughout the Scene, and a Thoughtfulness of Countenance.

Upbraiding. The Arms thrown forwards; the Palm of the Hands turn'd outward; the Fingers open, and the Elbows turn'd inward to the Breast; shew Upbraiding and Despite.

Anger. The left Hand struck suddenly with the right; and sometimes against the Breast; denotes Anger.

Threats. Threatening is express'd by raising the Hand, and shaking the bended Fist; knitting the Brow; biting the Nails, and catching back the Breath.[40]

In *The Loves of Mars and Venus* alone, Weaver catalogued more than twenty specific passions that he represented in the ballet.[41] The descriptions suggest that the movement for each passion was designed around a static pose in which the parts of the body were carefully placed.

Unlike either Sir Thomas Elyot, who never questioned the obvious *resemblance* between the curtsy and the virtue of honor, or Sir John Davies, for whom the galliard naturally indicated masculine characteristics, Weaver saw himself as scrupulously contriving a set of elements to create a specific effect. He believed that the "justness" of a performance could be determined by a choreographer and by viewers able both to discriminate between the event in the world and the event on the stage and to compare the two. In the court ballets, where the similitude of gesture to event remained unquestioned, *resemblance* was a cause for commentary but not the kind of examination Weaver proposed.

Balanchine's choreography contains many rhetorical and pantomimic gestures like those of eighteenth-century choreographers. These range from highly explicit gestures of conspiracy, or pleading, or playing an instrument to the more general motions of regarding or offering one's hand to another dancer. These gestures, however, all confirm the nobility of actors, actions, and the ballet vocabulary itself rather than functioning as definitive versions of social interaction. They seem to say, "Yes, you are looking at the ballet" rather than "See how it is that one can greet another person." For twentieth-century audiences uninterested in the rhetoric of movement, these gestures are less striking than they might have been for eighteenth-century audiences. We have no gestural science analogous to the rhetorical studies of the eighteenth century, nor are we a society newly committed, as the eighteenth century was, to picturing itself.

Interest in mimed gestures developed rapidly in the early part of the eighteenth century. But choreographers attracted to the pantomime because of its potential to represent social behavior were equally engrossed in the development of more abstract, intricate steps based on forms of social dance. While the pantomime offered beautiful and accurate imitations and facilitated the use of more complex plot structures, the fancy footwork of the minuet, gavotte, or saraband offered visual excitement and the opportunity to display physical accomplishment. By 1700 a lexicon of basic steps and positions for these dances was well established throughout Europe.[42]

This lexicon differed from that of the Renaissance social and concert dances in three important ways. First, it accentuated the hierarchical organization of positions and steps, conceiving of some as building blocks for other, more complex, actions. Arbeau's Renaissance manual, for example, describes various steps from which a given dance is composed but seldom discusses the relative difficulty of the steps. Pierre Rameau's treatise on social dance, *The Dancing Master* (1725), not only arranges steps in order of increasing complexity and difficulty but also distinguishes between steps and positions—positions being identified as the basic placements of the legs and arms that "give a correct proportion to the steps, so that the body is maintained in a perpendicular line."[43] Second, the eighteenth-century lexicon isolated and then paired various positions of the arms and legs to enhance the body's capacity for geometric designs. Guidelines for arm positions in the court performances had focused on a graceful accord of steps, torso, and arms more than on specific prescriptions for arm or head positions. The eighteenth-century lexicon developed a more arbitrary relationship among these parts of the body and consequently a greater repertoire of possible positions.

And finally, this lexicon modified the appearance of the movement to suit the dance's new location on the proscenium stage. Steps no longer preserved the three-dimensional roundness of the era of the court dances. Instead, they exploited the two-dimensional vertical plane by extending arms and legs further away from the central body into space and by increasing the number and kinds of elevation and jumps. This difference between court and proscenium lexicons is clearly evident in the drawings from Arbeau's manual of 1581 and from Rameau's illustrations of similar positions in 1725. Whereas Arbeau's figures gently suggest a bodily spherics, Rameau's dancers boldly inscribe themselves in the vertical plane.

This concern with the body's design-ability, however, did not begin to approximate the abstract segmentation of body parts characteristic of today's ballet. In comparison with Balanchine's remarkable extensions, inversions, and elevations of body parts, the eighteenth-century performances would seem diminutive and strangely upright: tiny beats of the feet and flicks of the wrist ornamented modest yet intricate turns and jumps as dancers bobbed up and down along their designated paths. The body, never as distinctly jointed or as radically compartmentalized as in Balanchine's dances, maintained an integral wholeness, a subtle complexity of movement patterns appearing only at the extreme periphery of the body. Each body did, however, as in Balanchine's dances, fill the visual field with its designs and patterns.

Many of the steps in the concert vocabulary derived from social dance compositions of the period, although their complexity was usually augmented for concert presentation.[44] Unlike Balanchine's dances, which bear almost no resemblance to contemporary social dance forms, the eighteenth-century social and concert forms not only had a common lexicon but also the same aesthetic concern with physical appearances. In *The Dancing Master*, Rameau illustrates just how important the visual details of bodily comportment could be:

I have made an Observation, which seems to me very just, on the Manner of carrying the Head; which is, that a Woman, how graceful soever she may be in her Deportment, may be differently judged of: For Example; if she holds it upright, and the Body well disposed, without Affectation, or too much Boldness,

Plates 258 and 244 from Pierre Rameau's *The Dancing Master* (1725).

Deuxieme attitude pour le Contretems de Coté

Figure preste à faire le piroëté

they say there goes a stately Lady; if she carries it negligently, they accuse her of carelessness; if she pokes her Head forward, of Indolence; and in short, if she stoops, of Thoughtlessness, or want of Assurance.[45]

In the Renaissance, correspondences like these between carriage and character were usually based on a single quality common to both, whereas Rameau asserted the connection solely on the basis of appearance. The stooped head made a person appear thoughtless, not because it developed out of thoughtlessness, as we might interpret it today, or because the two shared the quality of being lowered, as they might have deduced in the Renaissance, but because the mental and physical conditions could repeatedly be observed occurring together.

Greue droiĉte,
o v
Pied en l'air droiĉt.   **Greue gaulche,**
o v
Pied en l'air gaulche.

Ruade droiĉte.   **Ruade gaulche.**

Ru de vache droiĉt. Ru de vache gaulche.

Poſture droiĉte.   **Poſture gaulche.**

Pages 45–47 from Thoinot Arbeau's
Orchésographie (1581).

Because in social as well as concert dance the body's movement conformed to and was evaluated in terms of ideal forms, dancing, like the art of rhetoric, was approached as an effective method for improving one's appearance and, consequently, one's identity. In the Renaissance courts, dancing was advocated because it instilled gracefulness in its practitioners and because it fostered harmony in social interactions. The eighteenth-century aristocracy, in contrast, seems to have danced and sponsored concerts of dance to improve the way they looked. Rameau writes that "if [dancing] do not completely eradicate the defects with which we are born, it mitigates or conceals them." [46] Rameau's matter-of-fact approach to self-improvement should not be taken to imply any deception on the part of dancers. Like that of Balanchine's dancers, the eighteenth-century dancers' identity seemed to hinge on their dedication and skill in performing movement.

This emphasis on skill allowed the eighteenth-century social dancers to improve themselves by dancing. It also allowed professionals to resolve the contradictions inherent in their new role as human beings who represented other humans in the dance. Whereas in the court performances dancers behaved in a kingly or a foolish way but seldom portrayed the thoughts and feelings of a king or a fool, in the proscenium ballets dancers depicted the king or the fool as a real person. Diderot, in *The Paradox of Acting*, conceived of the resultant dilemma in these terms: the performer could effectively express such sentiments as anger, astonishment, or love without feeling even a trace of the sentiments themselves. [47] Although Diderot and the performers he wrote about may have puzzled over their task, they knew how to respond: the dancer's job was to perform the movement as brilliantly as possible, be it a complicated *cabriole-entrechat* series or a look of astonishment or despair.

For the eighteenth-century choreographers, as for Balanchine, the choice of an appropriate subject matter was key to the presentation of a brilliant image, and these subjects came from diverse sources, including the myths of classical antiquity. Balanchine, however, selects a topic appropriate to the music he has chosen, one that can sustain the elaboration of beautiful sequences of movement. The eighteenth-century choreographers chose topics that could support, in their scenic diversity and fast-moving action, numerous virtuoso displays of dancing skill as well as the dramatic tableaus of social life. Topics that included festivals, ceremonies, games, duels, or even social dance scenes offered a solution to the demands for fast action and drama, and indeed many, although certainly not all, ballets of the period referred to these social events.

One early proscenium ballet, *Les Amants magnifiques* (1670), while retaining some features of the court dances, exemplified many concerns of the new period. Composed collaboratively, in the manner of the court dances, by Jean-Baptiste Lully, Molière, Pierre Beauchamp, and Gasparo Vigarini, it emphasized visual splendor. Molière's *avant-propos* summarized the subject:

The king, who desires the extraordinary alone in all he undertakes, proposes to give his court a divertissement which should be composed of all that theatre might offer; to encompass so vast a diversity of elements, His Majesty has chosen as subject two rival princes, who in rural sojourn in the Vale of Tempe, where are celebrated the Pythian games, regale a young princess and her mother with all possible gallantry.[48]

This scenario, similar to that of the court ballets in its lack of development, nonetheless focused on the encounter between two princes and one princess and, through its sung dialogue and mimed scenes, presented these characters as idealized versions of real people. The ballet culminated in an approximation of Greek games that included virtuoso dancing by athletes, warriors, and slaves, presided over by the god Apollo. Unlike the court dances, in which scenic diversity had celebrated balance and harmony, this early proscenium ballet displayed idealized characters from diverse social groups.

Louis XIV, who danced for the last time as Apollo in this ballet, had recently established the Academy of Dance, thereby institutionalizing the quest for perfection in dancing. The amateurs who danced with him in this ballet would continue to perform at court (where the aristocracy often introduced dancing masters' latest social dance compositions), but they would not perform the ballet in its new proscenium location. Subsequent public performances would draw on an academy of professionals trained by choreographers or by lead dancers.

Whereas topics for the court dances were chosen to transform social life into eternal structural ideals, those for the proscenium ballets were used as stately contexts for presenting contemporary social intercourse. Thus John Weaver's *The Loves of Mars and Venus*, like *Les Amants magnifiques*, utilized a classical setting and dressed dancers as Mars, Venus, Vulcan, and other minor mythical characters. In contrast to the court dances, however, the professional dancers performing without masks would have appeared not as gods, or symbols of order, but as people likened to gods. As Weaver clearly states, one of the purposes of *The Loves of Mars and Venus* was to display various human passions with decorum and dexterity to illuminate the audience's experience of them.

Weaver's description of the action, quoted here in full, gives a rich impression of the piece:

The Entertainment opens with a Martial Overture; at the Conclusion of which four Followers, or Attendants of Mars, arm'd with Sword, and Target, enter and Dance a Pyrrhic to a March; then follows a Warlike Prelude which introduces Mars attended by Gallus carrying his Sword and Buckler; he performs his Entry, and then joyns in Pyrrhic Mood with his Followers; wherein he appears engaged sometimes with two at a time, and sometimes with all four: At last he clears the Stage; which finishes the Entry, and the first Scene. . . .

SCENE II

After a Simphony of Flutes, etc., the Scene opens and discovers Venus in her Dressing-Room at her Toilet, attended by the Graces, who are employ'd in dressing her. Cupid lies at her Feet, and one of the Hours waits by. Venus rises, and dances a Passacaile: The Graces joyn her in the same Movement, as does also the Hour. The Dance being ended, the Tune changes to a wild rough Air. Venus, Graces, etc., seem in Surprize; and at the Approach of Vulcan, the Graces, and Cupid run off.

Enter to Venus, Vulcan: They perform a Dance together; in which Vulcan expresses his Admiration, Jealousie; Anger; and Despite; And Venus shows Neglect, Coquetry; Contempt; and Disdain.

SCENE III

With this last Action Venus quits the Stage in order to meet Mars; Vulcan remains, and moving up the Stage strikes at the Scene which opens to Vulcan's Shop, where the Cyclops are discover'd at Work; some at the Forge; some at the Anvil; some Hammering; and some Fileing; while Cupid is pointing his Arrows at the Grindlestone. Jupiter's Thunder; Mars's Armour; Neptune's Trident; Pallas's Spear, etc., are all laid on the Floor. A rough Consort of Musick is heard while they are at Work, adapted to the particular Sounds of the Shop; after which four of the Cyclops advance, and perform their Entry; with whom Vulcan joyns; and in the Dance, delivers Wire to the Cyclops to form a Net; and turns them in, to their Work, and the Scene shuts.

SCENE IV—A GARDEN

A Prelude of Trumpets, Hautbois, Violins and Flutes alternate; to which Mars with his Followers enter on one Side; and Venus, with Graces, etc., on the other. Mars and Venus meet and embrace; Gallantry, Respect; Ardent Love; and Adoration; appear in the Actions of Mars: An affected Bashfulness; reciprocal Love; and wishing Looks, in Venus; they sit on a Couch, while the four Followers of Mars begin the Entry; to whom the Graces joyn; and Afterwards Mars and Venus: At which time Cupid steals away the Arms of Mars and his Followers.

SCENE V

Vulcan is discover'd leaning in a thoughtful Posture on his Anvil; the Cyclops appears working the Net; they joyn it together; Vulcan dances. The Cyclops having finish'd, bring it forward, and shew it Vulcan, he approves of it, and they carry it off, etc.

SCENE VI

A soft Symphony of Flutes, to which the Scene draws and discovers Mars and Venus sitting on a Couch; Gallus sleeping; and Cupid playing; etc. Mars and Venus express by their Gesticulations, equal Love, and Satisfaction; and a pleas'd Tenderness which supposes past Embraces. Vulcan and Cyclops enter; the Net falls over Mars, and Venus, who seem slumbering, and being catch'd, appear in the utmost Confusion. An insulting Performance by Vulcan and the Cyclops. After which enter Jupiter, Apollo, Neptune, Juno, Diana, and Thetis.

Vulcan shows them his Prisoners. Shame; Confusion; Grief; and Submission, are discover'd in the Actions of Venus; Audacity, Vexation; Restlessness; and a kind of unwilling Resignation; in those of Mars. The Actions of Vulcan are of Rejoicing; Insulting; and Derision. Neptune intercedes with Vulcan for them. Vulcan at length condescends; and forgives them; and they are releas'd. Mars, with the rest of the Gods, and Goddesses, dance a Grand Dance, which concludes the Entertainment.[49]

Changes from scene to scene in the ballet were abrupt, visually contrasting, and stimulating. The most important function of the plot was not to develop the characters, or a sense of suspense, or even a causal logic between events but rather to compose and arrange human action for study and admiration.

In *Le Turc généreux*, the first act of the opera *Les Indes galantes* (1735), characters and plot resembled those of *The Loves of Mars and Venus*, but the setting was a Turkish isle in the Indian Ocean. The ballet, with music by Jean-Philippe Rameau, was first staged by Marie Sallé, one of the greatest ballerinas of the period, and was performed throughout the century. In the ballet, a generous Turk who rules the island has fallen in love with a captured French slave. Her French fiancé is eventually shipwrecked on the island as well. The Turk, after cruelly threatening the fiancé, finally decides to return the slave to him, and the ballet ends with combined celebrations by Turkish inhabitants and French sailors.

The engraving of the 1758 version choreographed by Franz Anton Hilferding van Wewen in Vienna provides a wonderfully vivid documentation of the final scene. In this illustration, ladies of the harem enter from the left, while the French sailors mass on the right. The Turk, center, is framed by the other principals and also by the arching backdrop. The set design and the distribution of the dancers are pleasantly asymmetrical and demonstrate the increasing complexity of spatial organization made possible by the proscenium stage. The same rethinking of spatial design that resulted in the development of the ballet lexicon produced the differentiated organization of dancers on the stage evident in this illustration. Just as parts of the body became more

Le Turc généreux (1758).

articulate and independent, so the placement of soloists and groups throughout the space became more diverse. In the court productions, large groups of dancers tended to perform in unison, while small groups featured dancers performing nonunison movement. The possibilities for two-dimensional tableaus in the proscenium ballets permitted small groups to perform independent activities simultaneously and to dance against the backdrop of larger groups. Individual sequences of steps and their paths through space were organized, in part, to achieve these striking visual compositions, each rapidly giving way to the next.

Given their concern with asymmetrical groupings of dancers who would highlight main actions, principal characters, and the center of the stage, choreographers seem to have operated with a logic like that of visual artists, and, in fact, writers throughout the period compared dance to painting. Noverre, for example, described the ballet as "a series of pictures connected one with the other by the plot."[50] Not only did the ballet look like pictures, but pictures could accurately represent the dance. Pierre Rameau, in the preface to his annotated ballet lexicon, assured his readers that after they consulted his drawings of dancers, "there should be no difficulty in placing the body in the correct position."[51] And Gregorio Lambranzi, an Italian commedia choreographer, assumed that he had adequately documented his ballets by summarizing the stage action, noting the opening phrase of the music, and providing a single picture of the event.[52] The correspondence between dance and picture seems to have been so obvious that the one was a perfectly satisfactory substitute for the other. But because pictures could not depict the intricate footwork of many dance steps, a system of notation, first devised by Pierre Beauchamp and Raoul Auger Feuillet, showed parts of the foot, positions, actions, and paths through space in a set of abstract figures. Even in these figures, however, the connection between dance and the visual arts remained clear. The lines indicating the steps suggested to a considerable extent the appearance of the danced steps themselves.

Scaramouche, Plate 26 from Gregorio Lambranzi's *New and Curious School of Dancing* (1716).

If the visual appearance of the dance influenced the dance's syntax, so did the music, and here the analogy to Balanchine is obvious. Even though the music for the eighteenth-century ballets was usually composed after the subject had been determined and the plot summarized, the choreographer fit both the steps and the distribution of dancers in space to the music much as Balanchine does—by correlating dancers or groups of dancers with musical instruments and themes and by constructing movement that parallels the variations, canons, or other contrapuntal devices of the music. The eighteenth-century composers, for their part, were careful to conform the music to each character and each type of dramatic interaction. The musical equivalent of the pantomime in choreography could be found in the use of hunting horns for hunting scenes or trilling piccolos for bird calls. Composers like Jean-Philippe Rameau, and later Christoph Gluck, also developed new

The Conclusion or Presenting Arms,
Plate XII, from Kellom Tomlinson's
*The Art of Dancing Explained by
Reading and Figures* (1735).

approaches to orchestration that encouraged choreographic experimentation with groups.

Unlike the choreographer of the court dances, who participated as one of a team of artists composing the performance, the eighteenth-century choreographer organized all the components of the event. These parts were to fit together, according to Noverre, like a "more or less complicated machinery."[53] The choreographer, as engineer, conferred with designers and composers to determine plot structure and setting and took into account, just as Balanchine does, the specific expertise of the dancers. Then he or she consulted the social dance repertoire and the schema for rhetorical and pantomimic gesture; the laws of design, proportion, and form of the visual arts; and the musical rendition of the plot. Out of these the choreographer fashioned a single perfect image.

Each of the arts copied the others in much the same way that Balanchine's dances render in visual terms the architecture of the music. Rather than translating single qualities from one art to another as the court dances had done, each medium in the proscenium ballets approximated the shape and form of the others. Where the Renaissance court performances supported a polyphony of discourses, some heard and some seen, the neoclassical ballets integrated these discourses into a homophonic event. This integration, however, was more metonymic than organic. It consisted of fitting together pieces of a puzzle or, in Noverre's words, "parts of a machine" to form a unified scene.

The image created by the choreographer allowed viewers both to achieve a certain distance from their own lives and to delight in a perfected rendition of their behavior. Where the court performances drew the audience into the allegorical world of the dance, the neoclassical ballets showed the world to the audience. Where the court dancer played the role of the knight or fool, the proscenium dancer showed these roles being played. Where the court dance encouraged the audience to contemplate humanity in relation to a universal order, neoclassical ballets celebrated individual and societal accomplishments.

The human being as a gifted maker of things in the world became the focus of the dance.

When the proscenium ballets detached dance and dancer from their allegorical moorings in the quotidian world, both could be viewed objectively. Nonetheless, these ballets stayed close to that world in a way that Balanchine's dances do not. In the eighteenth century the overlapping of social and rhetorical forms with the concert forms, and even the continuity between social dance skills and the expertise of professional dancers, gave the ballets a dual function. They improved their viewers by giving them not only an aesthetic experience but also a vantage from which to view society itself.

During the following century, exploration of the ballet lexicon dominated the concert dance tradition. The lexicon offered many possibilities for variation and ornamentation, and it held considerable appeal for the audience. Maintaining the balance between beauty and physical accomplishment, the steps of the lexicon were gradually enlarged. Higher elevations of leg lifts and leaps, longer balances, and new varieties of turns were developed, facilitated by the introduction of the toeshoe for the female dancer and lighter, shorter costumes for both sexes. Ballet masters such as Auguste Bournonville, Marius Petipa, and Enrico Cecchetti contributed substantial innovations to the lexicon and devised pedagogical techniques for its transmission, abstracting and purifying the lines of the body so that the dance no longer suggested idealized social behavior.

At the same time, new romantic subject matter was introduced that focused on the psychological identity and experience of characters and on their dream life. One of the most popular themes for these ballets was the impossible love of a mortal male for an enchanted or nonhuman female. Beginning with *La Sylphide* (1832) and continuing through *Giselle* (1841), *Coppélia* (1870), and *Swan Lake* (1896), the love between an ethereal, unattainable woman and an idealistic, devoted man was repeatedly explored. The ballet lexicon used to realize this theme, however, emphasized virtuoso performance and visual spectacle as much as or more than it explored dramatic characters in depth.

Not until the revolutionary break with the lexicon precipitated by Isadora Duncan did the concert dance tradition evolve a new paradigm, one in which self-expression superseded self-presentation. Psychological subject matter found authentic realization in the movement vocabularies of each choreographer. And audiences, for the first time, were asked to identify with dancer and dance and to feel rather than see their own life experiences on the stage.

In the name of what was both natural and divinely inspired, Isadora Duncan proclaimed a new era of dance beginning in 1903.[54] Born in California in 1876, she traveled as a teenager to Europe, where she dedicated herself to the project of reinventing Greek dance. Classical Greece had served as a model for choreographers in the court dance period and in the eighteenth century, but Duncan's choreographic vision did not depend as much on an understanding of Greek culture or mythology as on her conception of the Greeks' ideas about the soul and the body. Unencumbered by the artifices of society, Duncan's Greeks were both childlike and noble—spontaneous and honest in feeling and action. To her they represented the possibility of overthrowing the traditional academic European ballet in favor of a revitalized, expression-filled form in which the body could serve as medium for the divine expression of the human spirit.

To manifest her vision Duncan appeared alone on a bare, classically draped stage, wearing only a Grecian-style toga and dancing to music by the great composers of the nineteenth century—Beethoven, Tchaikovsky, Chopin, Schubert, and Wagner. For a soloist presenting an entirely new form of dance, her success was overwhelming. The continuous development of her simple phrases of movements, the seeming transparency of her mood and spirit, the generosity and conviction of

Expressionist Dance in the Early Twentieth Century

Isadora Duncan in *La Marseillaise*
(1916). Photo by Arnold Genthe.
Courtesy of the Dance Collection,
New York Public Library at
Lincoln Center.

her presentation contrasted sharply with the pose-oriented choreography of the late nineteenth-century ballets. Audiences were enraptured, moved to tears. This sympathetic description of Duncan's *La Marseillaise* by noted critic Carl Van Vechten gives some sense of her power:

She stands enfolded; she sees the enemy advance; she feels the enemy as it grasps her by the throat; she kisses her flag; she tastes blood; she is all but crushed under the weight of the attack; and then she rises, triumphant, with the terrible cry, *Aux armes, citoyens!* Part of her effect is gained by gesture, part by the massing of her body, but the greater part by facial expression. In the anguished appeal she does not make a sound, beyond that made by the orchestra, but the hideous din of a hundred raucous voices seems to ring in our ears. We see Félicien Rops's *Vengeance* come to life; we see the *sans-culottes* following the carts of the aristocrats on the way to execution . . . and finally we see the superb calm, the majestic flowing strength of the *Victory of Samothrace*. . . . At times, legs, arms, a leg or an arm, the throat, or the exposed breast assume the importance above that of the rest of the mass, suggesting an unfinished sculpture of Michael Angelo, an aposiopesis which, of course, served as Rodin's inspiration.[55]

At first glance, Van Vechten's listing of the images evoked by Duncan's dance suggests a pantomime. But as he begins to analyze the impact of her performance, he evaluates not her accurate rendition of each scene but its force, a force created out of her ability to *replicate* rather than *imitate* the story of the French Revolution.

Although she was the most flamboyant and perhaps the most charismatic choreographer of her time, Duncan was certainly not the only one struggling to find new forms to express the concerns of her era and of the human soul. Loie Fuller, Maud Allen, Rudolf Laban, Ruth St. Denis, and Ted Shawn, among others, began work around the turn of the century on vocabularies and styles of movement that would respond to a new expressionist aesthetic.[56] They were followed in the 1920s and 1930s by a second generation of choreographers that included Laban's student Mary Wigman and St. Denis's and Shawn's students Doris Humphrey and Martha Graham.

After dancing in Shawn's company for several years, Graham left to begin her own experiments with choreography. Unlike earlier choreographers, who had begun their careers first by studying with and then performing in the works of already established artists, Graham and her contemporaries did not see themselves as contributing innovations to an existing lexicon but as creating entirely new vocabularies of movement, whose uniqueness would testify to the authenticity of their artistic impulses. In this sense, Graham cannot inherit the early modern dance in the way that Balanchine can identify his genealogical place in the ballet tradition. Instead, she is a pioneer among other pioneers, pursuing a goal defined not by social or historical circumstances but by psychological necessity. Nor is Graham separated socially or temporally from the origins of her own tradition, as Balanchine is. Because she partakes of early-twentieth-century dance both historically and philosophically, the following discussion of that period surrounds and includes Graham's work more than it draws analogies to it.

The early choreographers of the new expressionist dance took their role as pioneers seriously for several reasons, not least among them the relative lack of concert dance in America. In Europe, where there was a long-standing tradition of concert dance, the pioneers were received enthusiastically. In the United States, however, they worked to educate the public to the difference between dance as light entertainment—presenting stock characters and standard revues at traveling road shows, in burlesque theaters, and on Broadway—and dance as an art using new forms to arouse profound emotions about universal life situations. At a time when even concerts of ballet rarely occurred—and then only in major cities—the extensive touring by these pioneer choreographers helped establish dance as an independent performing art.[57]

Experimentation by these choreographers produced a wide variety of theatrical impressions. Where Duncan on stage was notably austere, St. Denis often created opulent sets with sculptures and scenic backdrops to simulate exotic locales like Egypt or India. Loie Fuller attached forty-foot-long silk scarves to her body in order to reproduce the spirit of a raging fire or a butterfly. And Maud Allen, as Salome, danced around a sculpted head of John the Baptist. As different as they were in setting and subject matter, all these dances focused on the danced character's internal experience. Rather than define the character, dance movement manifested an interior process undergone by the character during performance. Even when the dances featured spectacular stage settings or elaborate costumes, these were important not for their visual impact but for their clues to the characters' states of mind. They helped to establish an environment in which the choreographers could lay bare their concerns.

Technical advances in lighting and architectural revision in the theater facilitated the choreographers' project. During the nineteenth century, gas lighting allowed for greater control over levels of light on stage and in the auditorium; it was electric lighting, however, established in most American and European theaters by the 1880s, that allowed the audience to sit in complete darkness while highly specialized lights, capable of creating subtle changes in color and intensity, illuminated the stage. Audiences were encouraged to focus exclusively on the stage action, not only by the lighting but also by the configuration of the auditorium. To improve sight lines, theater designers eliminated the boxes bordering the proscenium and decreased the number of balconies. The main floor of the theater, designated for the nobility and for the production itself in the Renaissance and relegated to the working class in the eighteenth century, offered viewers by 1900 a single democratic perspective on the performance. In many theaters the proscenium arch was eliminated to achieve greater intimacy, with the stage as a boxlike, three-sided room whose fourth wall had been eliminated.[58]

All these changes invited the audience to look in on and become involved with the dancers and their expressive activities. Members of the audience were no longer spectators, clearly acknowledged within the conventions of the auditorium and by the dancers' own focus; they now became voyeurs, quietly regarding, and drawn into, the private world of the dancers. Scenery increased this sense of intimacy. Where backdrops in the eighteenth and nineteenth centuries offered panoramic vistas, perspectives, or grandiose architecture, settings for these dances reproduced an intimate clearing in the forest, a single room, a temple facade, or an impressionistic landscape.

Within the intimate confines of the stage, dancers seemed to undergo a powerful transcendental experience. No longer accomplished technicians presenting story and movement to an audience, they instead seemed transported by the occasion into the life of the character or into the dance itself. Their actions were vivid and full of passion, as if, unaware of either the performance context or the vocabulary of movements they had studied, they might transform feelings directly into actions. The choreographers themselves often danced the leading roles, further augmenting the persuasive power of the dances. That one person chose the subject matter of the dance, invented the vocabulary to express that subject, and then danced the final composition heightened the immediacy and authenticity in the dances.

Despite the dancers' passionate actions, the choreography was not intended to reveal their actual personalities. In the intimacy of the stage setting, the dancers' performance represented what the choreographers considered universal concerns. Human emotion assumed a central importance as subject matter, however, because specific human situations and feelings emblematized a universal human condition. Thus the dancers, while they clearly felt the emotions about which they were dancing, also became abstract embodiments of the emotions themselves. Dancers did not represent people, or even mythical or stereotypic versions of people, but rather the essential characteristics of a range of human feelings.

To represent such characteristics, according to John Martin, a major theorist of the period, the choreographer had to develop the dance

with such breadth of dimension and clarity of outline that it will awaken the spectator to recognition of its personal significance for him. Literal mimetics cannot accomplish this experience of identification, for they contain too much that is purely objective. The dancer's movements are abstract; that is, they have abstracted the essentials from a particular life experience, omitting all that is merely personal and without universal significance.[59]

Thus St. Denis, seated in mystic meditation for her dance *Radha* (1906), referred not to her specific interests in Hinduism and yoga but to what she saw as a universal experience of religious meditation and self-transformation. Duncan in *Mother* (ca. 1921) did not depict her specific feelings and attitudes toward motherhood or her own experience as a mother but the archetypal characteristics of a mother's experience. Whatever the theme, the choreographer tried to extract its essential features and present them as a metaphysics of human experience that transcended both culture and history.

Although the expressionist choreographers recognized that they were involved in forging a new genre of concert dance, the forms their dances took followed no shared or generalized formats like those of the story ballets or the court dances. Rather, the dances grew organically out of each choreographer's project of self-expression. All the choreographers, however, were absorbed in representing life by *replicating* in movement systemic relationships between feeling and behavior, between one emotion and the next, or between one person and another.

Duncan, St. Denis, Shawn, and Fuller all sought to relate the spiritual and the material in their dances. For Duncan the quest meant "long days and nights in the studio seeking that dance which might be the divine expression of the human spirit through the medium of the body's movement . . . I . . . sought the source of the spiritual expression to flow into the channels of the body filling it with vibrating light—the centrifugal force reflecting the spirit's vision."[60] Similarly, St. Denis recalls her first choreographic inspiration on seeing a poster image of an Egyptian goddess:

Here was an external image which stirred into instant consciousness all that latent capacity for wonder, that lay at the deepest center of my spirit. In this figure before me was the symbol of the entire nation, culture, and destiny of Egypt . . . the figure, its repose, its suggestion of latent power and beauty, constituting to my sharply awakened sensitivity a strange symbol of the complete

The cigarette poster that inspired Ruth St. Denis's first choreography. Courtesy of the Dance Collection, New York Public Library at Lincoln Center.

inner being of man. . . . It was, however, not merely a symbol of Egypt, but a universal symbol of all the elements of history and art which may be expressed through the human body.[61]

Both choreographers, defining spiritual experience as the nexus of several related feelings and profound insights, sought through the medium of dance to demonstrate the relationship among those feelings and between the spiritual and the bodily.

For Graham, Humphrey, and Wigman, dance was less a material manifestation of spirituality than an expression of the relationship between movement and a full range of psychological events, including those attributed to the unconscious. Wigman proclaimed that "every true composition should be a confession" in which the choreographer unmasked the inner workings of the psyche.[62] And Humphrey advised that "there is only one thing to dance about: the meaning of one's personal experience and this experience must be taken in its literal sense as action, and not as intellectual conception. Art, like religion, is based on events; physical manifestations which have been lived through and therefore represent action, emotion."[63] The strong, almost admonitory tone of Humphrey's statement, like that of Graham's dictum "movement never lies," suggests the arduous process of psychological and physical introspection these choreographers have undergone. Unlike Duncan and St. Denis, who had only to locate the source from which spiritual impulse could flow into movement, Graham, Humphrey, and Wigman necessarily scrutinized each motivation and each physical response to determine its validity. But their goal, like that of their predecessors, was to chart the organic progression from internal feeling to external form.

For all the expressionist choreographers, representation based on *replication* began with a journey inward. The subject matter of dances and its corresponding vocabulary of movement could be found only in the psyche itself. Even movement adapted from existing lexicons—from social, ethnic, or theater dance forms—participated in, and was transformed by, the individual choreographer's search for authentic physical expression. Reacting to the ballet academy, but also recognizing the new source of inspiration, choreographers oriented their investigations toward the primal origins of movement. They posited an original natural body in which form and feeling connected organically.

Both ancient and ethnic sources offered insights into the "natural" human being, uncorrupted by the demands of civilized life, whose body was simply the "luminous and fluid manifestation of the soul."[64] In studying these sources, however, the choreographers were less inclined to appreciate cultural difference than to confirm their own intuitions about a universal impulse to move. Thus Duncan discovered in Greek art a clue to the relationship between spiritual ecstasy and bodily form. St. Denis was similarly inspired by Hindu mythology, dance, and yoga. And Fuller sought to understand the primordial relationship between movement and light. Later choreographers based their vocabularies on fundamental principles of human motion, such as Graham's contraction and release, Humphrey's fall and rebound, or Wigman's space, time, and weight, adapted from Laban. Even the principles established by these later choreographers governed fundamental bodily experiences that related, ultimately, to psychological experience.

The choreographers' prescriptions for technical mastery of their vocabularies were consistent with their search for the origins of movement. Technique was not something to be acquired, as in the eighteenth and nineteenth centuries, but something to be discovered. The eighteenth-century choreographers had recommended that dancers practice *imitation* as the key to perfect representation. Those who executed the established gestures over and over learned to perform both the movements associated with feelings and the more abstract sequences until they were perfectly accurate. The eighteenth-century choreographers further believed that dancing, a manifestly social activity, improved an otherwise imperfect physical structure; however, Duncan and St. Denis, in particular, believed that one learned to move naturally and freely by ridding oneself of the tension and artifice of society.[65] This disburdening necessitated a return to such basic patterns as walking, skipping, running, falling, and turning and to movements based on breathing. Repetition of the basic exercises brought the dancer closer to an essential way of moving—a graceful, powerful style common to all human beings. Even Graham and Humphrey, for whom technical competence entailed a more formal cultivation of the body, believed that their study began with a return to the basic sources of movement.

If the search for new movement was primarily motivated by the choreographers' intuitions about what was natural, it was also encouraged by the science of movement popular at the end of the nineteenth century. The study of rhetoric that had influenced choreographers throughout the eighteenth century developed by the late nineteenth century into a study of elocution and expression that included gymnastics, dramatics, pantomime, interpersonal communication, and public speaking.[66] Chief among the researchers and teachers of expression

Isadora Duncan dancing in a Greek
amphitheater, 1904. Courtesy of the
Dance Collection, New York Public
Library at Lincoln Center.

was François Delsarte (1811–1871), who based a new system for analyzing movement on the belief that human physicality directly manifested human spirituality. In the United States in the late nineteenth century, Delsarte's system was used in the growing physical culture movement to inspire self-expression by cultivating relaxation, equilibrium, and flexibility—the attributes of a natural body—so that the body would immediately make clear a person's sentiments. Delsarte's theories also influenced dramatists and dancers attempting to decipher and represent human feelings.

Based on an occult interpretation of the Christian Trinity, Delsarte organized the human psyche into a triune system of functions—what he called the mental, the emotional, and the vital—and proposed an identical trinity in the structure and function of the human body. The head corresponded to mental activity, the torso to emotion, and the pelvis to vitality. The head, in turn, was divisible into its own mental, emotional, and vital zones—the upper forehead, the face, and the back of the head—as was each part of the body. Once all parts of the body had been identified with one of the three principles, patterns governing the interrelationships of the parts were determined. Body parts moving in opposition to one another were fundamentally vital, whereas those parts moving parallel to one another were mental. Successive movements, associated with the emotions, were, as Ted Shawn explains, of two kinds: "The Good, the True, the Beautiful, and all normal emotional expressions use successions—evil, falsity, insincerity, etc. use reverse succession." [67]

Both Shawn and St. Denis studied with several Delsarte teachers, and both were guided by Delsarte's principles in developing their movement vocabularies. An illustration of successive movement from Shawn's *Every Little Movement* outlines the relevance of Delsartian theory to expressionist dance:

Suppose someone in his room hears a knock on the door—an unexpected visitor. (1) On the command "Come in" the door is opened and the visitor is someone much loved, welcome, and he is glad to see her. The eye reports to the brain those facts—the brain sends out orders to be glad. So, successively, the eyes light up, the mouth smiles, the chest rises, the movement flows successively through the shoulder, elbow, and wrist into a welcoming gesture of the hands, and downward through the legs producing a walk which carries him towards the welcome visitor. (2) The same beginning situation leads to seeing that the unexpected visitor is one who for various reasons is not welcome, but tact, diplomacy, politeness, provide the need to be polite and *appear* to be glad to see the visitor. The eye reports to the brain, and the brain sends out orders, "You don't like this person, but you must not let him know it—welcome him cordially." So, he starts walking towards the visitor, his hand comes out first in a gesture of welcome, and gradually the reverse succession works inward, until eventually and at last there is a smile of welcome.[68]

In everyday life as well as in the danced representation of life, interior feelings guided the movements of the body into forms that could be identified by the serious student of human movement. According to Shawn, the choreographer wanting to express either genuine gladness or deceptive cordiality would first consider the flow of movement through the body and then apply the same principle, where appropriate, to the organization of groups of dancers moving in space. Thus strong, violent emotions should be expressed by an explosive expansion of the group, whereas fear or repulsion should be shown by a centripetal group pattern.

Rhetoricians of the eighteenth century had studied sets of correspondences between feeling and movement; Delsarte was concerned with analogous systems in both realms. The eighteenth-century choreographer John Weaver, following the rhetoricians' guidelines, based representations of anger on the concurrence of the behavior and the emotion—"The left Hand struck suddenly with the right; and sometimes against the Breast" meant anger. Although Weaver believed that the feeling of anger caused the physical movement, there was no underlying system that related the psychological to the physical. People felt as they moved. The choreographer, in turn, observed and then amplified the behavior in order to duplicate its visual features in the dance. In contrast, Delsarte proposed analyzing the systemic organization of each emotion or idea, which could then be *replicated* in a system of bodily poses and movements. According to his theory, the choreographer representing anger first needed to understand the vital agitation, the emotional assertion, and the mental judgment that formed the experience of anger. Then that choreographer could determine the corresponding physicalization of anger in the body's vital shoulder, emotional elbow, and mental wrist joints. In a "true" expression of anger, the movement would flow from the torso successively outward through the joints of the arm.

Although most expressionist choreographers did not engage in this detailed analysis, they were influenced by the Delsartian interpretation of bodily movement. Graham and Humphrey studied Delsarte's theories at the Denishawn school, and Humphrey eventually articulated her own principles of composition, which clearly evolved from Delsarte's approach. According to Humphrey, motion, as contrasted with repose, was inherently dramatic and expressive. To understand and enhance this expressiveness, one could analyze the design, rhythm, and dynamics of motion. For example, symmetrical design suggested a dull quiescence, whereas asymmetry indicated tension and conflict. Rhythms in the movement that followed the natural cycle of breathing suggested the calm, inevitable ebb and flow of human events, whereas metered rhythms that placed the body in a particular place at a particular time suggested more excitement. Dynamics combined the tempo of a rhythm with the tension of the body's muscular action to produce intensities of movement ranging from "the smoothness of cream to the sharpness of a tack."[69] To give the dance its shape, the choreographer needed only to determine the correspondences between the dance's theme and these three principles of movement.

The same set of assumptions informed Wigman's work. Her mentor Laban, although far more concerned with the precise description of the body in motion than with the Delsartian interpretation of body parts, nonetheless assumed that any manifestation of the principles of space, time, weight, or flow in movement resulted from psychological forces. From Laban's study of movement effort, Wigman derived principles of space, time, and energy in movement remarkably similar to Humphrey's. She referred to Laban's insights as the American choreographers referred to Delsarte—to clarify both the intention of their movement and its universality.

The expressionist choreographers' dedication to *replicating* human feeling resulted in scenarios far less complex than those of the nineteenth-century story ballets. Rather than depicting the adventures of characters, they tended to focus on portrayals in depth of a given moment in the character's psyche. Characters were shown progressing through a sequence of feelings that usually intensified, climaxed, and then died away. Most action grew out of a plausible, coherent development of emotional states rather than any attempt to present a story.

Ruth St. Denis's early solo *Radha* was typical in its subject matter and scenario: the curtain opened to reveal the interior of an elaborate Hindu temple. Priests entered and paid homage to the goddess Radha, seated on a pedestal upstage. St. Denis, as Radha, then stirred to life and came forward to begin "The Dance of Sight," the first of five dances dedicated to the senses, each more intensely seductive than the last. The performance culminated in a "Delirium of the Senses," an ecstatic whirling sequence ending in the dancer's collapse and a complete blackout on stage. The lights came back up on Radha meditating with a lotus blossom and then returning to her pedestal and her motionless *samadhi*.[70]

Ostensibly *Radha* portrayed a Hindu goddess tempted by earthly pleasures who finally renounced them for a life of religious meditation. But like the allegorical court dances of the Renaissance, Radha contained a deeper meaning founded on the tension between sensuality and asceticism, between material perceptions and mystical knowledge. Renaissance choreographers had concerned themselves with similar themes to locate the human being socially and morally within a universal plan. St. Denis, however, like other expressionist choreographers, not only defined the human condition as the focal point of the universe but also construed it in terms of psychological issues and concerns. By assuming the identity of Radha, she did not, like an eighteenth-century dancer, enhance the image of humanity, using her godly role as an attractive showcase for the individual person. Instead, she repre-

Ruth St. Denis in *Radha* (1904).
Courtesy of the Dance Collection,
New York Public Library at
Lincoln Center.

sented the relationship between spiritual and material desires as an ongoing struggle within every human being.

Another relationship that concerned expressionist choreographers was that of the individual to the social group. Doris Humphrey's *New Dance* (1935) took as its subject this relationship, attempting to create a utopian vision of human society in which individual desires and group needs would coincide. The dance consisted of seven sections: "Prelude," "First Theme," "Second Theme," "Third Theme," "Processional," "Celebration," and "Variations and Conclusion." The opening section, because it stated all the movement to be used throughout the dance but without apparent order or development, was meant to symbolize a random, nonhomogeneous collection of individuals. In the "First Theme" and "Second Theme" sections, Humphrey and her colleague Charles Weidman performed movement that was slowly taken up by the other female and male dancers, respectively. In the "Third Theme," the two groups moved together in processional toward a jubilant celebration of their newfound community. In the final section of the piece, the dancers swept around the stage in a pinwheel formation that allowed individual dancers to break away, perform solos, and then rejoin the group.

Humphrey summarized her intentions in the piece:

Whether it was my personal life within this world or my sense of technical sureness that impelled me into these three dances [*New Dance*, *Theatre Piece*, and *With My Red Fires*] is difficult to say. I believe it was both. Anyone could tell you what was wrong but no one seemed to say what was right. It was with this mental conflict that I approached *New Dance* first, determined to open up to the best of my ability the world as it could be and should be: a modern brotherhood of man. I would not offer nostrums and I could not offer a detailed answer. It was not time for that, but it was time to affirm the fact that there is a brotherhood of man and that the individual has his place within that group.[71]

The impact Humphrey envisioned would result not from the presentation of an idealized community but from the reconciliations—of male and female, individual and group, similarity and difference—that in

Humphrey's judgment underlay the successful establishment of any utopia. The nonspecific costumes, which distinguished the sexes of the dancers but not their historical or ethnic identity, and the set design, a cluster of portable boxes, both enhanced the abstractness of the dance movement and drew the viewer's attention to the movement phrases within the group. As dancers first watched and then participated in the statement of themes and the eventual integration of themes into a unified choreographic statement, the viewer could apprehend the thematics of community in any time or place.

In general, expressionist choreographers approached the subject matter of their dances as a set of dialectically related forces, between individual and group, as in Humphrey's dances, or between the spiritual and the material, as in St. Denis's. Humphrey spoke repeatedly about the importance of choosing a dynamic theme for the dance, claiming that only with conflict could the theme generate the dramatic tension essential to a good dance.[72] But even as the dance developed out of the tension inherent in the theme, it was nonetheless the occasion for a synthesis of the forces producing the conflict. These dances did not always conclude with an optimistic resolution; however, by demonstrating an organic relationship between antagonistic forces, they encompassed the tension between these forces as an inevitable part of the human condition.

The dance not only synthesized opposing forces in the subject matter but also reconciled the various antagonisms inherent in the creative process itself. The opposition between spontaneity and craft, cited frequently by all expressionist choreographers, was described by Mary Wigman in highly dramatic terms: "I knew that, without killing the creative mood, I had to keep the balance between my emotional outburst and the merciless discipline of a super-personal control, and thus submitted myself to the self-imposing law of dance compositions."[73] Once the initial phrases of movement had been discovered, the choreographer refined and abstracted them further while still sustaining their personal relevance and power. If the instinctual impulse burst forth unchecked, the dance would lack form and impact. If, on the other hand, the composition lost its personal motivation and urgency, the dance would become an academic exercise.

Both by treating body parts systematically and by treating individual dancers as systemic parts of one group, choreographers approached organically the integration of tensions inherent in the creative process and the subject matter. In the photo of Mary Wigman and her dancers, for example, the varying arm shapes suggest that each dancer's experience of a common concern is different: each portion of the arm, hand, and finger contributes its distinct message. At the same time, each body replicates that same message with respect to the group. Rather than indicate basic patterns, the arms appear to develop out of the dynamic balance within each body and within the group's body. Similarly, Graham's ensemble in *Primitive Mysteries* (1931), although it uses a more linear set of shapes for the dancers' bodies, still achieves an organic sculptural integrity, with each dancer's shape functioning expressively to enhance the dynamic presence of the whole. Whereas the disposition of dancers on stage in the eighteenth century created a panorama of social differences based on social class, gender, and technical accomplishment, the arrangement of dancers in expressionist pieces like these demonstrated the various parts of a single social organism.

The relationship between music and dance developed from similar organic principles. Music seemed to offer both a structure and an emotional development the choreographer could follow. Choreographers fitted movement to the rhythmic and dynamic properties of the music without actually *imitating* the music or attempting to make it visible.[74] Musical syntax guided them in developing their own thematic concerns. Humphrey summarized this relationship between music and dance: "Dance is the wordless art of the physical body, always speaking in its own ways of human beings, no matter how abstracted . . . it is not an independent art; it is truly female, needing a sympathetic mate, but not master, in music."[75] Music contributed the "mas-

Mary Wigman and dancers in the
1920s. Courtesy of the Dance
Collection, New York Public Library
at Lincoln Center.

Martha Graham and Company in
Primitive Mysteries (1931). Photo
1935 by Barbara Morgan. ©

culine" syntactic structure for the dance, focusing the dance as it elaborated its own version of the dramatic narrative but not subordinating it.

Beyond their frequent references to the importance of understanding music, choreographers said little about the procedures for sequencing the movements of the dance. These procedures, because they involved decisions that were felt, not reasoned, were ineffable. Unlike the eighteenth-century choreographers who seemed to delight in explaining their compositional strategies, the expressionist choreographers saw the process as too personal and also too inevitable to describe. They knew the movement was right because of the way it felt when performed or when envisioned.

As the choreographer's intuition, and to a certain extent the music, determined the dance's syntax, so too the choreographer's style determined the style of the dance. In the eighteenth- and nineteenth-century ballets, choreographers' stylistic innovations prescribed a new approach to the existing lexicon or additions to the lexicon that referred to a specific ethnic or historical culture. But style was equally associated with an entire nation's approach to art, as in the devotion of the English to pantomime, of the Russians to romanticism, of the Danish to simplicity and precision, and so forth. At the other end of the spectrum, style was identified with specific performers whose virtuosity allowed them to move in new ways. Throughout the period, style was an attribute of all these variations, from national to personal, that the ballet as an established tradition could undertake. The work of the expressionists, with its emphasis on the individual creativity of the choreographer, redefined style as one of the choreographer's principal messengers.

The burgeoning tradition of expressionist dances arose from an increased sense of the body's weight while moving, a preference for continuous movement through adjacent parts of the body suggesting a sinuous totality, and an emphasis on the torso as an independent area in which movement frequently began. But each choreographer used body parts and movement qualities differently. Duncan's humanism, evident in her weighted, full-bodied, robust commitment to movement, contrasted with St. Denis's mysticism, her more ethereal and delicate sensuality. Wigman's tensile central body and peripheral ornamentation lent her work a brooding intensity quite unlike Humphrey's lyricism, the result of a sequential flow of movement through the periphery of the body combined with the swinglike cycles of fall and rebound. Each choreographer's style helped define a particular artistic mission, a different version of both the world and the artist's role in it.[76]

From initial idea to final production, the choreographer's intensely personal search for the right expression oriented the realization of the dance. Unlike the court ballet choreographers, who collaborated extensively with composers and designers, the expressionists, although they might commission music and set design, controlled the form the dance took. Unlike the eighteenth-century choreographers who brought together the autonomous creations of composer and designer to make one display, expressionists approached each supporting art in terms of its functional role in the dance. In this Wagnerian integration of the arts, music provided both a cerebral structure and a spiritual power, while costumes and lighting indicated the dramatic context or occasion. Movement represented the whole range of individual feelings. The choreographer integrated the matter and motivation of each art into an organic whole—the dance.

Performers were not asked to master the dance or contribute innovations in form as much as to learn a new way of moving and, in so doing, to connect their personal histories to the archetypal life patterns of the dance. Konstantin Stanislavsky (1863–1938) only confirmed what dancers had already apprehended about the new dance: it was not enough to execute the movements of astonishment, anger, or rapture perfectly.[77] Rather, dancers had to feel these things fully during the performance or, more precisely, bring a full psychological involvement with the dance to each performance, so that the objectified, choreographed version of these feelings would come to life on the stage. Performers drew on their own pasts to identify with the danced version of human feeling and to experience the transcendental synthesis of personal sentiment and universal form.

In its various manifestations, expressionist dance offered viewers a similar transcendental experience. The audience, drawn into the dance by the power of its characters and its symbolic forms, no longer played the role of spectators or voyeurs but empathized with the dramatic action. As the process of identification between viewer and dance gathered momentum, the dichotomies of intellect and emotion, form and feeling, personal and universal dissolved, and the viewer was swept into the catharsis or ecstasy of the moment. The experience of the audience seemed to affirm the choreographer's belief in a universal human condition, for despite their different experience of the dance, all the viewers in the theater felt a communal involvement in it.

In withdrawing from Graham's company and dedicating himself to the presentation of his own work, Cunningham repeated the pioneering gesture of his mentor. However, unlike other third- and fourth-generation modern dancers—Valerie Bettis, Erick Hawkins, Hanya Holm, Pauline Koner, José Limón, Daniel Nagrin, Alwin Nikolais, Anna Sokolow, and Paul Taylor,[78] among others—who studied with Graham, Humphrey, or Wigman and then left to pursue their own artistic visions, Cunningham set out not to elaborate his own vocabulary of expression but to challenge the very idea of expression through movement. After collaborating with John Cage in New York and at Black Mountain College, he realized that his aesthetic interests required an altogether new way of conceptualizing choreography, one that could be described as *reflective* rather than *replicative* in its basic mode of representation.

Three related concerns soon became evident in his work: an anarchistic involvement with the conventions of expressionist dance, a desire to show the makings of a dance, and an absolute devotion to the activity of moving. By the early 1960s, Cunningham had made dances that took place in gymnasiums, lofts, and theaters-in-the-round. He

Objectivist Dance from the 1950s to the Present

had incorporated walking and other pedestrian gestures into his movement vocabulary. He had refused to coordinate music with dance movement and had used music devoid of apparent structure or emotional content. Above all, he had used chance procedures to organize the movements of some of his dances.

In effect, Cunningham's decisions turned expressionist dance inside out. His pieces challenged the organic connection between feeling and form by denying the expressionist choreographers' symbolism, their syntax, and their distinction between pedestrian movement and dance movement. In addition, Cunningham shattered the hallowed relationship between dance and music and thwarted viewers' expectations by providing no commentary on the human condition. While his dances exposed the workings of expressionist choreography, Cunningham's interests lay not with the conventions of choreography themselves but with the presentation of articulate movement. His radical actions were necessary to establish a new context for making and viewing dances about movement.

Isadora Duncan, one of the instigators of the previous upheaval in concert dance, had shocked audiences with her liberated use of the sensual body to present the dance's meaning. By contrast, Cunningham disturbed audiences with dances that emphasized the arbitrariness of any correlation between movement and meaning. Earlier representational conventions had developed out of a seemingly unquestioned correspondence between dance and world. John Weaver, for example, asserted that "the left Hand struck suddenly with the right" indicated anger, and expressionist choreographers, following Delsarte, represented anger as the intense, sudden successional flow of movement from torso through the joints of the arm. Cunningham, however, presented a world in which all such correspondences were equally arbitrary. In his dances all movements were treated as carefully composed physical articulations, and as such they took on a concrete, material existence. No longer evanescent forms through which ideals or feelings were expressed, they became the stuff of which dances were made. This materialization of dance movement liberated the senses, as in

Duncan's pieces, but even more, it liberated the art of composing dances.

Once the dance, and by extension the body, was disengaged from the structure of the musical accompaniment and freed from service to the expressive subject, it acquired a variety of choreographic options. Cunningham's use of chance procedures and his eclectic treatment of body parts may have set certain limits, but his methods were far from the only choices possible. The young choreographers and dancers who studied with Robert Ellis Dunn at Cunningham's studio in the late 1950s and early 1960s—they came to be known as the Judson Church group because they presented their work at the Judson Memorial Church in New York in the early 1960s—experimented with a variety of choreographic procedures ranging from chance to mathematical formulas to game structures to bricolage.[79] They expanded the dance lexicon to include commonplace tasks performed by people untrained in any dance techniques. They produced dances not only in galleries, lofts, and churches but also on rooftops, in parking lots, or in successive locations, so that the audience had to move from place to place.

Cunningham's dances had hinted at these possibilities, but it was the Judson choreographers in their own work throughout the 1960s and early 1970s who systematically challenged the existing vocabularies, frames, and artistic functions of the dance. Motivated in some cases by a strong social and political awareness, they sought to liberate the body and the dance from what they perceived as the psychological domination of the expressionists and the virtuoso orientation of the ballet. They used untrained performers, minimalist vocabularies, and a matter-of-fact style to suggest a continuum between art and life that would both make dance more accessible to the audience and challenge the elitist conception of art embodied in the rigorous physical or emotional demands on choreographers and dancers made by the traditions of ballet, by expressionist modern dance, and even to a certain extent by Cunningham's own work. To establish a more democratic relationship with the audience, one in which viewers would neither be seated according to the price of a ticket nor be told precisely where to look by

Trisha Brown Dance Company in
Group Primary Accumulation
(1973). Photos by Babette
Mangolte. ©

the frame of the proscenium, the dances were presented in theaters-in-the-round and other open settings.

Some of these dances tested the limits of art by including so many elements of ordinary life as to seem undifferentiated from it. For *Satisfyin' Lover* (1967), Steve Paxton recruited entirely untrained "dancers" who wore ordinary street clothes and walked in seemingly random configurations from one side of a space to another.[80] In Yvonne Rainer's *Room Service* (1963) performers transported furniture, and in *We Shall Run* (1963) they ran through the space while Hector Berlioz's *Requiem* played in the background. Other dances undermined the boundaries between art mediums. Visual artists like Robert Rauschenberg and Robert Morris frequently contributed pieces to the Judson performances and used Judson choreographers as performers. By transplanting the visual arts into the space and time of dance performance, they developed striking theatrical images as well as new insights into the human body and human movement. In one of Rauschenberg's pieces, for example, Steve Paxton propelled himself around the stage while lying on his stomach in a chicken coop on rollers and eating a plate of fried chicken. In another, Deborah Hay danced with her torso encased in a large birdcage filled with five white doves.

As nonsensical as they might seem, these experiments were carefully composed, producing powerful dramatic statements. They confirmed that any movement could be defined as dance, but they went beyond this conceptual stance in their aesthetic impact. In Rainer's *We Shall Run*, for example, the paths of running dancers were designed to create complex rhythmic and spatial configurations requiring intricate shifts of weight and direction. And Rainer's *Room Service*, by disengaging actions from their functional context, asked viewers to attend closely and perhaps for the first time to simple activities like moving a tire.[81] The care and detail with which dancers manipulated these objects gave their actions a trenchant eloquence that transcended both their pedestrian origins and the iconoclastic message of the dance. Similarly, Trisha Brown turned the activity of walking on its side by harnessing dancers so that they could traverse museum walls and sides of buildings.[82] In so doing, she offered a rich visual and kinesthetic image that was even more compelling than the intriguing idea of walking on walls. Having readjusted their movement to accommodate the new distribution of weight, dancers progressed across the surfaces with an eerie sureness, their form of travel uncanny yet familiar.

Even dances as suffused with symbolic connotations as Brown's *Rummage Sale and the Floor of the Forest* (1971)—in which dancers suspended in a rope gridwork above an actual rummage sale endlessly climbed in and out of various articles of clothing—insisted on the preeminence of bodily articulation. In this piece, the tedium of dressing and undressing and the inevitability and futility of the consumer's search for the perfect garment emerged as messages out of the consummately physical activity of changing clothes while suspended in the

Yvonne Rainer's *Room Service*
(1963). Photo by Peter Moore. ©

air. Because the dance created no symbolic world out of the rope grid-work and conveyed no message about the world to its audience, any commentary about the human condition was gathered and held together by a pedestrian activity occurring in a quotidian time and place. Adopting a point of view that could be described as more behavioristic than psychosocial, Brown's dances, like others of this period, *reflected* above all else their own physicality.

Of the choreography that came out of the Judson-related performances, Yvonne Rainer's *Trio A* (1966) formulated one of the most eloquent visions of the human body in motion. *Trio A*, a four-and-one-half-minute dance performed either by a single dancer or simultaneously by several dancers, was constructed using guidelines similar to those for minimalist sculpture.[83] Throughout its single sustained phrase, made from an eclectic blend of twists, swings, walks, bends, rolls, kicks, lunges, balances, crouches, and smaller gestural movements of the head and arms, no moves were repeated. The entire phrase occurred in the midrange of bodily extension, occupied a moderate amount of floor space, and maintained a uniform pace, neither fast nor slow, with no perceptible accelerations or decelerations. Perhaps its most striking feature was that it seemed to require a uniformly moderate effort, regardless of the complexity or difficulty of the movement. The dancer accomplished the phrase matter-of-factly but attentively, never once gazing out toward the audience.[84]

Instead of shapes and poses or organically developing phrases, *Trio A* offered only transitions, a continuous sequence of actions without pauses or dynamic changes of any kind. Instead of either masking the effort of performance under an aura of cool aplomb or highlighting the effort as evidence of the struggle to express, Rainer's *Trio A* gave bodily action a sense of accustomed economy:

The execution of each movement conveys a sense of unhurried control. The body is weighty without being completely relaxed. What is seen is a control that seems geared to the *actual* time it takes, the *actual* weight of the body to go through the prescribed motions, rather than an adherence to an imposed ordering of time. In other words, the demands made on the body's (actual)

Yvonne Rainer in *Convalescent Dance*, a version of *Trio A* (1967). Photo by Peter Moore. ©

energy resources appear to be commensurate with the task—be it getting up from the floor, raising an arm, tilting the pelvis, etc.—much as one would get out of a chair, reach for a high shelf, or walk down stairs when one is not in a hurry.[85]

Not only the unhurried weightiness of the body but also the combinations of bodily articulations worked to distort, even as they recalled, the conventional lines of design-oriented dance. Just when one saw a familiar dance shape, the configuration of the body would shift, sometimes to a foreign shape, sometimes to a commonplace shape that seemed oddly out of place in the dance. These fleeting glimpses of classical placement and design unsettled the eye, making the sequence difficult to follow. A similar denial of expressionist dance resulted from the irregular and broken flow of movement from one part of the body to another. The sustained, smooth transfer of weight in *Trio A* was reminiscent of the organic successivity of expressionist movement. The movement, however, never originated anywhere, and the dancer's consistently averted gaze tended to direct the viewer's attention rapidly and unpredictably from body part to whole body or from one body part to another distant part. These distorted allusions to already established forms, along with the shifts and changes in anatomical articulation set forth in the choreography, resulted in an overabundance of visual and kinesthetic images.

Like Cunningham's dances, *Trio A* reverberated with the logic of the bodies who performed it. But because of the medium range of dynamics and bodily extension maintained throughout the dance, the body was never presented as a cultivated entity. It was certainly not a showcase for ideal forms, as in Balanchine's dances, nor even a structure whose organization suggested a movement vocabulary, as in Cunningham's. Instead, the movement itself came to the foreground as intelligent human activity.

Trio A and the Judson performances of which it was a part contained a complex mixture of nihilistic and transgressive impulses, a quest for minimalist purity, a vigorous investigation of syntactic procedures, and a concern with the political relevance of the dance.[86] Underlying these sometimes conflicting concerns, however, and giving the dances their integrity was a commitment to and understanding of human articulation. By disjoining human movement from its pedestrian as well as choreographic and dramatic domains and by then representing it, newly ordered, the Judson choreographers, along with Cunningham, objectivized dance movement. They created the possibility for patterned movement to predominate as the subject matter and message of the dance, a possibility that choreographers like Trisha Brown and Lucinda Childs subsequently pursued as they chose such syntactic strategies as logico-mathematical or other structural formulations to serve as templates for organizing movement.

Brown, for example, in *Locus* (1976), used a brief autobiographical statement as the template for the movement sequence by assigning each letter of the alphabet to a point on an imaginary cube. She devised individual moves that incorporated the points on the cube in the order dictated by the spelling of the narrative. Brown has frequently used structures like this to cast body parts in unpredictable directions, to "cancel, interrupt, and disrupt" her inclinations to move.[87] The result could be described as an excogitation on gravity and momentum, the body slipping through the air as it folds and unfolds its parts.

If Brown during this period exposed the body's pattern-ability, Childs emphasized and continues to develop the patterns themselves—rigorous mathematical principles with which she organizes her dances. Her typical vocabulary of simple hops, skips, gallops, turns, walks, and runs has not offered a new vision of human articulation so much as it has allowed for multiple recombinations of and perspectives on individual moves. Each move can be seen in changing relation to others and at different locations in the performance space. Childs's description of her dance *Radial Courses* illuminates her primary concerns:

Radial Courses, 1976, is for four dancers spatially organized on four overlapping circles of the same size, which are equally distant from each other. There are three phrases, a walking phrase, and two skip hop phrases which are closely identical; however, in the second phrase there is an additional turn which throws the first phrase one beat out of sync with the second when they are executed simultaneously. While the walking phrase takes the dancer one half of the way around his or her given circle, the two skip hop phrases take him 3/4 of the way around. Thus the dancers start out at the same point but continually arrive at different points on their circles according to what combination of phrases they do or whether or not they shift from left to right in doing them. The pace of the dance is determined by the fastest possible walk that can be maintained.[88]

The patterns formed by courses of motion through the space, along with the varying views of each phrase attained by recommencing it at different locations, become the primary focus of the dance. As a result, viewers are encouraged to discern where and how they have seen individual moves before, or what the actual length of a phrase is, or what

Lucinda Childs Dance Company in
Radial Courses (1976). Photos 1977
by Babette Mangolte. ©

principles of substitution and recombination are at work. The movements, although elegantly performed, are just simple enough to suggest that an appreciation of their shapes and designs would be insufficient. The repetitions and variations highlight the dance's structure, so that the viewer can fathom the mathematical templates of the dance.

In Brown's more recent pieces, or in works by Douglas Dunn, a former member of Cunningham's company, both movement invention and the use of syntactic procedures have become increasingly complex. Phrases made from an eclectic vocabulary of movement are broken up, recombined, and performed by other dancers—in different spatial orientations, against a backdrop of contrasting material, and in retrograde—to produce a fast-moving, dynamically varied succession of kinesthetic events. Within this profusion of syntactic and anatomical gambits, the body takes on two related roles: it becomes an entity to jump or roll over, lift, carry, pull, support, or throw as one might any esteemed physical object; and it serves as a locus of postural and gestural articulation. The result—sometimes humorous—is a convergence of bodily logics. Parts of the body typically assumed to be non-weight-bearing or nontouchable easily, if unpredictably, take on those

roles. Unanticipated trajectories, landings, and traversals create stunning kinesthetic paradoxes as one compares what the body might have done with what it actually did.

The opulence of the movement and the formal spaces in which it is performed contrast with the more austere, minimalist concerns of objectivist dance in the late 1960s and 1970s. Settings for the dances, no longer composed from a bricolage of mundane objects, frequently rely on specialized technological innovations. The dancers' wide-ranging skills have also taken on a more virtuoso appearance. The significance of the dances, however, continues to center on the body's enunciations, their unexpected versatility, and their organization. And viewers continue to see an array of kinesthetic images that call for their active participation to grasp the intricate blending of vocabulary and syntax.

Objectivist dance, throughout its various stages, has asked dancers to explore freely their individual responses to the choreography. Movement quality, certain preferences for phrasing, and the size, shape, and anatomical structure of the body inevitably distinguish one dancer from another and give to each an identifiable personal style. Because the choreography focuses on the trace of the movement rather than the design, dancers' bodies do not conform to an ideal as much as they give the movement its distinctive impact. Differences in performance, however, become apparent within the stylistic logic of the choreography that demands a neutral execution of the movement as though it were a daily task. Although no more "natural" than Duncan's return to the Greeks, the straightforwardness of the dancers' performance does ally the dance with the quotidian world. And it presents the dancer as a human being—a practitioner of moving—rather than as a symbol for universal experience. Still, it would be misleading to say that the style of objectivist dance reflects that of the quotidian world. The clear, efficient directness of these dances bears little resemblance to the meandering, halting, even bumbling rhythms of commonplace activities. While they are as calm and effective as ironing, cooking, and carpentering, the dances exhibit an expert economy more properly associated with the movement of professional launderers, chefs, and craftspersons.

Trisha Brown Dance Company in *Locus* (1976). Photo 1977 by Babette Mangolte. ©

Lucinda Childs Dance Company in *Congeries on Edges for 20 Obliques* (1975). Photo by Babette Mangolte. ©

In its exploration of matter-of-fact style, objectivist dance embodies a seemingly paradoxical relation between human feeling and movement: by focusing on the performance of movement as a neutral activity, the dance allows feeling to appear tacitly at the margins of the body and the dance. Although human sentiment is not the subject matter of the dances, nor do the faces or bodies of the dancers give themselves over to the display of feeling, emotion nonetheless enjoys a full, rich presence in these pieces. The individual dancer who is not expressing archetypal experience can instead express the body both as a physical structure and as a subject. Because the dancer's self is not concerned with self-presentation—it does not tell the body how to move or how to express feelings—but rather participates fully in the activity at hand, that self creates an aperture through which it can be viewed. The subject-body thus presents itself as its own passionate message.[89]

Objectivist dances provide a similar opening on their own choreographic workings, sometimes through kinesthetic irony, the unexpected alliances of the anatomical and syntactic possibilities they present, and frequently through their treatment of the other mediums composing the performance. Brown has even incorporated into several of her pieces spoken dialogue that comments on the production of the choreography. Instructions like those in *Line Up* (1977) for varying the movement sequence are given by one dancer to the rest of the group, alerting the audience to some of the procedures governing the dance's composition. In another section of the same piece, dancers confer with one another about accomplishing the specific task of maintaining contact between the ends of six-foot-long poles as the dancers move under and around them. ("Hold up. OK. I'm on.") These verbal cues function similarly to Rauschenberg's sets for Cunningham's dances, where the bare brick wall at the back of the theater or the lowered boom of lights calls attention to the production of the event, asking viewers to comprehend not only the movement but also the circumstances surrounding and informing it.

Even though Brown's verbal commentary precisely describes events as they occur, the narrative remains strangely distant from the activity of the dance. Instructions like "Spill, Diane" or "Branch, Vicky" have an obvious effect on the dancers, but the commands fail to elucidate the variation being performed. Like Rauschenberg's sets, the commentary coexists alongside the dance, interacting with the choreography on logistic but not symbolic grounds. This gap between talking and dancing both requires viewers to suspend their reliance on the descriptive capacity of language and reinforces the materiality of the movement. A similar effect occurs in *Accumulation (1971) With Talking (1973) Plus Watermotor (1977)* when Brown recites excerpts from two stories about an early performance of the solo she is dancing at that moment without ever describing her movements with the words or illustrating her words with the movements. The independence of speech and movement produces the highly unusual effect of a talking person and a moving person existing simultaneously at the site of the

Trisha Brown in *Accumulation (1971) With Talking (1973) Plus Watermotor (1977)*. Photos 1978 by Babette Mangolte. ©

same body. Watching Brown, viewers experience the same tension evident in *Trio A* between the references to earlier dance forms and the insistence on simple physical articulation, but in Brown's piece, the disparity occurs between coincident discourses.

This autonomy of all the mediums of the performance, as much as their various reflections on the dance's circumstances, creates for the viewer a new autonomy as well. Unlike allegorical, neoclassical, or expressionist traditions, all of which fused in their individual ways the supporting arts of music, costume, and scenic design to present the viewer with a single message, objectivist dance actively dis-integrates the various mediums, thereby calling into question the viewer's role as receiver of a message. Whereas choreographers in prior traditions directed or collaborated with composers and visual artists, objectivist choreographers concentrate primarily on the movement and its organization. The choreography, when not guided or reinforced by the other mediums, becomes concrete and complete. It speaks its own language, and it alone provides the key to its interpretation.

The choreography thus creates spaces between its own message and the messages of the other mediums, spaces that make room for the viewer to watch the dance selectively. For any given performance, the viewer soon comprehends that the mediums are not saying the same thing in different ways but, instead, are developing their own statements. Viewers can track each statement and perceive correspondences between statements, but always with a sense of shifting from one discourse to another or of attending to two things at the same time. Inevitably, this process of selective attention reflects back on itself, giving viewers a sense of their own contribution to the dance's organization. It does not, however, entrap viewers in cycles of self-reflective awareness because the sheer physical impact of the dance continually recalls their interest.

With objectivist dance, choreographers have become artisans. Much like choreographers of the eighteenth century, and like Balanchine, they do the best job possible with the tools of their trade.

Whereas the "tools" of the neoclassical dance included music, costume, scenery, and, above all, perfect movement, the objectivist choreographers focus on compositional procedures and on inventing unprecedented movement. Still, like the neoclassical choreographers, objectivist choreographers make dances in which the appearance of the dance *is* its meaning. No deep significance, as in expressionist or allegorical dance, resides in the movement. The dances are about what they look like.[90] Objectivist dance, however, represents the human being in a new place in the order of things—as involved in a more particularized and, perhaps, a more humble existence. Because they simply present individual people in motion, the dances clearly do not presume to represent idealized experience or experience that might be common to all people. Instead, they cast the human being as a maker of patterns within a world of patterns and pattern makers. And although they insist on the validity of presenting articulate movement, they do not presume to tell the viewer what and how to watch. The patterns created by the dance are consciously and willfully composed as an assemblage of independent, individual offerings, one that includes the readings of the viewers themselves.

CHAPTER FOUR

Writing Dancing:

The Viewer as Choreographer

in Contemporary Dance

By giving ontological status to dance movement, Cunningham and the other objectivist choreographers enable the reading of dance I have undertaken here. Alternative theories about choreographic meaning have been proposed within expressionist and allegorical traditions, based on their assumptions about the intrinsic connection between movement and meaning, as well as within the neoclassical tradition where dance movement, although conceived as an artificial creation, nevertheless corresponds inevitably to other events in the world. Objectivist dances, however, refer to their own structured movement, and because of this they construe a fundamentally arbitrary relationship between movement and meaning. Once the relation between movement and its referent is questioned, the *how* of choreography as a system of codes and conventions becomes available for study, along with the different approaches to representation itself. This study was conducted in a theoretical way in chapter 2 and then in relation to a historical situation in chapter 3.

The aesthetic suppositions of objectivist dance informed not only the collection of the historical materials in chapter 3, but also their organization. Instead of tracing the development of a single form, I have recounted the history of dance as an assemblage of different choreographic projects. Renaissance choreographers might have approached the history of the dance as a fluid world of implicit moral analogies; eighteenth-century choreographers might have classified all historical dances as they conformed to various models; and expressionist choreographers might have assessed the evolution of dance as the integration of functionally distinct parts into an organic whole.[1] In the objectivist manner of Cage and Cunningham, I have presented a history of the dance that juxtaposes four ways of perceiving and organizing relations between things in the world. The dance reader, like the viewer of objectivist dances, chooses among them with a clear understanding of the conventions governing each approach.

Implicit in the act of attending to the conventions that give dance its meaning, however, the reader may find a fifth model for the choreographic process, one that reflects back on both the representational process in dance and the representation of dance in a book like this.[2] For even though the objectivist approach, the juxtaposition of discrete mediums, inspired the arrangement of the four models of dance presented here, it does not support, or in a sense even permit, the act of writing about dancing. Cunningham, especially, believes in the untranslatability of each medium; for him, dance speaks messages in its own language that can never be repeated in another. The writing of this book therefore must find its basis in another model of dance, one that assumes the autonomy of dance movement and the integrity of dance as a discipline but nonetheless permits parlance among mediums. This interdisciplinary approach to dance composition and its implications for the dance viewer are the focus of the discussion that follows. Although interdisciplinary choreographic techniques inform much of contemporary dance, I have chosen to illustrate their use by three widely divergent groups—the Grand Union, Meredith Monk and the House, and the Twyla Tharp Dance Company—because these three groups together define the contours of an interdisciplinary choreographic model.

Although dances conforming to this fifth model take an objectivist stance toward movement, they nonetheless counter the objectivists' contention that movement stripped of any symbolic references to the world is the dance's message.[3] Objectivist dance focuses on the body's movement, allowing any references to the world to accrue alongside the dance as a by-product of the body's motion. The reflexive choreography I am describing here assumes that the body will inevitably refer to other events, and because of this asks how those references are made. Whereas objectivist dance has laid bare the conventions governing representation to allow the body to speak its own language, reflexive choreography works with these same conventions to show the body's capacity to both speak and be spoken through in many different languages. Because these dances expose the representational process as part of the choreography, their message is concerned with the body's movement, but also with the process of messagemaking.[4] In commenting on their own production, these dances often address the issue of the viewer's hermeneutic role. Unlike objectivist dance, which asks viewers to perceive, more than it invites them to interpret, the choreography, reflexive dance involves viewers in the task of sorting through and synthesizing the multiple interpretations it identifies.

The impulse simultaneously to represent the world in dance and to show the act of representation animated the Judson Church group performances of the early 1960s.[5] This complex moment in the history of dance produced Yvonne Rainer's *Trio A*, a dance with clear objectivist intentions, as well as dances like Lucinda Childs's *Carnation* (1964) and David Gordon's *Random Breakfast* (1963), in which highly theatrical scenes both hinted at and debunked narrative sequence.

In *Random Breakfast*, for example, Gordon and his partner, Valda Setterfield, worked with a bizarre assortment of costumes and props, fashioning from them the possibility for narrative rather than an actual story. Setterfield appeared as a dowager-empress performing a striptease, as a classical dancer, and as a nun who "leapt upon a pair of child's bedsprings, slowly picked up six plastic washbaskets and knocked them down with a large ball, and shoved a cream pie in her own face."[6] Gordon intervened as a brash entrepreneur explaining how to make a successful modern dance, as a Spanish senora complete with strapless lace dress and mantilla, and as a shy young man in top hat and tails meandering around the stage to Judy Garland's "Somewhere over the Rainbow." Gordon's and Setterfield's characters followed one another as though they had some relationship, but viewers could discover no logical or causal connection between their actions. Even in the striptease, normally a predictable performance, Setterfield used repetition of the movements of undressing and a pragmatic style to recast the sensuous as ordinary, neutral. The Judson repertoire, like other dances in the 1960s, included such procedures as the surreal gathering of images and the juxtapositions of pragmatic and expressive gestures that bracketed the very idea of narrative and, along with it, the viewer's role in responding to narrative.

Influenced by the Judson aesthetic, works by the Grand Union and Meredith Monk show a systematic and sustained use of these reflexive techniques, whereas Tharp, especially in her recent work, adopts them more sporadically so that her work lacks Monk's and the Grand Union's paradigmatic integrity. Using reflexive choreographic conventions to construct and then deconstruct symbolic fields for the body and for the dance, Monk, like the Grand Union, shows how dance acquires meaning. In her own way, she incorporates into the performance the viewer's active search for meaning.[7] In contrast, Tharp's use of reflexive techniques initially suggests the possibility for a collaborative relationship with the audience, but because she neither sustains the techniques nor connects them to the subject matter of the dance, she ultimately closes off the dance from viewers and presents it as a *fait accompli*.[8] The following discussion expands on these differences, first by briefly describing the three groups' works in terms of frame, mode of representation, style, vocabulary, and syntax and then by examining each group's treatment of the relationship among the various mediums that contribute to the performance, as well as the relationship between subject and body and between the dance as a whole and its viewers.

The Grand Union, 1975. Photo by
Babette Mangolte. ©

The Grand Union was formed in 1970 by a collective of choreographers, most of whom had participated in the Judson concerts of the early 1960s.⁹ Although it underwent fluctuations and changes in membership, the group performed throughout the United States for six years and also toured Italy and Japan. Its performances were inconsistent and unpredictable. The members often chose music, collected costumes and props, and arranged the performance space for each concert at the last minute. Underlying these impromptu decisions, however, was a commitment to cultivating the liminal ground between art and life and to collaborating on dance not as a beautifully fashioned product but as a choreographic process.

Most Grand Union performances were presented in gymnasiums, galleries, or churches, places that afforded a theater-in-the-round viewing situation and a casual, makeshift atmosphere. Often, viewers entered to find the dancers already moving around: warming up, talking with one another, or arranging various props to be used that evening. The dancers' activity gradually evolved into the performance itself, although no specific beginning was announced. During the performance, dancers occasionally moved out into the seating area and frequently looked at or addressed audience members directly. They smiled, wiped the sweat away, scratched themselves, or rearranged clothing, all with matter-of-fact cordiality. Dancers acted independently—practicing a movement phrase, stretching, twirling a rope, carrying a ladder, or manipulating any of the mundane items scattered throughout the space. Sometimes they coalesced briefly in duets or trios before returning to their individual pursuits, or else a small group might persist in collaborating by proposing various structures for their heretofore unrelated activities.

Suddenly, out of a collage of movement, dialogue, costumes, props, and excerpts from popular music, a dramatic, archetypal vignette of American life would emerge—the hangman and the guilty cowboy, the surfer riding the breakers, or the all-American farm couple. The scene would then evolve predictably for a few moments—the cowboy would

The Grand Union, 1972. Photos by
Babette Mangolte. ©

accept the noose, the farmers complain about the drought—until interrupted by the metacommentary that appeared sporadically throughout the performance. This self-reflexive dialogue had a dual focus: the logistic and pragmatic details of accomplishing some effect and the performers' thoughts and feelings about their actions. The description of a typical scene exemplifies the multileveled commentary:

For instance, David Gordon and Nancy Lewis have been acting out a B-movie scene: they are tenant farmers, worried about the rain and the crops. He is lying on his back, obviously incapacitated, and she is begging him to get up just this once to help her handle the crisis. They break character to discuss who is supposed to sing the climactic song, behaving as though this had all been scripted already—Lewis objects to singing it all by herself, Gordon assures her he'll join in on the chorus. He promises to turn over when she comes to the line about water. . . . Then, they're on, reassuming the frame . . . of the scene they've just been discussing. Steve Paxton has been assigned the role of the thunder, and as Lewis sings he carts a chair, a bucket of water, a tall standing fan, and a long silk scarf closer to them. Barbara Dilley moves in to sprinkle water from the bucket as Paxton holds the billowing scarf in front of the fan. The group cooperates to make the scene develop . . . and suddenly Gordon gets up and says, "I want to turn this into an up moment. Forget the farm, forget the crops; forget the drought. Let's think about surfers and sand. . . ." A Beach Boys record comes on. Paxton and Dilley move over to where Douglas Dunn has been dancing on top of a tall stool, they wrap the scarf around him, and now Dunn looks like he's riding the waves.[10]

The Grand Union developed four kinds of voices in their performances: those of the characters, of the actors playing the characters, of the choreographers or playwrights scripting the action, and of the stagehands. The effect created by their sudden shifts from one voice to another was both jarring and amusing. Comments ranged from poignant to banal, from insightful to self-indulgent. But the process, which produced an open, cooperative atmosphere among the dancers, also enabled a sustained self-scrutiny of the entire performance.

Metacommentary was only one of several techniques the Grand Union employed to create a self-reflexive and collaborative atmosphere. Another was improvisation: the dancers choreographed the dances as they performed them. Members of the company did share a knowledge of certain movements and phrases, material from previous performances, general aesthetic predispositions about matters of style, syntax, and the use of props and music; and assumptions about the constituents of an appropriate performance. They did not, however, know precisely what they would do at any given moment during the performance, and thus their work was endowed with an unusual spontaneity and openness. Sometimes the dancers' intentions collided, producing confusion; and sometimes improvisation gave rise to long periods of boring inactivity. But because the dancers never broke from their attentiveness to the activity of the moment, viewers always saw alert, articulate people appraising the situation and selecting actions that determined the course of events. Members of the audience were encouraged by what they saw to compare decisions the dancers made with decisions they themselves might make in a similar situation. Thus improvisation not only signaled the dance's production to the viewers but also elicited from them a participation that involved assessing the aesthetic decisions the artists made then and there.

And who were the artists? As one watched the members of the Grand Union watching the dance, embodying the dance, and commenting on it, each performer acquired a variety of personae. Performers became the dramatic characters whose lives they portrayed, as well as dancers executing specific movements, collaborators attempting to interest others in their current vision of the dance, and metacommentators giving a context to the entire project. None of these characters could be equated with the true identity of the performer. Just as a collage of contrasting dramatic contexts composed the dance, so the dance itself promoted a constantly shifting self-definition for all performers. Each time they talked or moved, their identities were necessarily determined anew.

This continual shifting of identities could be found more concretely in the Grand Union's use of such props as ropes, boxes, buckets, ladders, and scarves—all ordinary items out of which the dancers created the settings for their dramatic encounters. The rope was a jumprope or a kinetic sculpture; the ladder could be a hiding place or a soap box. Minutes later the rope might become both a lasso and a noose for the cowboy; the ladder, draped with scarves, became a wave for a surfer to ride. Because the ladder still looked like a ladder and the noose attached to no scaffold, these props preserved their own quotidian origins and emphasized the makeshift construction of the setting. Furthermore, the dancers consistently manipulated these objects with a pragmatic style that restated the meaning of the object as a concrete, physical structure. A lively tension was thus created between the props as a *reflective* representation of their own objective identity and their *resemblance* to or *imitation* of different worldly objects.

Movement maintained a similarly dual existence—as concrete physical articulations of the body and as gestures accomplishing some

The Grand Union, 1975. Photos by
Babette Mangolte. ©

expressive or pragmatic task. Frequently, sequences inventoried possible movements, as though the dancer were simply exploring a range of options for bodily articulation that could be performed using a moderate amount of space and effort. Such sequences might evoke verbal comment, especially when duets or trios attempted to coordinate their efforts. Dancers sometimes instructed each other—"Left foot first" or "Try putting your arm a little lower around my back"—as matter-of-factly as they moved. At other times, someone might yell, "Could you put the music on?" Then, to the highly charged rhythm and lyrics of Bob Dylan, Ike and Tina Turner, or Bob Marley, dancers would begin a minimalist version of social dancing, a version that, like the ladder-as-surfer's-wave, kept its identity as a physical event. Movements followed the meter of the music and sometimes cited vernacular dance steps and expressive codes, but the style was economical and understated. The contrast between hard-driving music and unruffled dancing commented drolly on the self-abandonment typical of rock and roll. Even when enacting social dramas, dancers deadpanned. An emphasis on the physicality of enunciating phrases like "Oh darling, what can we do in the face of so much misfortune?" and the reserve of the delivery undercut the viewer's attachment to the character or sympathy with the feelings expressed.

In both their use of props and their changing personae, the Grand Union showed clearly that cultural artifacts and human identity itself depend on context. Even more important, the Grand Union showed *how* the changes of identity occurred. Repeatedly, performers would persist in a given activity while those around them constructed a contrasting narrative. The individuals' activities would slowly take on new meaning as they became embedded in the new social context. Alternatively, the dancers might show that one set of activities could not redefine another set; as a result, two or more scenerios would coexist provocatively, distinct but never completely separate. For example, as one group of dancers rehearsed and commented on a duet involving a lift and the other worked out a suspenseful encounter between cowboy and hangman, each influenced the interpretation of events in the other. Comments of the dancers rehearsing the lift—"I've got too much of your weight at a weak point on my back"—would be infused with the symbolic content of the cowboy scene, while the matter-of-fact support of one body by another—a graphic illustration of the body's weight—lent an added meaning to the cowboy's situation. Such resonances as these, originating in the juxtaposition of movement that signified both itself and something else, pervaded the Grand Union's performance.

Despite their unmanageable length, their unwieldy form, and their self-indulgence, the Grand Union's dances endeared themselves to their viewers. The dancers committed outrageous acts that they mitigated by contrite and astute self-criticism. Wonderfully inventive, courageous, and unpredictable—but also fallible—they barely fit their diverse visions of dance into the collective format of their group improvisations, and the dances, as a result, seemed constantly to burst

The Grand Union, 1973. Photos by
Babette Mangolte. ©

their own seams. Yet the dances emphasized the value of cooperation in group activities and showed how cooperation determined the meaning of those activities. In a climate both supportive and ironic, the dancers developed a sense of community and extended it to include the audience as well.

Meredith Monk

Meredith Monk's career as dancer, choreographer, composer, singer, and actress dates to the mid-1960s, when she performed in the Judson Church concert series.[11] Since that time she and her company, named The House, have performed and toured extensively throughout the United States and Europe. Unlike the Grand Union, who told their stories with the restraint of devout ironists, Meredith Monk and her company approach storytelling with earnest, wholehearted commitment. Even in their seriousness, however, they manage to reflect back on their own performance. While the Grand Union used metacommentary, improvisation, and the polyvalency of gestures and props to refer to their own productions, Meredith Monk uses stop action, surrealist composition, and the juxtaposition of pedestrian and ritualized actions.

At many performances by Meredith Monk and The House, one enters the hall to find in a corner of the space a diminutive version of a living room—two chairs, an antique floor lamp, and a small rug—or perhaps a kitchen—a sturdy wooden table, chairs, mugs, and a teapot. These elements of familiar domestic scenes never occupy the entire performance space, as they would have in early twentieth-century drama, but rather assign a portion of the space to familial affairs. Family and ancestral heritage are consistent themes in Monk's work; the diminutive living room set suggests how the performance elaborates these themes. The set is one of several realms, depicted using only the most essential elements and arranged in a montage, through which both audience and performers journey.

Monk's characters are created out of a few pungent gestures that, like the floor lamp or rug in the living room set, are chosen carefully to

Meredith Monk and Ping Chong in
Paris (1973). Anonymous photo
1974.

Meredith Monk and the House in *Education of the Girlchild* (1973). Top photo 1973 by Peter Moore ©; bottom photo 1973 by Lorenzo Capellini. ©

evoke a richer drama than their limited physical range would otherwise imply. These characters, in historical, ethnic, fantastic, or mythical costume, populate the living room, sit around the kitchen table, and inhabit the other areas of the performance space, fabricating intimate tableaux of domestic family life, or work, or religious activities. Despite the vivid intensity of these powerfully condensed images, however, the characters are far from realistic.

They are unrealistic in part because they assemble in heterogeneous, almost absurd, groupings. At the beginning of *Education of the Girlchild* (1973), for example, five women of various ages, costumed in an assortment of white garments—nightgowns, petticoats, and dresses—sit at the kitchen table. They silently pantomime domestic tasks, converse, read, or listen to each other. Soon, they discover and are joined by a sixth character, a nervous, perky, South American peasant woman, in colorful clothes and a large red sombrero. She is immediately assimilated into the group at the table, participating in their conversation, their mundane tasks, and their meaningful glances, yet visually and symbolically she disrupts the coherence of the European or North American kinswomen. A similar effect is achieved in *Paris* (1974)—a duet evoking Paris garret life—by the simple addition of a mustache to Monk's womanly, if workmanly, garb: a voluminous peasant skirt, padded jacket, and workboots. She looks like a woman wearing a mustache, and in the series of subtle exchanges and nonexchanges between Monk and her male partner, the mustache both disassembles and augments the significance of her character.

Monk's groupings of characters are not only incongruous, but they also participate in scenes that are consistently interrupted. Pantomimed actions are arrested, with gestures suspended in midair, and then resumed. Groups might move and then stop in unison; some members of the group might move while others remain still; or individuals might interject idiosyncratic pauses into their own ongoing sequences. Some actions creep along at an abnormally slow pace, or they accelerate or decelerate, or else performers repeat, well beyond the number of times necessary, the functional task they imitate. The scenes filled with interrupted actions, moreover, follow one another in no logical sequence. Sometimes they seem to offer different perspectives on a central theme, such as the holocaust or the education of a young child. Sometimes they display the surreal syntax of dreams. The sequence of events, however, never manifests causal relations or temporal continuity. Even Monk's long solo from the second half of *Education of the Girlchild*, which takes as its subject matter the predictable maturation from youth to old age, reverses the sequence. Beginning as old woman and ending as young girl, Monk calls attention to narrative expectations while also recasting actions as ritual rather than theater.

The unfolding scenarios reveal that Monk's goal is not to document human social interaction but to represent human ceremonial forms. With repetition, she not only defamiliarizes individual gestures but also establishes the ritual format for events. Somewhat later in *Education of the Girlchild*, the six women leave their table and become involved in a peculiar rite of passage (identified as "A Test" by a large banner carried across the space). Veiled in gauzy fabric, they present themselves to a living sculpture—an altar piece—brought in by the banner carriers. Each woman in turn performs a different act of homage before the figure as it barks and shrieks nonsense orders, all the while growing in stature as it rises from a squatting to a standing position. Although none of the women's exchanges with the idol is identifiable as a prayer, the participants' solemn repetition of the form suggests a sacred rite.

After this Test, whose outcome is never clear, the women journey to a new location, each carrying a miniature symbolic object on her head—a branch, a little red house, a lizard, a chair, a globe. Eventually they become involved in yet another scenario, this time entitled "A Tale." The women, now wearing kerchiefs, dance with mincing prances, to a rhythmic cackle, their fingers curled, their faces cheery and animated. A figure with branches growing out of her head and small childlike puppets in place of hands appears enigmatically off to one

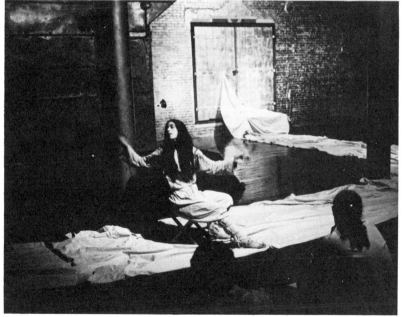

Meredith Monk in *Education of the Girlchild* (1973). Top photo by Philip Hipwell ©; bottom photo by Peter Moore. ©

side. Her presence seems to dispatch a small cavorting nymph, who, by throwing a hood over one of the women, captures her and takes her away. The nymph repeats the sequence with each of the women until Monk, who has throughout acted the part of a young girl, is left, chanting plaintively: "I still have my skin; I still have my mind; I still have my book; I still have my gold ring; I still have my feet; I still have my money; I still have my memory." Eventually she too is carried away.

Several other features in addition to the repetition of sequences contribute to the ritual aura of Monk's dances. From time to time, familiar archetypal figures appear: a robed figure carrying a scythe or a menacing, black-suited commandant. Long swatches of material unfurl, along which processions of characters travel. As scenes fade from one to the next, a ceremonial timekeeper often signals the transition. In *Education of the Girlchild*, for example, a Jewish immigrant couple

Meredith Monk and the House. Opposite page, *Vessel* (1971), Part 1; photo by Ruth Walz ©. This page, Parts 2 and 3; photos by Peter Moore. ©

Meredith Monk and the House
in *Quarry* (1979). Photo by
Johan Elbers. ©

slowly sweep across the space, tapping canes as they go. In *Vessel*
(1971), Part 3, a performer playing the French horn sounds a plaintive
fanfare as each new section begins. In *Venice/Milan* (1976) the familiar banner carriers appear, this time with ornate scrolls like those used
in melodrama or pantomime, to announce the next scene. These formal devices allude to their counterparts in authentic ritual even as they
undermine their own official status. The cane-tapping couple, for instance, seem lost, almost as though they had wandered in from another theater's cast. The French-horn player creates the appropriate
feeling of melancholy, but the sound of his flourish is more muted and
forlorn than that of a traditional fanfare. Solemnly repeating most ceremonial actions in a disarmingly pedestrian way, Monk's characters
seem to combine specific ethnic or historical references and archetypal
gestures with the childlike game of dressing up. The intermingling of
sacred and profane styles in Monk's work serves the same function as

the Grand Union's metacommentary—it gives viewers multiple interpretations, contrasting yet coexistent, of the stream of events.

Monk clearly intends her pieces to move their audiences deeply. Where the Grand Union engaged in self-critical play with images from popular culture, Monk and her company chart the territory of critical concerns: they examine our past, our life's work, human suffering, and dignified human conduct. If the Grand Union's dances were about the process of making, Monk's are about remembering. Her dances remind viewers of the passage of time and the importance of collective practices for commemorating events. When Monk summons images of war and oppression that evoke the horror of inhumanity, she proposes kinship as an antidote. Monk's conception of kinship extends beyond the family to all who respond to the human plight by engaging in ritual with solemnity and humility. Kinship thus defined encompasses the art event and its audience as well.

Twyla Tharp

Twyla Tharp's early choreography explored many of the same experimental issues that interested the Judson choreographers, the Grand Union, and Meredith Monk. Several of Tharp's dances, beginning with *Tank Dive* (1965), contrasted dance and pedestrian movement vocabularies and mixed trained and untrained performers. These dances, set in different environments, including the outdoors, questioned the relationship between particular movement styles or vocabularies and their context or occasion. Tharp could transpose movement from one context to another because she commanded a variety of syntactic procedures. Whether the movement was pedestrian or theatrical in origin, she could manipulate it using simple mathematical equations or principles based on theme and variation. The dances allowed viewers both to see the development of the spatial, temporal, and tensile characteristics of movement and to reflect on the origins and assumptions of several movement idioms. Sometimes, as in *The Bix Pieces* (1971), they offered even more.

Twyla Tharp in *When We Were
Young* (1981). Photo by
Martha Swope. ©

Among the dances of Tharp's early period, *The Bix Pieces* is undoubtedly the most striking and the most reflexive. In this three-part work for five dancers and an actress, Tharp conveys her motives for and intentions in choreographing the dance by superimposing her words on one section of the dance. The piece begins with a solo by Tharp, who manipulates a batonlike stick—is it a cane for soft-shoe dancing, a pointer, or the pride of a young majorette? Tharp continually drops it and receives another until, after an unsuccessful attempt to handle two batons at once, she exits. Five short dances, two duets, a trio, and two quartets follow, displaying a variety of dance forms: a bump-and-grind phrase gives way to a faster-paced disco measure; a sexy, floppy Raggedy-Ann style contrasts with the more proper style of social dance vignettes; ballet mingles with tap dance and fox-trot. In one quartet, a trio of dancers parodies a soloist's serious endeavors, although the dancers seldom acknowledge one another until a final quartet that includes a round of pantomimed greetings and handshaking. Overall, the style is casual, with movement conforming to the meter of the music but not its phrasing or melodic line. Underlying the effortless flow, one sees Tharp's typical expertise at arranging movement.

In the second section of the dance, a narrator appears with the dancers. Carrying Tharp's baton from the opening scene, she begins to comment, as though she were Tharp herself, on the origins of the dance. The jazz music and the atmosphere of the dance commemorate her father's youth, the narrator-choreographer explains. The approach to composition is nonlinear and nonpositional, she continues. As she goes on to describe individual moves, label them in French, and even call out numbers of phrases for the dancers to perform, the commentary and choreography balance precise explanation and metaphoric allusion. The words do not reduce the movement to mere illustration, for there is always far too much activity occurring at any given moment to permit a one-to-one identification. Moreover, the narrator's commentary ranges from specific analysis to remembrances and from remarks about the evolution of the piece to diary entries from the time it was composed, so that no single point of view emerges in the narrative.

Thus when the narrator mentions two major events in Tharp's life that occurred during the making of the dance—the birth of her son and the death of her father—and explains the appropriateness of the dance's rondo section to this succession of events, she connects personal experience and art making without imposing any simplistic causal explanations. In contrast with Balanchine, who denies the influence of the artist's life on art, or Graham, who would advocate a direct connection between the choreographer's feelings and the dance's message, Tharp here suggests a complex vision of artistic creation. She implies that when she choreographs, she is first and foremost involved in making a dance, not in expressing herself. But she also intimates that dances are suffused with the feelings of those who make and perform them and that such feelings are best shown and observed indirectly, peripherally to the main subject of the dance, the movement itself.

The coda of the dance is introduced by the narrator as a reworking of material in the first two sections. Speaking again as the choreographer, she claims that she can invent nothing new in dance except by rehandling extant material, and to prove the point she announces a concentrated version of the dance thus far. Performed to the music of Haydn, the final dance serves as an exquisite prism through which the viewer can review and reflect on the entire dance.

Since *The Bix Pieces*, Tharp has continued to explore choreographic conventions in ways that comment on both the role of the artist and the meaning of dance. In her diverse choreographic incarnations—as radical avant-gardist in the late 1960s and subsequently as the first "modern" dancer to compose for the ballet, for musical comedy, and for figure skating—she has challenged high art assumptions about the artist as extrasensitive witness to the verities of human existence. Her self-proclaimed interest in begging, borrowing, and stealing and her seditious experimentation with the idioms of popular culture have likewise set her apart as the rebellious creator of a new hybrid of dance forms. But with her first compositions for the ballet companies, beginning with *Deuce Coup* (1973), Tharp's work shifts from the experimental to the conventional and from thoughtful investigation to exhilarating entertainment.

Over the past ten years, Tharp has further expanded the repertoire of moves for her dances, using the lexicons of ballet, pedestrian movement, modern dance, baton, jazz, tap dance, social dance, pantomime, martial arts, computerized stick figures, and, most recently, boxing. Her dances also continue to reflect exquisite craftsmanship. The choreography intercalates moves from one lexicon into phrases from another or strings together moves from disparate traditions into complex sequences. Initially, the interruptions in form create abrupt shifts in the viewers' aesthetic expectations. These pieces, like her early works, invite viewers to decipher the origins of a given move or phrase and to assess its relationship to other moves from other lexicons. Eventually, however, the viewer sees all movements as equivalent, governed not by their respective aesthetic traditions but by their arrangement according to the syntactic principles of theme and variation, accumulation, retrograde, reversal, and so on. In Tharp's early work, the objectivist syntactic procedures that disengaged movement from its original context illumined the kinesthetic features of movement; these later dances use objectivist procedures to abstract the movement of various idioms still further, creating polished displays of the visual and rhythmic properties of movement.

Changes in the style of her dances have reinforced this shift in choreographic emphasis. In her early pieces, dancers maintained the casual, pragmatic style of objectivist dance, performing all movement with unassuming involvement in its kinesthetic identity. In recent years, however, the style has grown more complex. Sometimes the dancers' daring and precise execution of complex phrases offers a virtuoso illustration of the form of the movement. Sometimes, the dancers revert to a less obtrusive presentation of movement as fact. At other times, they offer a cool nonchalance—disdaining the glad-handing

The Twyla Tharp Dance Company
with Christine Sarry in *Deuce
Coupe* (1973). Photos 1983 by
Martha Swope. ©

rhetorical appeal of the ballet and the introspective angst of the early modern dance but also isolating themselves as absorbed practitioners of their craft or even members of a hostile elite.

At first glance, Tharp's formal treatment of such an eclectic vocabulary seems to eradicate the barrier between high art and popular culture, but the dances develop no themes to explain or justify the variety and choice of vocabulary. Instead, the dances present incidental narratives of romance and intrigue or nostalgic evocations of mood that offer pretexts for presenting technically demanding, glamorous, and seductive movement. Sumptuously costumed and set to hard-driving popular music, the dances take place in formal proscenium auditoriums and are performed by dancers of exceptional technical prowess from either Tharp's own company or a ballet company. Because the dances are, above all, beautifully choreographed and brilliantly performed, the popular allusions offer only titillating innovations on dance as spectacle.

Twyla Tharp Dance Company in *The Catherine Wheel* (1983). Photo by Martha Swope. ©

Similarly, Tharp's clever parodies of performance logistics remind viewers of the premises of the dance event itself, but they never develop either as a theme in the dance or as a commentary on the main action. The dancer falls down, or runs into a stage curtain while exiting, or steps out of the spotlight and continues soloing in relative darkness; or dancers enter with push brooms and sweep the debris of the previous act from the stage. Isolated moments like these appear throughout Tharp's dances, but they are overwhelmed by the intricate, sensuous, and demanding activity of dancing.

The recent, highly successful *Nine Sinatra Songs* (1984) encapsulates many of these features of Tharp's work. The dance's seven duets and two ensemble sections, performed to nine of Frank Sinatra's most popular songs, derive from the formal principles of ballroom dancing. Each duet alludes to a different dance form—tango, waltz, cha-cha, and so forth—and, consequently, depicts a different amorous relationship between partners. The movement in each dance closely resembles that of the ballroom forms, yet each transfer of weight, balance, dip, glide, and position of the arms and head seems to have been reconsidered and manipulated in some way. The steps are those of the tango or the fox-trot, but performed with a different tension or quality of effort. Phrases vary the spatial and temporal characteristics of the original ballroom choreography, presenting an extraordinary array of minute differences in the ballroom vernacular. We see a hundred ways to support a woman's swoon and countless variations on handholds, lifts, or changes of direction.

Those familiar with the protocol of ballroom dancing become increasingly aware that the dance consists of not only variations on but also parodies of ballroom forms. Dancers vacillate ever so slightly between two positions of the head, as if to say, "Oh dear, I can't remember how the head is held in this section" or "There are just *too* many regulations in this ballroom-dancing business." Alternatively, dancers participate with the music in developing a climactic peak but drop out at the last minute, replacing a dramatic lift or embrace with a more mundane stepping pattern. Or they imbue a neutral moment in the

Twyla Tharp Dance Company in *Nine Sinatra Songs* (1984). Photo by Tony Whitman.

choreography or music with exaggerated desire, rejection, or flirtation. This playful mismatch between dancerly form and romantic content continues until the appearance of the "couple in red." Although the aura of restraint and irony persists, these two pull out most of the stops. Their torrid tête-à-tête culminates when the distraught supine woman is pulled to her feet by successive yanks from the overbearing, self-righteous macho man. The scene is so familiar and yet so thrilling.

Why so thrilling? Three related reasons seem plausible: first, this series of gestures blatantly resolves the tension between the sexes that has been developing throughout the dance—and both sexes are put in their "rightful" places; second, the duet transgresses the bounds of high culture by presenting something crude and lowbrow on the concert stage; and third, the choreography reintroduces and allows us to feel comfortable with traditional sex roles—roles we have come to question over the past twenty years—by means of nostalgia and irony. On the one hand, the dance seems to suggest that relations between

Sara Rudner in Twyla Tharp's *Eight Jelly Rolls* (1974). Photo by Tony Russell. ©

the sexes have always been like those in the duet. Furthermore, the dance glamorizes the traditional roles by aestheticizing the symbiotic association that is possible between masculine and feminine traits. The dancers look so wonderful that one cannot resist a moment's sentimental approbation of the good old days. On the other hand, the parody throughout the dance suggests that both the dancers and the audience "know better" than to take these traditional roles seriously. It is as if the distance from the situation implied by the role playing could liberate one from the oppressive structures of power implicit in the roles themselves.

The dance concludes with an ensemble in which all the couples reappear and mingle on the ballroom floor. The glorious costumes by Oscar de la Renta emphasize the distinctiveness of each couple, and the choreography isolates them from one another. Couples glide by, reiterating phrases from their earlier duets and providing a feast of contrasting colors and movement motifs. The final section neither develops further the characters of the partners, nor establishes the group as a collective, nor shows that the dancers are aware of one another's existence. The formal conclusion reassures viewers that the dance is about spatial design, rhythm, and dynamics rather than contemporary sex roles or romance. Its chic, understated circumvention of a narrative ending allows viewers one last reverie.

In *Nine Sinatra Songs*, as in most of her work over the past ten years, Tharp's self-referential statements—the eclectic vocabulary, ingenious parody, and disaffected style—poke fun at dance traditions without actually commenting on the dances in which they occur. Although they highlight the conventions by which dance is made and thus affirm the fictionality of dance in general, they fail to sustain a reflexive inquiry. Many of the movements work as in-jokes, puns, or parodies whose decoding requires an extensive knowledge of the concert dance tradition. Others are witty ornaments that engender either a homey accessibility or a playful naughtiness. But even as they celebrate diversity and satirize their own origins, Tharp's dances deny the viewer access to their own workings. They present the choreographic process for consumption rather than for collaboration.

Writing Bodies and Subjects

Following in the wake of Cunningham and the Judson era, the Grand Union, Monk, and Tharp have all necessarily addressed the issue of the relationship between body and subject, but they have answered the question "Who dances?" differently. The Grand Union and Monk have systematically refrained from enacting any of the traditional relationships between the body and the act of expression. Where their choreography momentarily suffuses movement with the expressive tension or virtuoso bravado of an inner self, these movements are soon shown to be hypothetical constructions by the understated calm and pragmatism that pervade the dances as a whole. In the dances of the Grand Union, the pragmatic stance adopted by the performers provided a vital contrast for the other bodies and subjects they explored, whereas in Monk's dances, a pragmatic style is a continuous and integral part of each character's actions. Both groups' dances, however, divest the subject of any sovereign claims over the body, whether it is performing the most banal task or the most artful gesture. The dances thus direct attention away from any specific image of the body and toward the process of constructing all bodies.

Tharp's choreography, on the other hand, indulges in and then backs away from a command of subject over body. This ambivalence toward the subject-body dichotomy results in a cultivated distance, a studied cool toward both body and subject. Instead of exploring the capacity of dance to create the body, Tharp's work seems to take advantage of that capacity, embracing stereotypic roles for the body while maintaining a sense of detachment.

In the same way that the Grand Union and Meredith Monk create a mutable body and subject, so they develop an interdisciplinary approach to the arts. The relation between dance, music, costume, and scenic design in their pieces is not coincidental as it is in the multimedia objectivist model. Instead of allowing events in each medium to speak for themselves in separate languages, the pieces establish a dialogue among mediums and thus affirm the possibility of conceptual resonances among disciplines. Each in a different way, the Grand Union and Monk reproduce the nonhierarchical, nonorganic interaction between body and subject by situating dance as one discourse among many. And perhaps what makes their performances most remarkable is that each offers a distinctive yet comprehensive strategy for interdisciplinary work.

Monk, in particular, explicitly describes the way she "thinks" between disciplines. She applies the techniques of one medium to the material of another: "I'm working like a filmmaker. I don't know why. That seems to be the way I think; the flash forward section in the first part [of *Vessel*] is an example. I'm doing live movies." [12] Monk's cinematic conception of the performance affects both the composition and editing of scenes in her work. Similarly, her attention to the sound of her pieces bespeaks an interdisciplinary attitude. As she explains, again using her piece *Vessel* as an example, one should be able to hear the performance, not the music at the performance. "*Vessel* is structured like a piece of music; you *hear* how the piece is structured as much as you see it. . . . If I don't teach people to hear in this piece then I feel I've failed, because I believe that hearing—absolute expansion of auditory perception—is what the piece is about." [13] This interdisciplinary thinking detaches the activities of seeing, hearing, and kinesthetically sensing from their traditional responsibilities in the arts. Presented with the unfamiliar medium of "live movies" or "painterly soundscapes," viewers extend their perceptual acuity beyond that required to see dance or listen to music.

The Grand Union also promoted this revitalization of the senses, but unlike Monk, with her cross-disciplinary conjunctions, they emphasized the sensate by continually restating the physicality of all human actions. Verbal pronouncements and phrases of movement were as concrete as the props that filled the performance space. Enunciating a sentence was shown to involve the same human capacity to articulate as climbing a ladder. Each gesture, in turn, was as palpable and material as a bucket of water or a feathered hat. This pragmatic view of human artifacts and actions jumbled the familiar hierarchies that deprive speech of its sensuality and movement of its mindfulness and permitted, instead, an extraordinary bricolage of expressive forms.

Tharp's choreography, in contrast, remains as coolly distant from music and design as subject from body. Her performances almost conform to a neoclassical model in which all mediums fit together like pieces of a puzzle. Tharp, however, is careful to separate the pieces. Choreographic and musical structures, for example, overlap to a certain extent, with dance and music sharing meter or mood for limited periods of time. But then the two mediums diverge—the sound drops out and the dancing continues, or the dancing develops a pulse at odds with the meter of the music, or the two contrast in dynamics or orchestration. These discrepancies point up the capacity found in both dance and music to articulate temporal forms while still demonstrating the autonomy of the two disciplines. Similarly, the clever disjunctures between dance and stage set—the dancer "accidentally" runs into a curtain or steps out of the light—effectively separate the dance from its perfectly framed setting. They underscore the importance of the setting to the success of the performance, yet they also emphasize how arbitrary the dance's relation to its context can be. Where the neoclassical frame and setting said to its audience, "Picture this," Tharp's use of the stage has the effect of saying, "Here we all are, picturing again." Thus Tharp's work, while seeming to create new connections between the arts, tacitly affirms the traditional boundaries between mediums.

By developing an interactive rapport between body and subject and between the arts, the Grand Union and Meredith Monk allow viewers to collaborate in interpreting the performance. The techniques that interrupt narratives give viewers access to the making of the stories. Metacommentary, improvisation, surreal juxtaposition, and polyvalent props and gestures establish for viewers a kaleidoscope of perspectives on the narrative. At the same time, the treatment of both the subject-body and the arts provides viewers with examples of a methodology for organizing and interpreting the narrative's multiple points of view. This methodology privileges working together, patience, alertness, the willingness to negotiate, and the ability to play around with things.

Thus viewers at a Grand Union concert could watch both the story and the making of the story. They could choose from among levels of commentary and individual dancers' versions of the piece and even place their own imagined responses to situations alongside those of the dancers. But they would also see (because the improvisational techniques practiced by the Grand Union made it only too clear) how each individual's decisions became part of the group's efforts, how individual initiatives could be thwarted or transformed, and how, ultimately, all interpretations including their own would be woven together into one collective fabric.

Meredith Monk's audiences experience a similar collectivizing impulse. Her dances also bring viewers into the making of the story by presenting surreal or abstract groupings of characters in open-ended, nonlinear developmental sequences that suggest a range of possible meanings. More through their location and their adaption of ritual structures than through improvisation, however, these dances remind viewers that their interpretive actions are not entirely solitary or individual. The parking lots, churches, or lofts where Monk presents her work frame the audience as part of the action so that they see themselves as a defined group participating in the event. The ritual format likewise gives the audience a functional role as members of the community who witness the action. Where the Grand Union's play spilled over into the audience, Meredith Monk's rituals encompass the audience. And where the Grand Union presented models for resolving conflict between individual and group by invoking an ironic metacommentary, Meredith Monk presents such models by appealing to a larger context of which the performers and viewers form but a small part.

In Tharp's dances the distance between body and subject and between different mediums is equally present in the separation between the dance and its audience. Unlike the concerts by the Grand Union and Monk in which the audience becomes a relatively immobile gathering of performers, Tharp's dances preserve distinct roles for viewers and performers. Viewers are presented with glossy objects whose craft delights and whose technical prowess impresses. These objects, however, are not completely impenetrable. The witty puns and reflexive pointers permit viewers to enter and become part of the performance, although their role is highly complex. At one level, these dances leave the audience scrambling for the best interpretation, competing to give the ultimate evaluation of the dance in the same way that the dancers vie for positions on a scale of technical competence. At another, the dances ask viewers to succumb to a genuine nostalgic glimpse of some former era, to be wrapped up in its flavor and mood. At still another, they ask viewers simply to perceive the dance's formal properties as sophisticated manipulations of the intrinsic spatial and temporal features of movement. Caught in this triple message, viewers take an ironic stance, responding as viewers of expressionist or neoclassical events might have responded, but without "really meaning it."

The Grand Union also asked viewers to adopt an ironic attitude toward the dance and the world, but for them irony was iconoclastic, a tool for unmasking the idols of popular culture. Tharp's dances accomplish just the reverse: they develop irony as a means of indulging in fantasies of popular culture, including traditional stereotypes of sex roles, without having to endure the consequences. Furthermore, where the Grand Union guided their ironic sensibilities toward collective group awareness, Tharp's dances ask each viewer to undergo the project of ironic distancing individually.

The Grand Union was only partially successful in imparting a collective reflexive consciousness, especially to viewers unfamiliar with the historical and aesthetic context of the performances. The Grand Union's concerts looked more like theater or even like grown-ups at play than like dance, and the dancers never managed to incorporate the virtuoso display of movement skills that is so frequently a part of dance into their ongoing reflexive discourse. Moreover, they were disturbingly ambivalent about direct audience participation. They seemed almost to invite the audience to join in, and yet they completely ignored the occasional viewer who courageously entered the performance space.[14] Viewers not only lost any familiar choreographic signposts that would have helped them assess the new images before them, but they were also given mixed directions about how to act. This ambivalence on the part of the Grand Union might have aroused the same sense of isolation that Tharp's dances sometimes inspire, especially in newcomers who undoubtedly sensed that other members of the audience felt right at home.

It could as easily be said of Meredith Monk's performances as of the Grand Union's that they do not qualify as dance, that they occur, instead, at the interstices of existing mediums. One critic wrote after seeing Monk's 1971 performance of *Vessel* that it is "a major work in an art form for which there is no proper name."[15] But if Monk's work is not dance, what is? Like any major innovation, her pieces redefine the boundaries of the medium of dance and, even more important, give a new perspective from which to evaluate the medium. Whether or not they are ultimately regarded as dance is less significant than their timely message about how meaning in dance is made.

If the Grand Union and Monk blur boundaries between mediums, they also blend the roles of choreographer, dancer, and viewer. Thus the dancers were the choreographers in the Grand Union performances, and in Meredith Monk's company dancers actively collaborate in the making of the pieces by offering suggestions and demonstrating possible options for the sequence of events. Monk's dancers also improvise the choreography for parts of their performance. Although not to the extent supported by the Grand Union, Monk's dancers do determine specific timing, sequence, and placement of activities within the overall draft of the piece. Similarly, the roles of choreographer and dancer merge with the role of the viewer in many respects. Viewers are given the opportunity to see themselves as part of the performance when they are asked to move to new locations, or when they are seated in theaters-in-the-round or such environments as the bleachers in the vacant lot of *Vessel*. They also participate in the creation of the event by choosing what to watch in a dance that is open-ended and delivers no single message. And as viewers determine the placement and significance of events for themselves, choreographers assume some of the critical perspective normally assigned to the audience. That is, the choreographers are located both inside the dance, composing it, and outside, evaluating it. In the case of the Grand Union, this dual role became evident in the different layers of metacommentary; for Monk, it manifests itself in the interdisciplinary thinking that produces her pieces.

While the Grand Union and Monk have taken reflexive representation toward interdisciplinary inquiry, Tharp has gone another route. Her pieces contain the familiar look of dancing, and they maintain distinct roles for choreographer, dancer, and viewer. Her use of choreographic reflexivity does not result in a sustained critique of how dances acquire meaning, like that in performances by the Grand Union and Monk. Instead, the reflexive tactics displace the dancing ever so slightly from its foundation in the concert dance tradition. In doing so, they define a location from which to survey and contemplate that tradition, but they give the viewer no assistance in evaluating concert dance or their own place in it. They turn and walk away from their viewers, even as they leave an interpretive door ajar.

Works by the Grand Union and Monk, then, suggest possible approaches to a dance that viewers not only *read* but also *write*. Unlike Tharp's dances, which time and again extend a collaborative hand to their viewers only to withdraw it, works by the Grand Union and Monk expand the role of the viewer required by any of the dance forms that have been discussed here to include the making of the dance itself. Reading dancing, as defined throughout this study, is the activity of attending to the dance as a set of choreographic conventions. This process inevitably permits both a more active participation in and a fuller response to the dance than would simply watching it. Writing dancing, viewers become involved in the choreography itself, helping determine the response they make, so that they become immersed along with the choreographer and dancers in a playful yet critical interpretive practice.

Underlying the possibility of a written dance is a new vision of the body as a locus of intelligent and passionate human gesturings. If choreographers like those who made up the Grand Union, Monk, and Tharp remind us that self-definition depends on the human being's social circumstances, they also demonstrate that each of us is multiple bodies. The body can be a voice through which the interior feelings and desires of the subject are made manifest, or it can simply enunciate itself. It can house a lexicon of abstract forms, or it can serve as the site at which images of the world come into being. Or it can comment on its own capacity to signify any of these things.

When the body is allowed to develop a polyvalent significance, dance likewise becomes a practice or activity rather than a contained object. Its dancing-ness comes to the foreground so that dance proliferates from a single phenomenon into countless different forms for making meaning. The body, no longer the stylus, the parchment, or the trace, becomes the process itself of signing, a process created mutually by all those—choreographers, dancers, and viewers—engaged in the dance. In this world of writing dancing, the body of this text could, as if in counterpoint with the writing body, leap off the two-dimensional page: it could turn, lunge, twist, kick, suspend . . . and with a final gesture—was it "Going my way?" or "Thumbs up"?—vanish.

NOTES

1. For the dance *How to Run, Kick, Pass, and Fall* (1965), Cage performs his composition *Indeterminacy*, in which he sits at a table on the apron of the stage in front of the proscenium drinking a bottle of champagne and telling humorous stories, each one minute in length.

2. Cunningham's *Changes: Notes on Choreography* (New York: Something Else Press, 1968) includes many of his working notes for *Suite by Chance*, arranged, like everything else in the book, by chance in a collagelike format.

3. In his preface to *Mythologies* (New York: Hill & Wang, 1972), Roland Barthes writes:

The starting point of these reflections was usually the feeling of impatience at the sight of the "naturalness" with which newspapers, art and common sense constantly dress up a reality which, though it is the one we live in, is undoubtedly determined by history. In short, in the account given of our contemporary circumstances, I resented seeing Nature and History confused at every turn, and I wanted to track down, in the decorative display of *what-goes-without-saying*, the ideological abuse which, in my view, is hidden there. (p. 11)

Following Barthes, I have attempted in *Reading Dancing* to disengage the body and the dance from their "natural" habitat and to reconstitute them as part of a cultural and historical situation.

4. Doris Humphrey, *The Art of Making Dances* (New York: Grove Press, 1959), p. 159.

5. See Suzanne Langer, *Feeling and Form: A Theory of Art* (New York: Scribner, 1953), and *Philosophy in a New Key* (Cambridge: Harvard University Press, 1957); John Martin, *The Dance* (New York: Tudor, 1946), and *Introduction to the Dance* (1939; New York: Dance Horizons, 1968); Curt Sachs, *World History of the Dance* (1937; New York: W. W. Norton and Company, 1963).

6. Doris Humphrey summarizes the attitudes toward dance of most of the early twentieth-century choreographers:

The dancer believes that his art has something to say which cannot be expressed in words or in any other way than by dancing. He recognizes that he is the lineal descendant of those ancients who expressed their innermost feelings in dance and gestures long before language became common.

He is, in a sense, a throwback. He is aware of that but believes that his art is rooted so deeply in Man's fundamental instincts that he can read back into His unconscious remembrance before the atrophy of civilization set in and moved Him profoundly without a word being spoken. (*The Vision of Modern Dance*, ed. Jean Morrison Brown [Princeton, N.J.: Princeton Book Company, 1979], pp. 58–59)

7. In *Feeling and Form* Langer makes an excellent case for the concept of dance movement as symbol. She describes how in dance composition the "feeling shown" evolves into the "feeling represented":

Implicitly there is always the recognition of created dance forces, impersonal agencies, and especially of controlled, rhythmicized formally conceived gesture begetting the illusion of emotions and wills in conflict. Writers who fill their introductions or opening paragraphs with statements committing them to a daily round of emotions enough to kill any normal person, and to spontaneous exhibits of them on schedule, do not talk about any specific emotions and feelings when they enter into discussion of specific dance problems, but almost invariably speak of setting up tensions, exhibiting forces, creating gestures that *connote* feelings or even thoughts. (pp. 184–85)

Yet Langer never goes beyond the insight that dance functions as a system of representation to examine how choreographers might devise movement or determine the sequencing of such movement.

According to Martin's theory of dance, "That portion of our emotional overcharge which we have not learned to shunt into intellectual paths, we vent either directly into play as primitive men do, or else through the vicarious channels of art" (*Introduction to the Dance*, p. 136). Although Martin argues that choreographers must craft these impulses into phrases of choreographed movement, the techniques of the choreographic craft are not as important as the viewer's ability, because of an innate sense of kinesthetic empathy with moving bodies known as "inner mimicry," to directly receive the dance's message.

Sachs comes the closest to an analysis of compositional forms in his description of basic spatial arrangements and basic steps for world dances such as circular dances, braided dances, and so forth. But his argument traces these forms to the social workings of the primitive societies in which they occur, and thus the forms themselves are reduced to an expression of societal needs. Their status as purely formal conventions and the human being's capacity to respond to them as such are dismissed in Sachs's functionalist argument.

8. In a recently published set of interviews, Cunningham describes in great detail his procedures for composing dances. See *The Dancer and the Dance*. Merce Cunningham in conversation with Jacqueline Lesschaeve (New York: M. Boyars Publishers, 1985).

9. Roman Jakobson, in his famous essay "Linguistics and Poetics," in *Style in Language*, ed. Thomas Sebeok (Cambridge: MIT Press, 1960), pp. 85–121, proposes an interpretive quadrant that shows the relationship between the formal organization of a text and its author, reader, and literary context:

The text, in a sense, exists at the vacant center of the forces that conspire to produce it. Jakobson argues, however, that the formal codes and conventions out of which the text is created take precedence over the other forces involved in its production, that the codes themselves tell us about the author, the relation of the text to other texts, and the viewer's experience of the text. For a lucid explanation of this aspect of Jakobson's theory, see Fredric Jameson, *The Prison-House of Language* (Princeton, N.J.: Princeton University Press, 1972), pp. 202–8.

Reading Dancing draws heavily on Jakobson's formulation of the text. To apply his interpretive strategies to dance, I have amended his quadrant to include the performer—one element that distinguishes the performing arts from literature and the visual arts—so that the dance can be approached as follows:

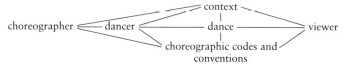

In the first chapter, I have tried to give a broad overview of the relations among the choreographic conventions, the choreographer, and the dancer; in chapter 2, I focus specifically on describing the conventions themselves. In chapter 3, I elaborate on the relations between the conventions and their context, and here I deviate from Jakobson's use of the model in two ways. First, Jakobson's classical formalism defines context as the set of artistic forms preceding and surrounding a work of art. In the case of dance, such a context would include other dances and genres of dance as well as the methods for teaching choreography and dancing. Insofar as I have implemented this idea of context, I have examined not other dances but the related arts of rhetoric and physical education. And I have done so, because I am specifically concerned with elucidating the conception of the body that informs the dance. I believe that such a conception can be apprehended only at the points of contact between related discourses. Second, I would argue that Jakobson's interpretive quadrant as he formulates it should be seen as embedded in a larger social and historical context that gives rise to the artistic context and to the conventions themselves. To avoid the debates that necessarily arise from privileging form over context or context over form, however, I have brought a sense of the historical setting to my analysis, thus apposing formalist and historicist concerns (see n. 1, chap. 2). Finally, in chapter 4 I examine the viewer's experience or relation to the conventions, but with the added historical perspective provided by chapter 3.

10. See especially Lincoln Kirstein, *Dance: A Short History of Classical Theatrical Dancing* (New York: Dance Horizons, 1935), and *Movement and Metaphor* (New York: Praeger, 1970).

11. This study approaches both writing and dancing as systems of *signs*. As developed by the Swiss linguist Ferdinand de Saussure (1857–1913), the sign is a unit of meaning in language composed of two parts: a sound or acoustical element called the signifier and a conceptual element, the signified. Saussure further argues that the relationship between signifier and signified is arbitrary: that is, there is no intrinsic connection between the way a word sounds and the concept or entity to which it refers. The work of anthropologist Claude Lévi-Strauss applies the concept of the sign to social institutions such as kinship, totemism, myth, architecture, and the visual arts. In the wake of his efforts to use the sign as a model for a variety of cultural phenomena, it becomes possible to conceive of dance movement as sign. Thus dance movement can be seen as a product of the physical movement of the body, the signifier, and the worldly events or concepts referred to by the movement, the signified. See Lévi-Strauss, *Tristes Tropiques*, trans. John Weightman and Doreen Weightman (London: J. Cape, 1973), *The Savage Mind* (Chicago: University of Chicago Press, 1966), and *The Raw and the Cooked*, trans. John Weightman and Doreen Weightman (New York: Harper & Row, 1969).

Yet the sign, as conceived by Saussure and Lévi-Strauss (and also Jakobson, see n. 9, above) relies on a fixed pairing of signifier and signified that fails to take account of historical or cultural context. As a consequence, Lévi-Strauss's research maintains a synchronic orientation, one that is ultimately directed toward confirming the universalist hypothesis that the human mind and language are organized around oppositional categories and relationships. Similarly, anthropological studies of dance using the same structuralist methods have tended to focus on the existence and identification of structural units in the dance rather than on questions of meaning, function, and representation. See, for example, Adrienne Kaeppler, "Method and Theory in Analyzing Dance Structure with an Analysis of Tongan Dance," *Ethnomusicology* 16, no. 2 (May 1972): 173–217; and Gyorgy Martin and Erno Pesovar, "A Structural Analysis of the Hungarian Folk Dance (A Methodological Sketch)," *Acta Ethnographica* 10 (1961): 1–40.

By contrast, semiological studies such as those conducted by Umberto Eco and Roland Barthes in his early work use the sign as a structural model for a variety of cultural artifacts and events, but they focus special attention on the nature of the coded relationship between signifier and signified. Eco, Barthes, and others have suggested several types of relationship, including the *index*, the *icon*, and the *symbol*, where indexical relations are based on cause and effect, iconic relations on shared likeness, and symbolic relations on shared essence. These studies suggest that dance movement can create meaning in many different ways, and thus they allow us to look at the dance not in terms of what it is trying to say but in terms of *how* it delivers the message. See Umberto Eco, *A Theory of Semiotics* (Bloomington: Indiana University Press, 1976); and Roland Barthes, *Elements of Semiology*, trans. Annette Lavers and Colin Smith (New York: Hill & Wang, 1978), "The Structural Analysis of Narratives," in *Image, Music, Text*, trans. Stephen Heath (New York: Hill & Wang, 1978), pp. 79–124, and *S/Z*, trans. Richard Miller (New York: Hill & Wang, 1974).

Still, a semiological analysis does not directly address the issue of the relationship between the sign and its context. And this, I believe, is what Barthes, in his later work, and also Jacques Derrida prepare the way for when they suggest that the sign should be seen as a coupling of signifier and signified that occurs always in a specific cultural and historical moment. The meaning of the sign (or, as Derrida calls it, the gram) is therefore inseparable from its occasion. See Derrida, *Of Grammatology* (Baltimore: Johns Hopkins University Press, 1976); Gregory Ulmer's explication of Derrida in "The Object of Post-Criticism," in *The Anti-Aesthetic: Essays on Postmodern Culture*, ed. Hal

Foster (Port Townsend, Wash.: Bay Press, 1983), pp. 83–100; and Barthes, *Writing Degree Zero* (New York: Hill & Wang, 1953), *S/Z*, and *Barthes by Barthes* (New York: Hill & Wang, 1977).

In a sense, *Reading Dancing* charts this progression from structuralist to post-structuralist theoretical positions as it moves from a structuralist account of four contemporary choreographers through a semiological analysis of choreographic conventions to a historical consideration of those conventions, resulting in a polyvalent notion of the body and the subject. For an incisive and comprehensive critique of structuralist uses of the sign, and one that argues persuasively for a concept of the sign similar to the one I have used here, see Teresa De Lauretis, *Alice Doesn't: Feminism, Semiotics, Cinema* (Bloomington: Indiana University Press, 1984).

CHAPTER ONE

Reading Dance

1. I have selected these four choreographers because their ideas and work most closely correspond to four paradigms of dance making, which, in turn, derive from literary theory. As contemporary literary theory has focused on the question of how texts can have meaning, it has examined not only how words refer to other signs in the world but also how language indicates the modality of relationships between worldly things as signs. This power of language to imply the organization of things, known to the classical Greek and Roman rhetoricians, became a major topic of study in eighteenth-century linguistic philosophy. Giambattista Vico (1668–1744), one of the most influential theorists of the period, determined four principal figures of speech, or tropes, that embodied the fundamental relationships that one thing in the world could have with another. These four tropes, from which all others can be derived, are metaphor, metonymy, synecdoche, and irony. A number of contemporary theorists—Kenneth Burke, Michel Foucault, Hayden White, and others—have adopted these tropes as a way of categorizing and commenting on literary texts and other social phenomena.

See Kenneth Burke, "Four Master Tropes," in *A Grammar of Motives* (New York: Prentice-Hall, 1945), pp. 503–17; Michel Foucault, *The Order of Things: An Archaeology of the Human Sciences* (New York: Pantheon Books, 1971); and Hayden White, "Interpretation in History," *New Literary History* 4, no. 2 (Winter 1973): 281–314, "Foucault Decoded," in *Tropics of Discourse*

(Baltimore: Johns Hopkins University Press, 1978), pp. 230–60, "Michel Foucault," in *Structuralism and Since*, ed. John Sturrock (Oxford and New York: Oxford University Press, 1979), pp. 81–115, and "The Value of Narrativity in the Representation of Reality," *Critical Inquiry* 7, no. 1 (Autumn 1980): 5–27.

I have found these tropes to be a powerful analytical tool for understanding both the choreographer's relationship to the body and to the dance and the dance's relationship to the world and to its viewers. The following brief summary of their application to dance gives an overview of the four models for dance making as they are presented in chapter 1 through a consideration of Hay, Balanchine, Graham, and Cunningham.

In a dance where the trope of metaphor predominates (changing a word from its literal meaning to one analogous to it), the dance functions as an analogy to the world, and the dancer's body is likewise seen as analogous to his or her sense of self, or subject. The choreographer's task is to translate worldly events into movement, while the viewer's role is to find in the movement its allegorical significance. Alternatively, a metonymic form of dance (substitution of cause for effect, part for whole, etc.) improves upon, as it replaces, the world to which it refers. The body substitutes for the subject, offering the best version of the subject it can. The choreographer decides how to "make the world over" into the image of the dance, just as viewers must discern and evaluate the selections made by the choreographer and the technical perfection of the results. Where dance functions in the manner of synecdoche (substitution of a whole for the part, essence for attribute, etc.), the dance becomes a special voice speaking to the world about essential things. In the same way, the body serves as a representative of the subject. Here the choreographer must transform personal experience into universal condition, and the viewer must similarly find the personal significance in a universal statement. Finally, under the trope of irony (expressing through the play between surface and depth meanings a meaning directly opposite of that apparent), the dance becomes another of the many activities that make up the world. The body is simply the subject, and yet it isn't. The choreographer, by focusing on the physical articulations of the body, may still express dramatic content, but this message will be one of several the viewer can choose. (These definitions of the tropes are adapted from Richard Lanham's *A Handlist of Rhetorical Terms* [Berkeley and Los Angeles: University of California Press, 1968].)

The four tropes also give rise to the four modes of representation described in chapter 2 (see pp. 65–75) and to the historical examples cited in chapter 3. In chart form:

Literary Trope	Choreographic Mode of Representation	Contemporary Choreographic Example	Historical Examples
Metaphor	Resemblance	Hay	Late Renaissance European court spectacles (1550–1650)
Metonymy	Imitation	Balanchine	Neoclassical proscenium theater ballets (1680–1760)
Synecdoche	Replication	Graham	American expressionist modern dance (1890–1950)
Irony	Reflection	Cunningham	Contemporary, postexpressionist experimental dance (1950–present)

2. My approach here follows Roland Barthes's "ethnographic" account of Japan, *The Empire of Signs*, trans. Richard Howard (New York: Hill & Wang, 1982). In his first chapter, Barthes states that he intends to "isolate [a] somewhere in the world *faraway*" and find there "a certain number of features (a term employed in linguistics), and out of these features deliberately form a system. It is this system which I shall call: Japan" (p. 3). Barthes's purpose in evoking Japan as a system of signification exemplified by a few well-chosen social customs and artifacts, or mine in treating the (not-so-faraway) choreographers in the same way, is not to provide new insights into their symbolic world so much as to search out "the very fissure of the Symbolic" (p. 4). By this I take Barthes to mean that he hopes to explore and even to portray the possibility of an epistemic foundation utterly foreign to the West by comparing, and it is always necessarily an act of comparison, the significance given by the Japanese to certain cultural symbols with our own Western treatment of analogous symbols. I am attempting to accomplish a similar kind of "ethnography" by isolating and then comparing the four choreographic projects as discrete cultural systems, systems created from a combination of what the choreographers have written and said, what has been written about them, and my own observations and experiences watching their dances and studying dance in their traditions.

3. Throughout the book I have used the term *subject* to refer to the "I" or the "self" of the person dancing. I have chosen to speak of the dancer's subject rather than the more commonly used "dancer's self" to signal a theoretical position that holds that the self is not a natural or fixed entity but rather a process constituted by various cultural and historical circumstances. Barthes summarizes a wealth of recent anthropological, historical, and philosophical research on this matter when he says, "The 'I' which approaches the text is itself already a plurality of other texts, of infinite, or more precisely, lost codes

(origins are lost. . . . Subjectivity is generally thought of as a plenitude with which I encumber the text, but in fact this faked plenitude is only the wash of all the codes which make up the 'I,' so that finally, my subjectivity has the generality of stereotypes)" (*S/Z*, trans. Richard Miller [New York: Hill & Wang, 1974], p. 10).

What follows, then, is an attempt to "de-naturalize" our notions of the self and our assumptions about the body. In this study, I try to show how the body and the subject are formed—how they come into being—through participation in a given discourse, in this case the dance classes, rehearsals, and performances of a particular choreographer. This approach was originally inspired by readings in the anthropological research on the question of body and subject definitions. Two memorable studies that have had a "de-naturalizing" effect are Maurice Leenhardt's account of early-twentieth-century New Caledonia, *Do Kamo* (Chicago: University of Chicago Press, 1979), and Geneviève Calame-Griaule's massive study of Dogon theories of language, the body, and human articulation, *Ethnologie et langage: La Parole chez les Dogon* (Paris: Gallimard, 1965).

Barthes's treatment of the subject and body is equally insightful. His examination of the body relies heavily on the distinction between conscious and subconscious experience as it has been redefined by Lacan. As John Sturrock in his essay "Roland Barthes" has observed:

[Barthes] has chosen the word "body" to describe the source of these vital and characteristic determinants of a writer's language where others might have used "the subconscious". . . . In pre-Freudian days, the writer's self could be conceived of as a sort of shock-proof kernal, standing above and outside language; but now it has become much more a plaything of language, for as soon as the writer sits down to write he is dislocated and transformed by what Barthes also calls "verbal pulsations." These are the voice either of his "body," his psychic case-history so to speak, or of language itself—those unsolicited associations of signifiers to which we are all of us subject. (*Structuralism and Since*, pp. 68–69)

But if Barthes, following Freud and Lacan, has conceived of the body as a sign for the structure of the unconscious, he has also, following the Russian formalist and structuralist traditions, approached the body as a locus of mindful human articulations. In "Lesson in Writing" (*Image, Music, Text*, trans. Stephen Heath [New York: Hill & Wang, 1978], pp. 170–78), for example, Barthes analyzes the Bunraku puppet theater as a "text" composed of three separate "writings"—the expressive movements of the puppets, the pragmatic motions of the puppeteers, and the vocal gestures of the singer-narrator. It is this vision of the body's movement as an act of writing that I have chosen to emphasize in *Reading Dancing*.

4. Deborah Hay (b. 1941) began her dance career at the Judson Church performances and with Merce Cunningham's and James Waring's companies in the early 1960s. Her own choreographic interests in those years revolved around pedestrian activities and objects and made use of large groups of untrained dancers. Her approach to choreography reflects her devotion to t'ai chi ch'uan and her concern with informal contexts for dancing, as documented in Deborah Hay and Donna Jean Rogers, *Moving through the Universe in Bare Feet: Ten Circle Dances for Everybody* (1974; Chicago: Swallow Press, 1975). In 1976 she moved to Austin, Texas, where she has continued to pursue her community-oriented, ritualistic vision of dance with her own company and where she is currently working in collaboration with composer Pauline Oliveros. In addition to her book, her written works include "Deborah Hay," in *Contemporary Dance*, ed. Anne Livet (New York: Abbeville Press, 1978), pp. 120–33; "Dance Talks," *Dance Scope* 12, no. 1 (Fall–Winter 1977–78): 18–22; and *Tasting the Blaze*, with Tina Girouard and Pauline Oliveros (Austin, Tex.: Futura Press, 1985). Works about her include Sally Banes, "Deborah Hay: The Cosmic Dance," in *Terpsichore in Sneakers* (Boston: Houghton Mifflin, 1980), pp. 113–32; Bill Jeffers, "Leaving the House: The Solo Performance of Deborah Hay," *Drama Review* 23 (March 1979): 79–86; Michael Kirby, "The Objective Dance," in *The Art of Time* (New York: Dutton, 1969), pp. 103–13; and Don McDonagh, "Deborah Hay," in *The Complete Guide to Modern Dance* (New York: Doubleday, 1976), pp. 385–89.

5. Hay, "Dance Talks": 18.

6. Hay and Rogers, *Moving through the Universe*, p. 231.

7. Ibid., pp. 29, 60.

8. Hay, "Dance Talks": 21.

9. I am struck by certain parallels between Hay's work and that of visual artist Robert Irwin. Both seem to be similarly concerned to establish a continuum between daily life and their art, and both develop a "presence" in their work by devoting considerable time to aspects of their pieces that are not seen but rather support what is seen. For a lucid account of the evolution of Irwin's aesthetic, see Lawrence Weschler's biography, *Seeing Is Forgetting the Name of the Thing One Sees* (Berkeley and Los Angeles: University of California Press, 1982).

10. Hay, "Dance Talks": 21.

11. From a class with Deborah Hay, July 1982, Wesleyan University, Middletown, Conn.

12. George Balanchine (1904–1983) entered the school of the St. Petersburg Imperial Ballet at the age of ten. He became a member of the Marinsky

Ballet, where he performed and choreographed several ballets, and then assumed the role of *maître de ballet* for Diaghilev, touring Europe for four years. He came to America in 1932 to found the School of American Ballet. Balanchine firmly established the ballet in America, developing a unique style of dancer and of movement in the hundreds of works he created. Works by him include "Notes on Choreography," *Dance Index* (February–March 1945): 20–31; *Balanchine's New Complete Stories of the Ballets*, with Francis Mason (New York: Doubleday, 1968); and *Choreography of George Balanchine: A Catalogue of Works* (New York: Viking Press, 1983). Major works about him include Lincoln Kirstein, *The New York City Ballet* (New York: Knopf, 1973); Nancy Reynolds, *Repertory in Review: Forty Years of the New York City Ballet* (New York: Dial Press, 1977); Bernard Taper, *Balanchine: A Biography* (New York: Macmillan, 1974); *Dance Perspectives*, no. 55 (Autumn 1973); and Merrill Ashley and Larry Kaplan, *Dancing for Balanchine* (New York: Dutton, 1984).

13. Balanchine's knowledge of music and his ability to make musical structure visible in his choreography are a major focus of virtually all critical writings about him.

14. Taper, *Balanchine*, pp. 8–9.

15. Joseph Mazo, *Dance Is a Contact Sport* (New York: Saturday Review Press, 1974).

16. Balanchine, "Notes on Choreography": 21.

17. Ibid.: 22.

18. Ibid.: 23.

19. Igor Stravinsky and Robert Craft, *Themes and Episodes* (New York: Knopf, 1966), p. 24.

20. Taper, *Balanchine*, p. 266.

21. Ibid., p. 9.

22. Edwin Denby, quoted in Taper, *Balanchine*, p. 104.

23. Mazo, *Dance Is a Contact Sport*, p. 90.

24. Martha Graham (b. 1895) began studying dance in 1916 at the Denishawn School in Los Angeles. She performed in the Denishawn company and then with Ted Shawn until 1923. With the founding of her own company in 1929, she began to develop a powerful, cohesive dance lexicon and an equally dynamic theory of choreography. In collaboration with Louis Horst, Isamu Noguchi, Aaron Copland and many other great artists of her generation, she has created more than two hundred major works dealing primarily with mythical themes and settings. Graham maintains a school in New York and continues to present new work and to tour annually. Works by her include

"The American Dance," in *Modern Dance*, ed. Merle Armitage and Virginia Stewart (New York: E. Weyhe, 1935), pp. 101–6; "How I Became a Dancer," *Saturday Review* 48, no. 35 (August 28, 1965): 54; and *The Notebooks of Martha Graham* (New York: Harcourt Brace Jovanovich, 1973). Works about her include Merle Armitage, *Martha Graham* (Los Angeles: Merle Armitage, 1937); LeRoy Leatherman, *Martha Graham: Portrait of the Lady as an Artist* (New York: Knopf, 1966); Don McDonagh, *Martha Graham: A Biography* (New York: Praeger, 1973); Marcia Siegel, *The Shapes of Change* (Boston: Houghton Mifflin, 1979), pp. 175–209; and Walter Terry, *Frontiers of Life: The Life of Martha Graham* (New York: Thomas Y. Crowell, 1975).

25. *Cave of the Heart*, choreographed in 1946, is one of Graham's strongest and, from the point of view of this study, most typical works. It is based on the Greek tragedy of Medea.

26. Barthes has written about the theater that operates with assumptions similar to Graham's:

The Italian stage is the space of this deceit, everything there is taking place in a room surreptitiously thrown open, surprised, spied on and relished by a hidden spectator; a theological space, that of the moral failing: on the one side, under a light of which he pretends to be unaware, the actor, that is to say, gesture and speech; on the other, in the darkness, the public, that is to say, consciousness and conscience. ("Lesson in Writing," p. 173)

Out of his objections to this romantic (organic) conception of art, Barthes has created a powerful alternative, based on a set of oppositions between what he calls works and texts, or the readerly and the writerly. According to Barthes, the readerly work, the equivalent of Graham's choreography, suffocates the reader with its single, intended message, whereas the writerly text offers its reader the opportunity to participate in the creation of its meaning (see n. 7, chap. 4).

My interpretation of Graham's work and of the expressionist tradition in dance (see chap. 3, pp. 145–67) is heavily influenced by Barthes's analysis. Rather than elaborate a single alternative to this powerful model of dance making, however, I have tried to neutralize it and at the same time point up what is valuable in it by presenting it as one of four or, as I suggest in chapter 4, five alternatives.

27. Martha Graham, "A Dancer's World," transcript of the film *A Dancer's World*, published in *Dance Observer* (January 1958): 5.

28. Martha Graham, "Martha Graham Is Interviewed by Pierre Tugal," *Dancing Times* (October 1950): 22.

29. Martha Graham, "Martha Graham Speaks," *Dance Observer* (April 1963): 53.

30. From a class with Martha Graham, June 1969, Graham School, New York City.

31. Graham, "How I Became a Dancer": 54.

32. Graham, "A Dancer's World": 5.

33. Graham, "Martha Graham Is Interviewed by Pierre Tugal": 22.

34. Graham seems to advocate an approach to the danced character similar to Konstantin Stanislavsky's theory of acting. See Stanislavsky, *Building a Character*, trans. Elizabeth Reynolds Hapgood (New York: Theater Arts Books, 1949), and *Stanislavsky on the Art of the Stage*, trans. David Magarshack (1950; New York: Hill & Wang, 1961).

35. Graham, "A Dancer's World": 5.

36. Merce Cunningham (b. 1919) began his career as a member of the Martha Graham Company. After meeting John Cage, working with him at Black Mountain College in the early 1950s, and attending the lectures on Zen Buddhism given by D. T. Suzuki in those years, Cunningham initiated and then developed an entirely new approach to choreography. In addition to collaborating frequently with Cage, Cunningham has worked with an exceptional number of composers and visual artists, including David Tudor, Christian Wolff, David Behrman, Gordon Mumma, Robert Rauschenberg, Jasper Johns, and Remy Charlip. His concerts have been largely of two kinds: formal presentations of discrete pieces and experimental collages, called events, made from sections of several pieces. He directs a school in New York City and continues to choreograph, perform, and tour extensively. Works by Cunningham include *Changes: Notes on Choreography* (New York: Something Else Press, 1968); *The Dancer and the Dance*, Merce Cunningham in conversation with Jacqueline Lesschaeve (New York: M. Boyars Publishers, 1985); "The Function of a Technique for Dance," in *The Dance Has Many Faces*, ed. Walter Sorell (New York: World Publishing, 1951), pp. 250–55; and "Choreography and the Dance," in *The Creative Experience*, ed. Stanley Rosner and Lawrence E. Abt (New York: Grossman Publishers, 1970), pp. 173–86. Works about him include Carolyn Brown, et al., "Time to Walk in Space," *Dance Perspectives* no. 34 (Summer 1968); *Merce Cunningham*, ed. James Klosty (New York: Saturday Review Press, 1975); Don McDonagh, "Merce Cunningham/New Concerns and New Forms," in *The Rise and Fall and Rise of Modern Dance* (New York: Mentor Books, 1970), pp. 53–73; and Calvin Tomkins, "An Appetite for Motion," in *The Bride and the Bachelors* (New York: Viking Press, 1965), pp. 239–96.

37. "An Appetite for Motion" is the apt title of Calvin Tomkins's essay on Merce Cunningham in *The Bride and the Bachelors* (see n. 36 above).

38. Merce Cunningham, "A Video Event," May 10, 1984, and May 11, 1984.

39. Ibid.

40. Cunningham, "The Function of a Technique."

41. Ibid., p. 250.

42. Ibid., p. 251.

43. One of the main premises of this book is that Cunningham's approach to choreography points up the arbitrary nature of the relationship between dance movement, the signifier, and that to which it refers, the signified. And as a result, his work accomplishes for dance what recent literary criticism has referred to as "the death of the author." This phrase serves as shorthand for a shift in theories seeking to explain the significance of a text away from a search for the author's intended meaning and toward the interpretation of a text based on the codes and conventions that convey its meaning. That is to say, the dance itself rather than the choreographer suggests an interpretive itinerary for the viewer. This emphasis on choreographic conventions and the viewer's active role in interpreting them allows us to rethink the nature of the choreographer's involvement in the dance. By noticing how a choreographer implements conventions, the viewer becomes familiar with that choreographer's identity, not in biographical terms but in artistic terms, as the person who has engaged in the process of making a dance. Thus choreographer, dancer, and viewer, as they interact with choreographic conventions, each become endowed with an identity unique to the occasion of the performance. For summaries of the "death of the author" in literary theory, see especially Roland Barthes, "From Work to Text," in *Image, Music, Text*, pp. 155–64; and Michel Foucault, "What Is an Author?" trans. James Venit, *Partisan Review* no. 4 (1975): 603–14.

44. Cunningham, *Changes*, n.p.

45. Ibid.

46. Carolyn Brown, "Merce Cunningham," in *Merce Cunningham*, ed. James Klosty, p. 22.

47. Ibid., p. 24.

48. Carolyn Brown, et al., "Time to Walk in Space," *Dance Perspectives* no. 34 (Summer 1968): 32–33.

49. Cunningham, "The Function of a Technique," p. 255.

50. The concert was *Episodes*, premiered May 14, 1959. Martha Graham choreographed the first half of the work and Balanchine the second. The incident is reported in Taper, *Balanchine*, pp. 17–18.

51. Taper, *Balanchine*, p. 213.

52. Cunningham, "The Function of a Technique," p. 251.

53. Graham, "How I Became a Dancer": 54.

54. Graham tells this story on the videotape of the Martha Graham Dance Company 1976, originally telecast on the Dance in America series, April 7, 1976.

55. My approach to understanding the viewer's experience of the dance in this study is similar to that of Selma Jeanne Cohen in her book *Next Week, Swan Lake* (Middletown, Conn.: Wesleyan University Press, 1982), and it differs markedly from the statistical survey of viewer response developed by Judith Lynne Hanna in her recent book *The Performer-Audience Connection* (Austin: University of Texas Press, 1984). Hanna interviewed members of the audience at actual performances and attempted to correlate their socioeconomic background and their responses to a set of questions about the emotional values attributed to specific parts of the body, qualities of movement, and general kinds of movement seen in the dance. In contrast, I am concerned with a hypothetical viewer created out of a particular interaction with a set of choreographic conventions. My approach is hermeneutical rather than sociological, and my observations about viewers' responses are designed not to pinpoint the reactions of particular viewers at a single concert but to suggest types of responses that grow out of the dance's ability to require that we attend to it in a specific way. In this sense, *Reading Dancing* can be seen as a systematization, using literary theory, of the issues of style, genre, and identity raised by Cohen in her work.

56. See Jonathan Culler's discussion of literary competence in *Structuralist Poetics* (Ithaca, N.Y.: Cornell University Press, 1975), pp. 113–30.

1. From among the various interpretive methodologies that exist today—Marxist, psychoanalytic, semiological, and so forth—I have chosen for this analysis of dance composition what could be called a formalist strategy that makes use of semiological theory, because it seems to estrange the body most completely from our commonplace assumptions about it. A semiological analysis of dance necessarily regards the body as a location of human signifying practices; this removes the body from its status as physical object and imbues it with the capacity for intelligence and passion. A psychoanalytic interpretation would also view the body in this way, yet because its predominant focus would be the relation between the body and desire, it could easily become confused with existing theories of the dance, such as Martin's or Sachs's,

which often associate the body with unconscious or libidinal motivations but treat the body as a physical instrument or vehicle for these motivations. A semiological approach, then, offers a timely antidote to existing theories of the dance and can also serve as a foundation for other contemporary interpretive models. In particular, I see this study as compatible with a feminist, sociological, or political analysis of dance, which, in explaining such phenomena as private and public thought, individual and group relations, and the distribution of power among social groups, would consider the issues discussed here: the relationship between body and subject, choreographer and dancer, and dance and audience.

Raymond Williams, for example, in his book *The Sociology of Culture* (New York: Schocken Books, 1981), makes a case for the compatibility of a formal semiological approach with sociopolitical methods of inquiry. To illustrate his argument, he discusses the introduction of the soliloquy as a theatrical device, commenting as follows:

These new and subtle modes and relationships [between author, actor, and audience] were in themselves developments in social practice, and are fundamentally connected with the discovery, *in dramatic form*, of new and altered social relationships, perceptions of self and others, complex alternatives of private and public thought. It is then true that what has been discovered, and can later be analysed, in the form can be shown to be relatively associated with a much wider area of social practice and social change. New conceptions of the autonomous or relatively autonomous individual, new senses of the tensions between such an individual and an assigned or expected social role, evident in other kinds of contemporary discourse but evident also in analytic history of the major social changes of this precise period, are then in clear relation with the "device".

But it is not necessary to explain the device as their consequence, taking first the sociology and then the form. This may often appear to be the order of events, but it is often also clear that the formal innovation is a true and integral element of the changes themselves: an articulation, by technical discovery, of changes in consciousness which are themselves forms of consciousness of change. Thus to analyze the soliloquy in English Renaissance drama is necessarily, first, a matter of formal analysis, but not as a way of denying or making irrelevant a social analysis; rather as a new and technically rigorous kind of social analysis of *this* social practice. (p. 142)

By examining the choreographic conventions or devices of American concert dance, this study complements broader sociological and political inquiries into contemporary American culture in the manner outlined by Williams in this passage. In chapter 3 of this book I have indicated, to a limited extent, how formalist and sociological concerns could be brought together.

2. Such dances, created throughout the 1960s by Cunningham and the Judson choreographers, are discussed in more detail in the last part of chapter

3 and in chapter 4. The aggressive experimentation with all aspects of dance composition undertaken by these choreographers is, as Foucault would say, what sets the conditions for the possibility of knowledge in this study. See Michel Foucault, *The Order of Things: An Archaeology of the Human Sciences* (New York: Pantheon Books, 1971), p. xxii.

3. *Cave of the Heart* (1946), choreography by Martha Graham; *Dance for 3 People and 6 Arms* (1962), choreography by Yvonne Rainer; *Orpheus and Eurydice* (1936), choreography by George Balanchine; *Juice* (1969), choreography by Meredith Monk.

4. My point here is not that choreographers always choose events in the world to transform into dance. Following the arguments of the new literary criticism, developed in the United States and England during the 1940s and 1950s, I am more than willing to agree that art must be approached as autonomous. Because all art events are part of a tradition of similar events with specific formal structures and points of view, it is misguided to assume that art events necessarily comment on events in the world or that artists even consider what their works are about in worldly terms. At the same time, however—and this is one of the responses that semiotics and post-structuralist criticism have made to the new literary criticism—art inevitably evokes images of the world. Its organization is such that any given art event is oriented in two directions simultaneously: it refers to itself as an artistic event and to the cultural and social circumstances of which it is a part. It is this second direction that I am addressing in my formulation of the four modes of representation. I am concerned with the ways in which dance can make reference to the world, and I attempt to illustrate these ways by describing four choreographic treatments of the same worldly event.

5. As I mentioned in the notes to chapter 1, these four correspond to the literary tropes of metaphor, metonymy, synecdoche, and irony. The trope of metaphor, for example, is related to the representational mode of *resemblance*, in which distinctive qualities of things in the world are translated into similar characteristics in the dance movement. In this mode, a relationship such as that between mother and child might be represented by two dancers, one moving with strong, weighty qualities and shaping her movement to the lighter, quicker perambulations of the other dancer. In contrast, the trope of metonymy is related to the mode of *imitation*, wherein the visual characteristics of events in the world are transferred into formal geometric designs that are then taken up in the dance movement. Here the dancers would look like and be costumed as a mother and child, and their movement would delineate behavior typical of mother and child, for example, playing, disobeying, scolding,

comforting, protecting, and so forth. The trope of synecdoche and its related mode of *replication* would represent mother and child in terms of the systematic organization of various aspects of their bond. Thus feelings of affection and desire as well as the longing for separation and independence would manifest themselves in an ebb and flow of soft, embracing movement and stronger, isolating gestures. The choreography would show the cyclic nature of these contrasting impulses as dancers moved apart and were drawn back together, the full expression of each motivation giving rise to its opposite. The mode of *reflection*, related to the trope of irony, would show none of the characteristics of mother and child, or at least not explicitly. As the name implies, reflection simply mirrors the activity of moving in the motion of the dance. Dancers absorbed in the task of executing movement might occasionally approximate qualities or behave in ways that remind the viewer of a mother and child, but only in brief phrases, unsupported by the overall development of the dance.

6. E. H. Gombrich's notion of visual schemata is especially helpful in understanding how *imitative* representation functions in dance. Gombrich proposes that learned conventions of visual representation, or schemata, are employed in the making and viewing of paintings, allowing us to identify a correspondence between real world and painted image. These schemata streamline and clarify the basic features of the worldly image in a way similar to that in which *imitation* in dance transforms worldly events into choreography. See *Art and Illusion* (New York: Pantheon Books, 1956), especially pp. 63–90.

7. Originally titled *Apollon Musagête*, the ballet has been restaged several times. The description I give here is based on recent versions of the dance that begin with Apollo alone on the stage.

8. According to Annabelle Gamson, one of the foremost revivalists of Duncan's work, in a personal communication with the author, Wesleyan University, October 1982.

9. This conception of style derives from Roland Barthes's discussion of style in *Writing Degree Zero* and Michel Foucault's comments about the surrealist writer Raymond Roussel. Foucault remarks: "Style is the possibility, at once hidden and indicated, under the sovereign necessity of the words used, of saying the same thing, but differently" (quoted in Hayden White, "Michel Foucault," in *Structuralism and Since*, ed. John Sturrock [Oxford and New York: Oxford University Press, 1979], p. 87). See Michel Foucault, *Raymond Roussel* (Paris: Gallimard, 1963). I have also found helpful Anya Peterson Royce's discussion of style in *The Anthropology of Dance* (Bloomington: Indiana University Press, 1977), pp. 154–74, and E. H. Gombrich's essay "Style," in the *International Encyclopedia of the Social Sciences*, vol. 15, ed.

David Sills (New York: Macmillan and Free Press, 1968), pp. 352–61.

10. See Rudolf von Laban, *The Mastery of Movement* (London: Macdonald and Evans, 1960); *Choreutics* (London: Macdonald and Evans, 1966); *Modern Educational Dance* (London: Macdonald and Evans, 1968); and Rudolf von Laban and F. C. Lawrence, *Effort* (London: Macdonald and Evans, 1947).

11. A concise description of these correlations between movement and psychological motivation can be found in Marion North, *Personality Assessment Through Movement* (Boston: Plays, Inc., 1975).

12. Doris Humphrey, *The Art of Making Dances* (New York: Grove Press, 1959), pp. 74–76.

13. The structuralist method I am using here entails analyzing the dance in small parts. Such a method yields information about the principles governing the organization of the dance at the same time that it obscures the impact of the flow of action. Although this approach robs the dance of some of its most significant attributes, its continuity and dynamism, it does not ultimately conflict with an appreciation of the continuity of the activity; it merely affords us access to the codes that regulate the sequencing of movement, the use of the body and its specific parts, and the orientation of the dancers in the performance space.

14. See Kay Ambrose, *Ballet Student's Primer* (New York: Knopf, 1966); Gail Grant, *Technical Manual and Dictionary of Classical Ballet* (New York: Dover, 1967); and Horst Koegler, *The Concise Oxford Dictionary of Ballet* (London: Oxford University Press, 1977), for contemporary examples of dictionaries of the ballet lexicon.

15. Mary Wigman, "Reminiscences of Mary Wigman: Dance Scene in the Late 1920's," *Dance News* (June 1973): 4.

16. Yuri Lotman has suggested that the collision or conflict between different principles of organization contributes both energy and meaning to the text. See Lotman's *The Structure of the Artistic Text* (Ann Arbor: University of Michigan Press, 1977).

CHAPTER THREE

Readings in Dance's History

1. The nature of that relationship may be more precisely expressed as follows: Hay maintains a metaphorical relation with the Renaissance dances by *resembling* them. Balanchine's relation to the eighteenth century is metonymic, or *imitative*. Graham, as emblematic of expressionist dance, stands in synecdochic relationship to it. And Cunningham retains an ironic distance from his objectivist descendants.

2. This chapter can be seen as an "archeology of dance" similar in approach to the "archeologies" of the penal system, mental illness, sexuality, and the human sciences undertaken by Michel Foucault. See *The Birth of the Clinic*, trans. A. M. Sheridan Smith (New York: Pantheon Books, 1973), *The Order of Things: An Archaeology of the Human Sciences* (New York: Pantheon Books, 1972), *Discipline and Punish: The Birth of the Prison*, trans. Alan Sheridan (New York: Pantheon Books, 1978), and *The History of Sexuality*, trans. Robert Hurley (New York: Pantheon Books, 1978).

In these works Foucault examines the epistemological assumptions that inform the organization of the various institutions and social practices that define criminality, insanity, sexuality, and the human and natural sciences. Foucault has, in general, separated each of his histories into three separate periods—1400 to 1650, 1650 to 1800, and 1800 to some time in the early twentieth century. He further intimates the existence of a fourth, contemporary, period whose structures and limits are only vaguely discernible to us from our position in it. Foucault treats these historical periods as distinct cultures, or strata, and he makes no attempt to link them causally or developmentally. This approach allows him to examine in great detail the epistemic organization of human signifying practices in each period without his having to determine a narrative framework in the evolution from one set of beliefs to another. It also allows him to challenge notions of progress and organic development implicit in more traditional histories (see n. 1, chap. 4).

In his analysis of Foucault's work, Hayden White observes that the four epistemic periods Foucault has described elaborate the four literary tropes proposed by Giambattista Vico (see n. 1, chap. 1). Thus in the late Renaissance, the trope of metaphor predominated; in the classical age, metonymy; and in the romantic nineteenth century, synecdoche. In our contemporary world, the predominant trope is irony. See "Foucault Decoded," in *Tropics of Discourse* (Baltimore: Johns Hopkins University Press, 1978), pp. 230–60, and "Michel Foucault," in *Structuralism and Since*, ed. John Sturrock (Oxford and New York: Oxford University Press, 1979), pp. 81–115.

My reading of dance history in chapter 3 borrows heavily from Foucault's work, especially *The Order of Things*, and also from White's analysis of Foucault. Like Foucault, I am interested in the epistemological underpinnings of choreography in each historical period. Following White, I assume that the mode of representation—the tropological equation that allows art to represent life—offers the primary entry point into each period's epistemological organization.

3. In their writings on Renaissance dance and history, Margaret Mc-

Gowan and Frances A. Yates argue that interest in fusing all the arts led to the birth of the court ballet and gave dance a new role as a medium for aesthetic pursuits. See Margaret McGowan, *L'Art du ballet de cour en France: 1581–1643* (Paris: Éditions du Centre National de la Recherche Scientifique, 1963); and Frances A. Yates, *The French Academies of the Sixteenth Century* (London: The Warburg Institute, University of London, 1947).

4. In describing the epistemic organization of the human sciences in the Renaissance, Foucault writes:

Up to the end of the sixteenth century, resemblance played a constructive role in the knowledge of Western culture. It was resemblance that largely guided exegesis and the interpretation of texts; it was resemblance that organized the play of symbols, made possible knowledge of things visible and invisible, and controlled the art of representing them. The universe was folded in upon itself: the earth echoing the sky, faces seeing themselves reflected in the stars, and plants holding within their stems the secrets that were of use to man. (*The Order of Things*, p. 17)

Foucault's notion of *resemblance* or, as he often refers to it, "similitude" largely influences the use of the term throughout this chapter. But Foucault seems to imply in the organization and chapter titles of *The Order of Things* that *resemblance* lies outside the boundaries of the practice of representation as we know it in Western culture, and thus it may provide evidence for some "Other" ordering of knowledge prior to the birth of "modern" civilization. To avoid Foucault's dichotomy between modern and premodern culture, and between Western culture and the "Other," I have treated *resemblance* as one of four approaches to representation.

5. In France, the performances were often open to any who would wait in line to be admitted to the large halls of the palaces where the productions were staged. Having been informed by proclamation of the time and place, the title, and the commemorative occasion, the crowd arrived several hours before the event; upon gaining entrance, they rushed to the galleries for a good view. In England, the events were attended primarily by the aristocracy, although commoners certainly knew of the productions and many commoners either danced professionally in the antemasque roles or helped backstage with the scenery and costumes. In Italy, where the performances took place in segments as the intermission features between acts of plays, the audience was composed of aristocracy and commoners alike, all of whom paid to attend. Despite these and many other differences in structure and style, I have attempted to identify and analyze common, generic features of the *intermezzi*, the masques, and the ballets that, by the end of the sixteenth century, could be found in the fêtes of almost every court throughout Europe.

6. In describing the responsibilities of the Renaissance stage manager, performance organizer M. de Saint-Hubert stresses the importance of discouraging performers from promenading through the audience before the dance. See his "How to Compose a Successful Ballet" (1641), ed. A. J. Pischl, and trans. Andrée Bergens, *Dance Perspectives* no. 20 (Winter 1966).

7. Sir John Davies, "Orchestra, or a Poem of Dancing," in *The Poems of Sir John Davies*, ed. Robert Krueger (Oxford: Clarendon Press, 1975), p. 101. Much of the courtly literature in Davies's time is concerned with dance, especially dance as a metaphor for the amorous encounter. Arguments that uphold the virtuous and noble characteristics of dance compete with arguments that accuse dance of lascivious, immoral tendencies. Davies's poem contains both arguments. The young noble assiduously courting the woman of his desire uses as his rationale every positive interpretation of dancing; she counters by citing its negative attributes. Both interpretations, however, depend on the selection of single attributes in the dance that *resemble* (see n. 5, chap. 2) moral virtues and vices. For a comprehensive review of the courtly literature on dance, see Ann Wagner, "Dance as Virtue: An Analysis from the Sixteenth Century Courtesy Literature," *Proceedings of the Society of Dance History*, comp. Christena Schlundt (1983): 37–47, and "Dance as Vice: An Analysis from the Sixteenth Century Courtesy Literature," *Proceedings of the Society of Dance History*, comp. Christena Schlundt (1984): 84–95.

8. Guillaume Colletet, *Le Grand Ballet des effects de la nature* (Paris: Jean Martin, 1632), p. 1.

9. Louis XIII believed in these numerical correspondences so strongly that he appointed a numerical interpreter whose job it was to explain people's characters on the basis of the number and location of letters in their names. See McGowan, *L'Art du ballet de cour en France*, p. 99.

10. Archange Tuccaro, "Trois dialogues de l'exercise de sauter et voltiger en l'air" (Paris: 1599), p. 36. Author's translation.

11. See Yates, *The French Academies of the Sixteenth Century*, pp. 36–75.

12. See "*Les Fées des forests de S. Germain, ballet de cour*" (1625), ed. and trans. John H. Baron, *Dance Perspectives* no. 62, (Summer 1975).

13. Pierre de Brach (1548–ca. 1604), choreographer of *Le Masquerade du triomphe de Diane*, published this description of the ballet in his *Les Poèmes* (Bordeaux: 1576), p. 183. Author's translation.

14. Costumes, props, and even some patterns for the choreography were chosen after consulting texts that purported to explain ancient Egyptian and classical symbolism. According to Roy Strong, a copy of *Hieroglyphica*, supposedly written by the ancient Egyptian Horus Apollo, was brought to Florence in 1419. It was translated into the book *Emblemata* by Andrea Alciati,

which appeared in many editions. This and other manuals on emblems were complemented by lavishly illustrated mythologies, including Lilio Gregario Giraldi, *De deis gentium varia et multiplex historia* (1548); Piero Valenano, *Hieroglyphica sire de sacris Aegyptorium literis*; Vincenzo Cartan, *Le imagini de i dei degli anticho commentarii* (1566); Natale Conti, *Mythologiae*; and Cesare Ripa, *Iconologia*. See Strong, *Splendor at Court* (Boston: Houghton Mifflin, 1973), pp. 58–62.

15. Since the dance could represent all social life, explain the nature of all things, and manifest the political and philosophical aspirations of humankind, it was important to choose subjects to realize these goals, or so argued Claude François Menestrier in *Remarques pour la conduite des ballets* (Lyon: J. Molin, 1668).

16. M. de Saint-Hubert, "How to Compose a Successful Ballet," p. 28.

17. Both Stephen Orgel and Roy Strong in their analyses of Renaissance masques and court spectacles emphasize the political motivation and rationale for the performances and identify many ways in which the spectacles reiterated and reinforced the reigning distribution of power. See Orgel, *The Jonsonian Masque* (Cambridge: Harvard University Press, 1965), "The Poetics of Spectacle," *New Literary History* 2, no. 3 (Spring 1971): 367–89, and *The Illusion of Power* (Berkeley and Los Angeles: University of California Press, 1975); and Strong, *Splendor at Court*.

18. See McGowan, *L'Art du ballet de cour en France*, pp. 69–84, for a more complete description of the performance.

19. For descriptions of this ballet, see McGowan, *L'Art du ballet de cour en France*, pp. 101–15; and Strong, *Splendor at Court*, pp. 54–56.

20. Occasionally, the court dances deviated from the presentation of noble and sage figures involved in heroic exploits. Some, like the ballet *Les Fées des forests de S. Germain* (1625), offered an inverted vision of cosmic order. This ballet in five acts satirized the five virtues necessary for the gentleman at court: skill in music, sport, prudent decisions, warfare, and dance. The five sections of the ballet mocked courtly virtues by presenting incompetent, exaggerated attempts to behave properly. In the many burlesque scenes, dancers attempted to accompany themselves on musical instruments, lackeys and apes played at roulette together, demifools and daydreamers wandered through a thoughtless ballet, warriors without arms or heads engaged in combat, and *bilboquets*, dancers dressed as cup-and-ball toys, executed exquisite capers.

The cosmic order underlying these antics, however, remained unchallenged and unchanged. The ballet was arranged symmetrically, with an eccentric yet powerful fairy entering at the beginning of each act. An equal number of dances were performed in acts 1, 2, 4, and 5 and fewer in act 3, the only act in which a minor key predominated in the music. The virtue of music in act 1 was balanced against the virtue of dance in act 5, and sport in act 2 was paired with warfare in act 4. Jacqueline the Skillful, Fairy of the Simpletons, reigned during the pivotal act 3, and the blows of her wand that symbolically turned the ceiling into the floor recapitulated the simple inversion of cosmic order proposed in the ballet. Such burlesques became increasingly popular in the early seventeenth century. On the surface they debunked all social regulations, but their satiric commentary depended on and thus recreated the cosmic order. See Baron, ed., *Les Fées des forests de S. Germain.*

21. Foucault certainly implies this conception of the subject in his writings about the period, but for a more comprehensive and detailed analysis, see Stephen Greenblatt's elegant treatment of the Renaissance subject in *Renaissance Self-Fashioning* (Chicago: University of Chicago Press, 1980).

22. See Domenico da Piacenza, *De arte saltandi e choreas ducendi* (Paris: Bibliothèque Nationale de Paris, Ms. it. 972); Antonio Cornazano, *The Book on the Art of Dancing*, trans. M. Inglehearn and P. Forsyth (1455; London: Dance Books, 1981); Michel Toulouze, *L'Art et instruction de bien danser* (1486; London: Emory Walker, 1936); Otto Kinkeldy, *A Jewish Dancing Master of the Renaissance: Guglielmo Ebreo* (Brooklyn: Dance Horizons, 1929); Antonius de Arena, *Ad suos compagnones* (Paris: Chez Philippes Gaultier, 1533); Fabritio Caroso, *Il Ballarino* (Venice: Francesco Ziletti, 1581); Thoinot Arbeau [Jehan Tabourot], *Orchésographie*, trans. Cyril W. Beaumont (1588; Brooklyn: Dance Horizons, 1968); and Sir Thomas Elyot, *The Book Named the Governor* (1531; New York: Teachers College Press, 1969).

23. Elyot, *The Book Named the Governor*, pp. 166–72.

24. Ibid., p. 163.

25. Arbeau cites the Canary dance as one such example: "Some say this dance is common in the Canary Isles. Other, whose opinion I should prefer to share, maintain that it derives from a ballet composed for a masquerade in which the dancers were dressed as kings and queens of Mauretania, or else like savages in feathers dyed to many a hue" (*Orchésographie*, p. 179).

26. Dancing master Guglielmo Ebreo, quoting his own teacher Domenico, offered this advice on dancing, which, although formulated for social dances of the fifteenth century, still provides an excellent summary of the aesthetics of syntax and style in the sixteenth century concert forms. He proposed six qualifications of dancer and dance that continued to guide the court performances: (1) the dance should consist of the elegant alternation between motion and repose; (2) the dance should offer a moderate display of dynamics, avoiding all extremes; (3) both dancer and dance should keep time to the music; (4) the dancer should develop a graceful posturing, the ability to adapt

the body to the movements of the feet; (5) the dancer should remember the steps in their order; and (6) the dancer should fit the steps to the size of the room (Kinkeldy, *A Jewish Dancing Master of the Renaissance*, pp. 8–11).

27. Saint-Hubert writes that "one must fit the dancing and the steps to the airs and the entrées so that a vine-grower or a water-carrier will not dance as a knight or a magician" ("How to Compose a Successful Ballet," p. 29).

28. Davies, "Orchestra, or a Poem of Dancing," p. 108.

29. Mark Franko argues persuasively that the laws of moderation—the discipline and restraint evident in the style of the movement and its syntax—as well as the general rules of bodily comportment reinforced and enhanced this omnipresent sense of a controlling order. See *The Dancing Body in Renaissance Choreography (1416–1589)* (Birmingham, Ala.: Summa Publications, 1986).

30. In 1661, Louis XIV established the Académie de la Danse that made it possible for dancers to pursue performance as a profession, and he subsequently commissioned Pierre Beauchamp to collect, organize, and devise a notation system for existing dance steps. Both this system and improved versions of it were well known throughout Europe by the end of the century.

31. For a more detailed account of these changes, see Margarete Baur-Heinhold, *The Baroque Theatre* (New York: McGraw-Hill, 1967); Oscar G. Brockett, *History of the Theatre* (Boston: Allyn and Bacon, 1968); and Thomas E. Lawrenson, *The French Stage in the Seventeenth Century* (Manchester: University of Manchester Press, 1957).

32. See Frederick Penzel, *Theatre Lighting before Electricity* (Middletown, Conn.: Wesleyan University Press, 1978); and Brockett, *History of the Theatre*.

33. See Shirley Wynne, "Complaisance, An Eighteenth-Century Cool," *Dance Scope 5*, no. 1 (Fall 1970): 22–35.

34. Voltaire wrote more than one poem "diplomatically" evaluating the competing principal ballerinas:

Ah, Camargo, que vous êtes brillante!
Mais que Sallé, grand Dieu, est ravissante!
Que vos pas sont léger et que les siens sont doux!
Elle est inimitable et vous êtes nouvelles!
Les nymphs sautent comme vous,
Mais les Graces dansent comme elle!

35. Jean Georges Noverre, *Letters on Dancing and Ballets*, trans. Cyril W. Beaumont (1760; Brooklyn: Dance Horizons, 1966), p. 16.

36. One of the most comprehensive examples is John Bulwer's *Chirologia*

and Chironomia (1654; Carbondale: Southern Illinois University Press, 1974).

37. Examples include Charles Le Brun's *Method of Delineating the Passions* (1667), Gérard de Laresse's *Groot Schilderboek* (1707), and Father Franciscus Lang's *Dissertatio de actione scenica* (Monachii Typis Mariae Magdalenae Riedlin, 1727).

38. John Weaver, *The History of the Mimes and Pantomimes* (London: Jacob Tonson, 1728), pp. 11–12.

39. Lucian of Samosata (born ca. A.D. 120) wrote dialogues on theater and dance. See *Lucian* (Cambridge: Harvard University Press, 1955).

40. John Weaver, *The Loves of Mars and Venus* (London: W. Mears, 1717), pp. 4–5.

41. Weaver's representations of the passions underscore the historical specificity of the meaning of movement. His descriptions, especially of the movements for jealousy or upbraiding that would have little or no meaning for us today, provide a delightful confirmation of Barthes's assertion that the "natural" is a cultural category. Similarly, Weaver's and Noverre's willingness to write about their work, when compared with the silence cultivated by choreographers of Graham's generation, points up the "unnaturalness" of the choreographer's role. In addition to several carefully annotated scores, Weaver's writings about dance include *An Essay Towards an History of Dancing* (London: Jacob Tonson, 1712), *Anatomical and Mechanical Lectures upon Dancing* (London: Jacob Tonson, 1721), and *The History of the Mimes and Pantomimes.*

42. See Raoul Auger Feuillet, *Orchésographie* (Paris: 1700), trans. John Weaver (1706; Farnborough, England: Gregg International, 1971); and Kellom Tomlinson, *The Art of Dancing Explained by Reading and Figures* (1735; London: Gregg International, 1970).

43. Pierre Rameau, *The Dancing Master*, trans. Cyril W. Beaumont (1725; New York: Dance Horizons, 1970), p. 5.

44. For an excellent analysis of these social dance performances and their relation to the concert vocabulary, see Wendy Hilton, *Dance of Court and Theatre: The French Noble Style, 1690–1725* (Princeton, N.J.: Princeton Book Company, 1981).

45. Rameau, *The Dancing Master*, p. 40.

46. Ibid., p. xii. Here Rameau is reiterating Erasmus, who wrote two centuries earlier: "Ordered and natural gestures give grace: if they don't eliminate faults, at all events they attenuate and mask them" (*De Civilitate* [1532]), translation by Mark Franko in *The Dancing Body in Renaissance Choreography*. Still, I would argue that the two statements are based on different sets of criteria for assessing and improving one's bodily "defects." Just as the rhetorical manuals in Rameau's time began to include illustrations, so his observa-

tions about bodily comportment reflect an increasing emphasis on purely visual features and a concern with ideal visual forms. For a comprehensive analysis of the relationship between Renaissance dance and rhetoric, see Franko, *The Dancing Body in Renaissance Choreography.*

47. Denis Diderot, *The Paradox of Acting*, trans. Walter Herries Pollock (ca. 1778; New York: Hill & Wang, 1957).

48. Quoted in Lincoln Kirstein, *Movement and Metaphor* (New York: Praeger, 1970), p. 86.

49. Weaver, *The Loves of Mars and Venus*, pp. 3–7.

50. Noverre, *Letters on Dancing and Ballets*, p. 9.

51. Rameau, *The Dancing Master*, p. 2.

52. Gregorio Lambranzi, *New and Curious School of Theatrical Dancing*, trans. Derra de Moroda (1716; New York: Dance Horizons, 1966).

53. Noverre, *Letters on Dancing and Ballets*, p. 33.

54. Duncan delivered her first manifesto, "The Dance of the Future," as a lecture in Berlin in 1903. Published in Leipzig the same year by Eugen Diederichs, it is included in her collected writings, *The Art of the Dance* (New York: Theatre Arts, 1928), pp. 54–63.

55. Carl Van Vechten, *The Dance Writings of Carl Van Vechten*, ed. Paul Padgette (Brooklyn: Dance Horizons, 1974), p. 25.

56. It is tempting to include Vaslav Nijinsky's name in this list of choreographers because many of his choreographic concerns are consonant with the description of expressionist dance that follows. The fact that he was trained within and performed and choreographed for the ballet community, however, creates complications that cannot be explained adequately in the kind of broad overview of choreographic epistemes presented here.

57. Ruth St. Denis was undoubtedly the choreographer most influential in educating the American public. St. Denis traveled the vaudeville circuits year after year, offering entertainment—something between the burlesque's familiar showgirl dances and the "high art" performances that she and later modern dance choreographers presented in major city centers—that informed viewers of the aesthetic aspirations of the new American dance. See Suzanne Shelton, *Divine Dancer: A Biography of Ruth St. Denis* (Garden City, N.Y.: Doubleday, 1981); and Nancy Lee Chalfa Ruyter, *Reformers and Visionaries. The Americanization of the Art of Dance* (New York: Dance Horizons, 1979).

58. See William O'Dea, *The Social History of Lighting* (London: Routledge & Kegan Paul, 1958); Jacques Rouché, *L'Art théâtrical moderne* (Paris: Librairie Bloud et Gay, 1924); and Brockett, *History of the Theatre.*

59. John Martin, *Introduction to the Dance* (1939; New York: Dance Horizons, 1968), p. 89.

60. Isadora Duncan, *My Life* (New York: Garden City Publishing, 1927), p. 75.

61. Ruth St. Denis, *An Unfinished Life* (New York: Harper & Brothers, 1939), p. 52.

62. Mary Wigman, "On Composition" (Dresden: Mary Wigman School of the Dance, n.d.), p. 7.

63. Doris Humphrey in *Doris Humphrey: An Artist First*, ed. Selma Jeanne Cohen (Middletown, Conn.: Wesleyan University Press, 1972), p. 252.

64. Duncan, *The Art of the Dance*, p. 51.

65. Ruyter makes this point in *Reformers and Visionaries*, p. 84.

66. For an insightful summary of late-nineteenth-century developments in the art of rhetoric, see Ruyter, *Reformers and Visionaries*, pp. 17–30.

67. Ted Shawn, *Every Little Movement: A Book about François Delsarte* (Pittsfield, Mass.: Eagle Printing, 1954), p. 35.

68. Ibid.

69. Doris Humphrey, *The Art of Making Dances* (New York: Grove Press, 1959), p. 97.

70. See Shelton, *Divine Dancer*, pp. 59–67, for a detailed description and analysis of *Radha*.

71. Doris Humphrey, quoted in Sali Ann Kriegsman, *Modern Dance in America: The Bennington Years* (Boston: G. K. Hall, 1981), p. 284.

72. Humphrey, *The Art of Making Dances*, pp. 39–41.

73. Mary Wigman, "My Teacher Laban," *Dance Magazine* (November 1956): 27.

74. Even in works like Ruth St. Denis's music visualizations, in which the choreography follows the structure of the musical score in virtually every respect, the intention was quite different from that in Balanchine's dances or in neoclassical dance. St. Denis and all the expressionists believed that they were conveying through the dance spiritual qualities or motivations evoked by the music but equally evident in the body's motion. Thus their project was not to *imitate* musical forms but to *replicate* in dance a system of feelings they believed existed in the music.

75. Humphrey, *The Art of Making Dances*, p. 132.

76. These extraordinary innovations in movement quality were, in part, what prompted John Martin to formulate his concept of "inner mimicry" as he did:

Since we respond muscularly to the strains in architectural masses and the attitude of rocks, it is plain to be seen that we will respond even more vigorously to the action of a body exactly like our own. We shall cease to be spectators and become participants in the movement that is presented to us, and though to all outward appearances we shall be sitting quietly in our chairs, we shall nevertheless be dancing synthetically with all our musculature. (*Introduction to the Dance*, p. 53)

77. See Konstantin Stanislavsky, *Building a Character*, trans. Elizabeth Reynolds Hapgood (New York: Theater Arts Books, 1949), and *Stanislavsky on the Art of the Stage*, trans. David Magarshack (1950; New York: Hill & Wang, 1961).

78. Paul Taylor's choreography in the 1950s and 1960s was on a par with Cunningham's—highly innovative in its use of syntactic procedures and anti-expressionist in its desire to show the makings of a dance. In his subsequent work, however, he has returned to the more traditional concerns of expressionist and even neoclassical traditions, so that now only a small number of his works show an objectivist approach to composition.

79. Robert Ellis Dunn's composition classes at the Cunningham Studio in the early 1960s provided an important gathering place and a supportive context for exploring these new approaches to composition. See Berenice Fisher, "Master Teacher Robert Ellis Dunn: Cultivating Impulse," *Dance Magazine* (January 1984): 84–87; and Sally Banes, *Democracy's Body: Judson Dance Theatre, 1962–1964* (Ann Arbor, Mich.: UMI Research Press, 1983).

80. Actually, the score for *Satisfyin' Lover* is complex, involving detailed lists of simple actions for six separate groups of people. See Steve Paxton, "*Satisfyin' Lover*," *0 to 9* no. 4 (June 1968): 27–30.

81. See Rainer's scores for these dances in her book, *Work 1961–73* (Halifax and New York: Press of the Nova Scotia College of Art and Design and New York University Press, 1974).

82. These dances were part of a series of performances called *Equipment Pieces* that Brown choreographed between 1968 and 1971. For a detailed review of the entire collection of dances, see Sally R. Sommer, "Equipment Dances: Trisha Brown," *The Drama Review* 16 (T-55, September 1972): 135–41.

83. See Yvonne Rainer, "A Quasi-Survey of Some 'Minimalist' Tendencies in the Quantitatively Minimal Dance Activity Midst the Plethora, or an Analysis of *Trio A*," in *Work 1961–73*, pp. 63–75.

84. See also Sally Banes's lengthy and informative description of *Trio A* in *Terpsichore in Sneakers* (Boston: Houghton Mifflin, 1980), pp. 44–54.

85. Rainer, *Work 1961–73*, p. 67.

86. Jill Johnston persuasively describes the Judson Church performances of this period as

a beautiful mess. Within that mess certain hard-core positions were taking shape and certain works were undeniably extraordinary. After a period of some confusion and dispersion, the movement regained its momentum and is now in the process of enlarging, elaborating, and consolidating the dimension of its early promise. It is no longer so much a rebellion as a serious extension of novel positions. (*Marmalade Me* [New York: Dutton, 1971], p. 95)

87. Trisha Brown, lecture-demonstration at Wesleyan University, Fall 1983.

88. Lucinda Childs, "Lucinda Childs," in *Contemporary Dance*, ed. Anne Livet (New York: Abbeville Press, 1978), p. 71.

89. A similar phenomenon can be seen occasionally in the video or film demonstrations of sports events. The athlete viewed in slow motion or close up while completely absorbed in strenuous activity is a subject-body passionately engaged.

90. Samuel Beckett writing on James Joyce's *Finnegans Wake* could as easily be describing objectivist dance when he says: "Here form *is* content, content is form. You complain that this stuff is not written in English. It is not written at all. It is not to be read—or rather it is not only to be read. It is to be looked at and listened to. His writing is not *about* something; *it is that something itself*" (Samuel Beckett, "Dante . . . Bruno . . . Vico . . . Joyce," in *James Joyce / Finnegans Wake: A Symposium* [New York: New Directions, 1972], p. 14).

CHAPTER FOUR

Writing Dancing

1. Elsewhere I have argued that, in fact, the histories of dance written in the eighteenth century differ from early twentieth-century histories in much the same way that the dances of the two periods contrast with one another. See "On Dancing and the Dance: Two Visions of Dance's History," in *Proceedings of the Society of Dance History*, comp. Christena Schlundt (1983): 133–41. For a comprehensive analysis of the historical specificity of historical methods, see Hayden White, *Metahistory* (Baltimore: Johns Hopkins University Press, 1973), and "The Value of Narrativity in the Representation of Reality," *Critical Inquiry* 7, no. 1 (Autumn 1980): 5–27.

2. In chapter 4, I have avoided the term *postmodernism* just as I have throughout this study purposefully avoided the use of such period terms as *modern, romantic, baroque*, and so forth, that are typically employed in dance history and criticism. My reason is twofold: first, definitions of these terms in dance are vague and often contradictory, and their correlations to the other arts raise complex issues that are beyond the scope of this book; second, I

want to continue to emphasize that *Reading Dancing* is not a history of dance but rather a theory about dance. The models, allegorical, neoclassical, expressionist, objectivist, and reflexive, that I propose do not account for all dance occurring in any historical period, nor are they necessarily evident in any given dance. Rather, they are outlines of paradigmatic approaches to making and viewing dances.

3. In suggesting a fifth paradigm for dance making based on a reflexive representational practice, I am following a distinction Yvonne Rainer makes in a recent article entitled "Looking Myself in the Mouth—Sliding Out of Narrative and Lurching Back In, Not Once but . . . Is the 'New Talkie' Something to Chirp About? From Fiction to Theory (Kicking and Screaming) Death of the Maiden, I Mean Author, I Mean Artist . . . No, I Mean Character A Revisionist Narrativization of/with Myself as Subject (Still Kicking) via John Cage's Ample Back," *October* 17 (Summer 1981): 65–76. Rainer argues that Cage's and Cunningham's insistence on the autoreferentiality of sound and movement resulted in performances that denied or at least ignored the political and ideological significance of the body. Rainer suggests that by returning to narrative structures in which the body would necessarily refer to things other than itself while disrupting those narrative structures as they unfold in the performance, the performance can unmask the body's ideological message and thus allow viewers to contemplate the body as a signifying practice.

4. Umberto Eco gives an elegant description of this impulse to refer simultaneously to the message and its making in *A Postscript to "The Name of the Rose"* (New York: Harcourt Brace Jovanovich, 1984).

5. For a detailed survey of the Judson group dances, see Sally Banes, *Democracy's Body: Judson Dance Theatre, 1962–1964* (Ann Arbor, Mich.: UMI Research Press, 1983).

6. David Gordon, "It's About Time," *The Drama Review* 19, no. 1 (T-65, March 1975): 45.

7. Roland Barthes makes a distinction between "works" of art, which are classical and monolithic in stature, the product of a single, clearly intended point of view, and "texts," which he claims are more pluralistic and open-ended and invite an extemporized collaboration with their readers. The monolithic, or readerly, work relegates the reader to the role of consumer while the writerly text offers the reader the possibility of helping to produce it:

Why is the writerly our value? Because the goal of literary work (of literature as work) is to make the reader no longer a consumer, but a producer of the text. Our literature is characterized by the pitiless divorce which the literary institution maintains between the producer of the text and its user, between its owner and its consumer, between its author and its reader. This reader is thereby plunged into a kind of idleness—he is intransitive;

he is, in short, *serious*: instead of function himself, instead of gaining access to the magic of the signifier, to the pleasure of writing, he is left with no more than the poor freedom either to accept or reject the text: reading is nothing more than a *referendum*. Opposite the writerly text, then, is its countervalue, its negative, reactive value: what can be read, but not written: the *readerly*. We call any readerly text a classic text. (*S/Z* [New York: Hill & Wang, 1974], p. 4)

This distinction between readerly and writerly texts, much evident in the dances of the Judson choreographers, serves as a background for my analysis of contemporary dance in this final chapter. I realize that Barthes's division of texts into readerly and writerly camps raises more questions than it answers, but still I find it a useful concept, particularly when it is applied to the aesthetic issues at stake in the choreographic investigations of the 1960s and 1970s.

8. *Fait Accompli* is the apt title of one of Tharp's recent works, which had its premier at the Brooklyn Academy of Music in the winter of 1984. I include Tharp in this analysis of reflexive choreographic conventions because her implementation of them represents an emerging trend in contemporary dance, a kind of mainstream postmodernism in dance. Elsewhere I have analyzed the difference between her work and that of groups like the Grand Union and Meredith Monk by using Hal Foster's distinction between reactionary and resistive forms of postmodernism. See "The Signifying Body: Reaction and Resistance in Postmodern Dance," *Theatre Journal* 37, no. 1 (March 1985): 45–64.

Foster writes in the introduction to his volume of essays on postmodernism, *The Anti-Aesthetic: Essays on Postmodern Culture* (Port Townsend, Wash.: Bay Press, 1983), p. xii:

A postmodernism of resistance, then, arises as a counter-practice not only to the official culture of modernism but also to the "false normativity" of a reactionary postmodernism. In opposition (but not *only* in opposition), a resistant postmodernism is concerned with a critical deconstruction of tradition, not an instrumental pastiche of pop- or pseudo- historical forms, with a critique of origins, not a return to them. In short, it seeks to question rather than exploit cultural codes, to explore rather than conceal social and political affiliations.

Tharp's work, as an example of a reactionary postmodernism, shows how reflexive choreographic techniques can be used to impart a playful yet uncritical message, one that reinforces conservative values even as it leads ultimately to a profound sense of alienation. The resistive work of the Grand Union and Meredith Monk, on the other hand, seems to embody the play that Barthes so often referred to and created in his writing: a sustained, humorous, critical, and communal practice. My comparison of Tharp with the Grand

Union and Monk is designed, therefore, to enhance our ability to discriminate between reactionary and resistive forms.

9. The founding members of the Grand Union were Becky Arnold, Trisha Brown, Dong, Douglas Dunn, David Gordon, Nancy Green, Barbara Lloyd, Steve Paxton, and Yvonne Rainer.

10. Sally Banes, *Terpsichore in Sneakers* (Boston: Houghton Mifflin, 1980), p. 212.

11. Over the past ten years, Monk has developed at least three distinct kinds of interdisciplinary performances: concerts of her vocal compositions that pay special attention to the placement and movement of the musicians; cabarets that blend a musical score with striking theatrical images; and her dramatic theatre pieces that involve extensive acting, choreography, costuming, and set design in addition to the musical score. I consider this third category of performance in the analysis that follows.

12. Brooks McNamara, "*Vessel*: The Scenography of Meredith Monk (interview)," *The Drama Review* 16, no. 1 (T-53, March 1972): 102.

13. Ibid.: 96–98.

14. Richard Lorber makes this point in his review of a Grand Union concert, "The Problem with Grand Union," *Dance Scope* 7, no. 2 (Spring–Summer 1973): 33–34.

15. The unidentified critic is quoted by Brooks McNamara in "*Vessel*: The Scenography of Meredith Monk": 88.

SELECTED BIBLIOGRAPHY

Adorno, Theodor W. *Philosophy of Modern Music*. Translated by Anne G. Mitchell and Wesley V. Blomster. New York: Seabury Press, 1973.

Andrew, J. Dudley. "The Structuralist Study of Narrative: Its History, Use, and Limits." In *The Horizon of Literature*. Lincoln: University of Nebraska Press, 1982, pp. 99–124.

———. *Concepts in Film Theory*. New York: Oxford University Press, 1984.

Arnheim, Rudolf. *Art and Visual Perception*. Berkeley and Los Angeles: University of California Press, 1954.

Bachelard, Gaston. *The Poetics of Space*. Translated by Maria Jolas. New York: Orion Press, 1964.

Barthes, Roland. *Writing Degree Zero*. Translated by Annette Lavers and Colin Smith. New York: Hill & Wang, 1953.

———. *Mythologies*. Translated by Annette Lavers. New York: Hill & Wang, 1972.

———. *Elements of Semiology*. Translated by Annette Lavers and Colin Smith. New York: Hill & Wang, 1978.

———. *Critical Essays*. Translated by Richard Howard. Evanston, Ill.: Northwestern University Press, 1972.

———. *S/Z*. Translated by Richard Miller. New York: Hill & Wang, 1974.

———. *The Pleasure of the Text*. Translated by Richard Miller. New York: Hill & Wang, 1975.

Literary and Cultural Criticism

———. *Barthes by Barthes*. Translated by Richard Howard. New York: Hill & Wang, 1977.

———. *Image, Music, Text*. Translated by Stephen Heath. New York: Hill & Wang, 1978.

———. *The Empire of Signs*. Translated by Richard Howard. New York: Hill & Wang, 1982.

Becker, Alton L., and Aram A. Yengoyan, eds. *The Imagination of Reality: Studies in Southeast Asian Coherence Systems*. Norwood, N.J.: Ablex, 1979.

Benamou, Michel, and Charles Caramello, eds. *Performance in Postmodern Culture*. Madison, Wis.: Coda Press, 1977.

Benveniste, Emile. *Problems in General Linguistics*. Translated by Mary Elizabeth Meek. Coral Gables, Fla.: University of Miami Press, 1971.

Bloom, Harold. *A Map of Misreading*. New York: Oxford University Press, 1975.

Burke, Kenneth. "Four Master Tropes." In *A Grammar of Motives*. New York: Prentice-Hall, 1945, pp. 503–17.

———. *Language as Symbolic Action*. Berkeley and Los Angeles: University of California Press, 1968.

———. *A Grammar of Motives*. Berkeley and Los Angeles: University of California Press, 1969.

Callois, Roger. *Man and the Sacred*. Glencoe, Ill.: Free Press of Glencoe, 1959.

Clifford, James. "On Ethnographic Authority." *Representations* 1, no. 2 (Spring 1983): 118–45.

Culler, Jonathan. *Structuralist Poetics*. Ithaca, N.Y.: Cornell University Press, 1975.

———. "In Pursuit of Signs." *Daedalus* (Fall 1977): 95–111.

De Lauretis, Teresa. *Alice Doesn't: Feminism, Semiotics, Cinema*. Bloomington: Indiana University Press, 1984.

Deleuze, Gilles, and F. Guattari. *Anti-Oedipus: Capitalism and Schizophrenia*. Translated by Robert Hurley, Helen R. Lane and Mark Seem. New York: Viking Press, 1977.

Derrida, Jacques. *Glas*. Paris: Éditions Galilée, 1974.

———. *Of Grammatology*. Translated by Gayatri Chakravorty Spivak. Baltimore: Johns Hopkins University Press, 1976.

———. *La Verité en peinture*. Paris: Flammarion, 1978.

———. *Writing and Difference*. Translated by Alan Bass. Chicago: University of Chicago Press, 1978.

Eco, Umberto. *A Theory of Semiotics*. Bloomington: Indiana University Press, 1976.

————. "Semiotics of Theatrical Performance." *The Drama Review* 21, no. 1 (March 1977): 107–17.

————. *The Role of the Reader*. Bloomington: Indiana University Press, 1979.

————. *A Postscript to "The Name of the Rose."* Translated by William Weaver. New York: Harcourt Brace Jovanovich, 1984.

Elam, Keir. *The Semiotics of Theatre and Drama*. London: Methuen, 1980.

Erlich, Victor. *Russian Formalism*. New Haven, Conn.: Yale University Press, 1955.

Foster, Hal, ed. *The Anti-Aesthetic: Essays on Postmodern Culture*. Port Townsend, Wash.: Bay Press, 1983.

Foucault, Michel. *Raymond Roussel*. Paris: Gallimard, 1963.

————. *The Order of Things: An Archaeology of the Human Sciences*. Translation of *Les Mots et les choses*. New York: Pantheon Books, 1971.

————. *The Archeology of Knowledge*. Translated by A. M. Sheridan Smith. New York: Pantheon Books, 1972.

————. *The Birth of the Clinic*. Translated by A. M. Sheridan Smith. New York: Pantheon Books, 1973.

————. "What Is an Author?" Translated by James Venit. *Partisan Review* no. 4 (1975): 604–14.

————. *Language, Counter-Memory, Practice*. Translated by Donald F. Bouchard and Sherry Simon. Ithaca, N.Y.: Cornell University Press, 1977.

————. *Discipline and Punish: The Birth of the Prison*. Translated by Alan Sheridan. New York: Pantheon Books, 1978.

————. *The History of Sexuality*. Translated by Robert Hurley. New York: Pantheon Books, 1978.

————. *This Is Not a Pipe*. Translated by James Harkness. Berkeley and Los Angeles: University of California Press, 1982.

Fried, Michael. "Representing Representations: On the Central Group in Courbet's *Studio*." In *Allegory and Representation*, edited by Stephen J. Greenblatt. Baltimore: Johns Hopkins University Press, 1981, pp. 99–127.

Frye, Northrop. *Anatomy of Criticism*. Princeton, N.J.: Princeton University Press, 1957.

Geertz, Clifford. *The Interpretation of Cultures*. New York: Basic Books, 1973.

————. "Blurred Genres." *American Scholar* (Spring 1980): 165–79.

————. *Local Knowledge*. New York: Basic Books, 1983.

Gombrich, E. H. *Art and Illusion*. New York: Pantheon Books, 1956.

————. "Style." In *International Encyclopedia of the Social Sciences*, edited by David Sills. Vol. 15. New York: Macmillan and Free Press, 1968, pp. 352–61.

Greenblatt, Stephen. *Renaissance Self-Fashioning*. Chicago: University of Chicago Press, 1980.

————. "Filthy Rites." *Daedalus* (Summer 1982): 1–16.

————. "Invisible Bullets: Renaissance Authority and Its Subversion." *Glyph* 8 (1980): 40–61.

————. "Murdering Peasants: Status, Genre, and the Representation of Rebellion." *Representations* 1, no. 1 (Winter 1983): 1–29.

Harari, Josué, ed. *Textual Strategies*. Ithaca, N.Y.: Cornell University Press, 1979.

Henley, Nancy. *Body Politics: Power, Sex, and Non-Verbal Communication*. Englewood Cliffs, N.J.: Prentice-Hall, 1977.

Jakobson, Roman. "Linguistics and Poetics." In *Style in Language*, edited by Thomas Sebeok. Cambridge: MIT Press, 1960, pp. 85–121.

————. "What Poets Do with Words." A lecture by Roman Jakobson at the Center for Humanities, Wesleyan University, February 22, 1971.

Jameson, Fredric. *The Prison-House of Language*. Princeton, N.J.: Princeton University Press, 1972.

————. *Marxism and Form*. Princeton, N.J.: Princeton University Press, 1972.

————. *The Political Unconscious*. Ithaca, N.Y.: Cornell University Press, 1981.

————. "Postmodernism, or The Cultural Logic of Late Capitalism." *New Left Review* (July–August 1984): 53–94.

Kristeva, Julia. "Gesture: Practice or Communication." Translated by Jonathan Benthall. In *The Body Reader*, edited by Ted Polhemus. New York: Pantheon Books, 1978, pp. 264–84.

Lanham, Richard. *A Handlist of Rhetorical Terms*. Berkeley and Los Angeles: University of California Press, 1968.

Lévi-Strauss, Claude. *Structural Anthropology*. Translated by Claire Jacobson and Brooke Grundfest Schoepf. New York: Basic Books, 1963.

————. *The Savage Mind*. Chicago: University of Chicago Press, 1966.

————. *The Raw and the Cooked*. Translated by John Weightman and Doreen Weightman. New York: Harper & Row, 1969.

————. *Tristes Tropiques.* Translated by John Weightman and Doreen Weightman. London: J. Cape, 1973.

Lotman, Yuri. *The Structure of the Artistic Text.* Translated by Ronald Vroon. Ann Arbor: University of Michigan Press, 1977.

Matejka, Ladislav, and Irwin Titunik, eds. *Semiotics of Art.* Cambridge: MIT Press, 1976.

Mauss, Marcel. "Techniques sur le corps." *Economy and Society* 2, no. 1 (February 1973): 70–88.

Mink, Louis O. "History and Fiction as Modes of Comprehension." *New Literary History* 1, no. 2 (Spring 1970): 541–558.

Morgan, Robert P. "Musical Time / Musical Space." *Critical Inquiry* 6, no. 3 (Spring 1980): 527–38.

Olney, James. *Metaphors of Self.* Princeton, N.J.: Princeton University Press, 1972.

Ong, Walter. "From Allegory to Diagram in the Renaissance Mind: A Study on the Significance of the Allegorical Tableau." *Journal of Aesthetics and Art Criticism* 17 (1959): 423–40.

Onians, Richard B. *The Origins of European Thought.* New York: Arno Press, 1973.

Perloff, Marjorie. *The Poetics of Indeterminacy.* Princeton, N.J.: Princeton University Press, 1981.

Propp, Vladimir. *Morphology of the Folktale.* Translated by Laurence Scott. Austin: University of Texas Press, 1968.

Rainer, Yvonne. "Looking Myself in the Mouth." *October* 17 (Summer 1981): 65–76.

Ricoeur, Paul. "The Model of the Text: Meaningful Action Considered as a Text." *Social Research* 38, no. 3 (Autumn 1971): 529–62.

————. *Time and Narrative.* Chicago: University of Chicago Press, 1984.

Said, Edward. "The Text, the World, the Critic." In *Textual Strategies,* edited by Josué Harari. Ithaca, N.Y.: Cornell University Press, 1979, pp. 161–68.

Spivak, Gayatri. "Revolutions That As Yet Have No Model: Derrida's *Limited Inc.*" *Diacritics* (December 1980): 29–49.

Sturrock, John, ed. *Structuralism and Since.* Oxford and New York: Oxford University Press, 1979.

Suleiman, Susan, ed. *The Reader in the Text.* Princeton, N.J.: Princeton University Press, 1980.

Turner, Victor. *The Forest of Symbols.* Ithaca, N.Y.: Cornell University Press, 1967.

———. *The Ritual Process.* Chicago: Aldine, 1969.

———. *Drama, Fields, and Metaphors: Symbolic Action in Human Society.* Ithaca, N.Y.: Cornell University Press, 1974.

Ullman, Stephen. *Semantics.* New York: Harper & Row, 1979.

Vico, Giambattista. *The New Science of Giambattisa Vico* (1744). Translated by Thomas Goddard Bergin and Max Harold Fisch. Ithaca, N.Y.: Cornell University Press, 1984.

White, Hayden. "Interpretation in History." *New Literary History* 4, no. 2 (Winter 1973): 281–314.

———. *Metahistory.* Baltimore: Johns Hopkins University Press, 1973.

———. *Tropics of Discourse.* Baltimore: Johns Hopkins University Press, 1978.

———. "Michel Foucault." In *Structuralism and Since*, edited by John Sturrock. Oxford and New York: Oxford University Press, 1979, pp. 81–115.

———. "The Discourse of History." *Humanities in Society* (Fall–Winter 1979): 1–15.

———. "The Value of Narrativity in the Representation of Reality." *Critical Inquiry* 7, no. 1 (Autumn 1980): 5–27.

Williams, Raymond. *Culture and Society.* New York: Columbia University Press, 1958.

———. *Key Words.* New York: Oxford University Press, 1976.

———. *The Sociology of Culture.* New York: Schocken Books, 1981.

Young, Richard E., et al. *Rhetoric: Discovery and Change.* New York: Harcourt, Brace & World, 1970.

Dance, Art, and the Body

Alexander, F. Mathias. *The Resurrection of the Body.* New York: Delta, 1969.

Ambrose, Kay. *Ballet Student's Primer.* New York: Knopf, 1966.

Arbeau, Thoinot [Jehan Tabourot]. *Orchésographie* (1588). Translated by Cyril W. Beaumont. Brooklyn: Dance Horizons, 1968.

Arena, Antonius de. *Ad suos compagnones, qui sont de persona friantes, bassas dansas et branlos practicantes novelles per quam plurimos mandat.* Paris: Chez Philippes Gaultier, 1533.

Armitage, Merle. *Martha Graham.* Los Angeles: Merle Armitage, 1937.

Armitage, Merle, and Virginia Stewart, eds. *Modern Dance.* New York: E. Weyhe, 1935.

Artaud, Antonin. *The Theatre and Its Double.* Translated by Mary Caroline Richard. New York: Grove Press, 1958.

———. *Antonin Artaud Anthology.* Edited by Jack Hirschman. San Francisco: City Lights Books, 1965.

———. *Selected Writings.* Edited by Susan Sontag. Translated by Helen Weaver. New York: Farrar, Straus & Giroux, 1976.

Ashley, Merrill, and Larry Kaplan. *Dancing for Balanchine.* New York: Dutton, 1984.

Austin, Gilbert. *Chironomia.* Carbondale: Southern Illinois University Press, 1966.

Baker, Robb. "Landscapes and Telescopes—A Personal Response to the Choreography of Meredith Monk." *Dance Magazine* (April 1976): 55–70.

Balanchine, George. "Notes on Choreography." *Dance Index* (February–March 1945): 20–31.

———. "Mr. B. Sees Himself as Cook, Carpenter and Choreographer." *Dance Magazine* (January 1958): 34–35.

———. "An Interview with Ivan Nabokov and E. Carmichael." *Horizon* (New York) (January 1961): 44–56.

———. "Balanchine Talks to *Dance and Dancers.*" *Dance and Dancers.* (London) (December 1962): 31–33.

———. *Choreography of George Balanchine: A Catalogue of Works.* New York: Viking Press, 1983.

Balanchine, George, with Francis Mason. *Balanchine's New Complete Stories of the Ballet.* New York: Doubleday, 1968.

Banes, Sally. *Terpsichore in Sneakers.* Boston: Houghton Mifflin, 1980.

———. *Democracy's Body: Judson Dance Theatre, 1962–1964.* Ann Arbor, Mich.: UMI Research Press, 1983.

Baron, John, ed. and trans. "*Les Fées des forests de S. Germain, ballet de cour*" (1625). *Dance Perspectives* no. 62, (Summer 1975).

Bartinieff, Irmgard. *Body Movement: Coping with the Environment.* New York: Gordon & Breach Science Publishers, 1980.

Baur-Heinhold, Margarete. *The Baroque Theatre.* New York: McGraw-Hill, 1967.

Beaumont, Cyril. *The Ballet As Seen by Théophile Gautier.* London: Beaumont, 1932.

———. *Michel Fokine and His Ballets.* London: Beaumont, 1935.

———. *The Ballet Called Giselle.* 1945. Reprint. Brooklyn: Dance Horizons, 1969.

Beiswanger, George, Wilfried A. Hofmann and David Michael Levin. "Three Essays on Dance Aesthetics." *Dance Perspectives* no. 55 (Autumn 1973).

Belo, Jane. *Trance in Bali*. New York: Columbia University Press, 1960.

Bennington College Judson Project. *Judson Dance Theatre: 1962–1966*. Bennington, Vt.: Bennington College, 1981.

Bertalà, Giovanna M., and Annamaria P. Tofani. *Feste e apparati Medicei da Cosimo I a Cosimo II*. Mostra di Disegni e Incisioni, Gabinetto di Disegni et Stampe degli Uffizi XXXI, 1969.

Birdwhistell, Ray. *Kinesics and Context*. Philadelphia: University of Pennsylvania Press, 1970.

Blacking, John, ed. *The Anthropology of the Body*. New York: Academic Press, 1977.

Blasis, Carlo. *An Elementary Treatise upon the Theory and Practice of the Art of Dancing* (1820). Translated by Mary Stewart Evans. New York: Dover Publications, 1968.

————*The Code of Terpsichore*. London: Edward Bull, 1830.

Boas, Franziska. *The Function of Dance in Human Society*. Brooklyn: Dance Horizons, 1944.

Bonnet, Jacques. *Histoire générale de la danse*. Paris: Chez d'Houry, 1724.

de Brach, Pierre. *Les Poèmes*. Bordeaux, 1576.

Brainard, Ingrid. "The Role of the Dancing Master in Fifteenth Century Courtly Society." *Fifteenth Century Studies* 2 (1979): 21–44.

————. *The Art of Courtly Dancing in the Early Renaissance*. West Newton, Mass.: I. G. Brainard, 1981.

Brecht, Bertolt. *Brecht on Theatre*. Edited and translated by John Willett. New York: Hill & Wang, 1964.

Brinson, Peter. *Background to European Ballet*. Leyden: Sijthoff, 1966.

Brockett, Oscar G. *History of the Theatre*. Boston: Allyn and Bacon, 1968.

Brown, Carolyn, et al. "Time to Walk in Space." *Dance Perspectives* no. 34 (Summer 1968).

Brown, Jean Morrison, ed. *The Vision of Modern Dance*. Princeton, N.J.: Princeton Book Company, 1979.

Bruhn, Erik, and Lillian Moore. *Bournonville and Ballet Technique*. Brooklyn: Dance Horizons, 1961.

Buckle, Richard. *Nijinsky*. London: Weidenfeld and Nicolson, 1971.

Bulwer, John. *Chirologia and Chironomia* (1654). Carbondale: Southern Illinois University Press, 1974.

Burckhardt, Jakob. *The Civilization of the Renaissance in Italy*. 1860. Reprint. London: Phaidon Press, 1951.

Burnham, Jack. *The Structure of Art*. New York: Braziller, 1971.

Caffin, Caroline, and Charles Caffin. *Dancing and Dancers of Today*. New York: Dodd, Mead, 1912.

Cage, John. *4'33"*. New York: Peters, 1962.

———. *Silence*. Cambridge: MIT Press, 1966.

Cahusac, Louis de. *La Danse ancienne et moderne*. Paris: Chez La Haye, 1754.

Calame-Griaule, Geneviève. *Ethnologie et langage: la parole chez les Dogon*. Paris: Gallimard, 1965.

Caroso, Fabritio. *Il ballarino*. Venice: Francesco Ziletti, 1581.

Castiglione, Baldassare. *The Book of the Courtier* (1528). Translated by Charles S. Singleton. New York: Anchor Books, 1959.

Childs, Lucinda. "Lucinda Childs: A Portfolio." *Artforum* 11 (February 1973): 50–56.

Christout, Marie-Françoise. "The Court Ballet in France: 1615–1641." *Dance Perspectives* no. 20 (Winter 1966).

———. *Le Ballet de cour de Louis XIV, 1643–1672. Mise en scènes*. Paris: A. et J. Picard, 1967.

Clarke, Mary, and Clement Crisp. *Ballet: An Illustrated History*. New York: Universe Books, 1973.

Cohen, Selma Jeanne. *The Modern Dance: Seven Statements of Belief*. Middletown, Conn.: Wesleyan University Press, 1965.

———. *Dance as a Theatre Art*. New York: Dodd, Mead, 1974.

———. *Next Week, Swan Lake*. Middletown, Conn.: Wesleyan University Press, 1982.

Colletet, Guillaume. *Le Grand Ballet des effects de la nature*. Paris: Jean Martin, 1632.

Committee on Research in Dance. Research Annual VI. *New Dimensions in Dance Research: Anthropology and Dance—The American Indian*. The Proceedings of the Third Conference on Research in Dance. Edited by Tamara Comstock. New York: New York University, 1972.

———. Research Annual VII. *Reflections and Perspectives on Two Anthropological Studies of Dance*. Edited by Adrienne Kaeppler. New York: New York University, 1976.

Cooter, Roger. "The Power of the Body: The Early Nineteenth Century." In *Natural Order*, edited by Barry Barnes and Steven Shapin. Beverly Hills, Calif.: Sage, 1979, pp. 73–92.

Copeland, Roger. "The Politics of Perception: The Unnaturalness of Merce Cunningham." *New Republic* (November 17, 1979): 25–30.

Copeland, Roger, and Marshall Cohen. *What Is Dance?* New York: Oxford University Press, 1984.

Copland, Robert. *The Manner of Dancing Bace Dances* (1521). Sussex, England: Pear Tree Press, 1937.

Cornazano, Antonio. *The Book on the Art of Dancing* (1455). Translated by M. Inglehearn and P. Forsyth. London: Dance Books, 1981.

Croce, Arlene. *Afterimages*. New York: Knopf, 1977.

Cunningham, Merce. "The Function of a Technique for Dance." In *The Dance Has Many Faces*. Edited by Walter Sorell. New York: World Publishing, 1951, pp. 250–55.

———. *Changes: Notes on Choreography*. New York: Something Else Press, 1968.

———. *The Dancer and the Dance*. Merce Cunningham in conversation with Jacqueline Lesschaeve. New York: M. Boyars Publishers, 1985.

Darwin, Charles. *Expression of the Emotions in Man and Animals* (1872). Chicago: University of Chicago Press, 1965.

Davies, Sir John. *The Poems of Sir John Davies*. Edited by Robert Krueger. Oxford: Clarendon Press, 1975.

Davis, Martha. *Understanding Body Movement: An Annotated Bibliography*. New York: Arno Press, 1972.

———, ed. *Research Approaches to Movement and Personality*. New York: Arno Press, 1973.

———. *Towards Understanding the Intrinsic in Body Movement*. New York: Arno Press, 1973.

Dell, Cecily. *A Primer for Movement Description Using Effort-Shape Analysis*. New York: Dance Notation Bureau, 1970.

Denby, Edwin. *Looking at the Dance*. New York: Horizon, 1968.

———. *Dancers, Buildings, and People in the Streets*. New York: Horizon Press, 1973.

Diderot, Denis. *The Paradox of Acting* (ca. 1778). Translated by Walter Herries Pollock. New York: Hill & Wang, 1957.

Dieterlen, Germaine. *La Notion de personne en Afrique noire*. Paris: Colloques Internationaux du Centre de la Recherche Scientifique, 1973.

Dolmetch, Mabel. *Dances of England and France, 1450–1600*. London: Routledge & Kegan Paul, 1949.

———. *Dances of Spain and Italy, 1400–1600*. London: Routledge & Kegan Paul, 1954.

Domenico da Piacenza. *De arte saltandi e choreas ducendi*. Paris: Bibliothèque Nationale de Paris, Ms. it. 972.

Douglas, Mary. *Purity and Danger*. New York: Penguin, 1966.

———. "If the Dogon." *Cahier des etudes africains* 28 (1967): 657–72.

———. *Natural Symbols*. New York: Pantheon Books, 1970.

The Drama Review. "The New Dance Issue." 16, no. 3 (T-55, September 1972).

————. "The Post-Modern Dance Issue." 19, no. 1 (T-65, March 1975).

Duchamp, Marcel. *Notes and Projects for the Large Glass.* New York: Harry N. Abrams, 1969.

————. *Salt Seller: The Writings of Marcel Duchamp.* Edited by Michel Sanouillet and Elmer Peterson. New York: Oxford University Press, 1973.

————. *Duchamp du signe: Écrits.* Paris: Flammarion, 1976.

Duncan, Irma. *Duncan Dancer.* Middletown, Conn.: Wesleyan University Press, 1966.

————. *The Technique of Isadora Duncan.* Brooklyn: Dance Horizons, 1970.

Duncan, Isadora. *My Life.* New York: Garden City Publishing, 1927.

————. *The Art of the Dance.* New York: Theatre Arts, 1928.

————. *Yours, Isadora.* Edited by Francis Steegmuller. New York: Random House, 1974.

Dunn, Douglas, and Trisha Brown. "Dialogue: On Dance." *Performing Arts Journal* 1 (Fall 1976): 76–83.

Eisenberg, Abne and Ralph Smith. *Nonverbal Communication.* New York: Bobbs-Merrill, 1971.

Ekman, Paul. "Universal and Cultural Differences in Facial Expressions of Emotions." In *Nebraska Symposium on Motivation*, edited by J. Cole. Lincoln: University of Nebraska Press, 1971.

Ekman, Paul, and Wallace Friesen. "The Repertoire of Non-Verbal Behavior: Categories, Origins, Usage, and Coding." *Semiotica* 1:49–98.

Elyot, Sir Thomas. *The Book Named the Governor* (1531). New York: Teachers College Press, 1969.

Evans-Pritchard, Edward E. "The Dance." *Africa* 1 (1928): 446–62.

————. "The Nuer Conception of Spirit in Its Relation to the Social Order." *American Anthropologist* 55 (April 1953): 201–14.

Feldenkrais, Moshe. *Body and Mature Behavior.* New York: Humanities Press, 1969.

Feuillet, Raoul Auger. *Orchésographie* (1700). Translated by John Weaver. 1706. Reprint. Farnborough, England: Gregg International, 1971.

Fisher, Berenice. "Master Teacher Robert Ellis Dunn: Cultivating Impulse." *Dance Magazine* (January 1984): 84–87.

Fletcher, Ifan, and Selma Jeanne Cohen. *Famed for Dance: Essays on the Theory and Practice of Theatrical Dance in England.* New York: New York Public Library, 1960.

Flitch, J. E. Crawford. *Modern Dancing and Dancers.* Philadelphia: Lippincott, 1912.

Focillon, Henri. *The Life of Forms in Art.* Translated by Charles Beecher Hogan and George Kubler. New York: Wittenborn, 1948.

Fokine, Michel. *Memoirs of a Ballet Master.* Translated by Vitale Fokine. London: Constable, 1961.

Forti, Simone. *Handbook in Motion.* New York: New York University Press, 1974.

————. "Bicycles." *Dance Scope* 13, no. 1 (Fall 1978): 44–51.

Franko, Mark. *The Dancing Body in Renaissance Choreography (1416–1589).* Birmingham, Ala.: Summa Publications, 1986.

Fuller, Loie. *Fifteen Years of a Dancer's Life.* Brooklyn: Dance Horizons, 1913.

Gablik, Suzi. *Progress in Art.* New York: Rizzoli, 1977.

Gallini, Giovanni-Andrea. *A Treatise on the Art of Dancing.* London: Dodsley, 1762.

————. *Critical Observations on the Art of Dancing.* London: Dodsley, 1770.

Gautier, Théophile. *The Romantic Ballet.* Translated by Cyril W. Beaumont. London: Beaumont, 1947.

Geertz, Clifford. "Form and Variation in Balinese Village Structure." *American Anthropologist* 61 (December 1959): 991–1012.

Gellerman, Jill. "The Mayim Pattern as an Indicator of Cultural Attitudes in Three American Hasidic Communities: A Comparative Approach Based on Labananalysis." *Congress on Research in Dance. Essays in Dance Research Annual* no. 9 (New York: New York University, 1978), pp. 111–44.

Genthe, Arnold. *The Book of the Dance.* Boston: International Publishers, 1920.

Gibson, James J. *The Senses Considered as Perceptual Systems.* Boston: Houghton Mifflin, 1966.

Gordon, D. J. "The Imagery of Ben Jonson's *The Masque of Blackmere* and *The Masque of Beauty.*" *Journal of the Warburg and Courtauld Institutes* 6 (1943): 122–41.

————. "*Hymenaci*: Ben Jonson's Masque of Union." *Journal of the Warburg and Courtauld Institutes* 8 (1945): 107–45.

Goffman, Erving. *The Presentation of Self in Everyday Life.* New York: Anchor, 1959.

Gordon, David. "It's About Time." *The Drama Review* 19, no. 1 (T-65, March 1975): 43–52.

Graham, Martha. "The American Dance." In *Modern Dance*, edited by Merle Armitage and Virginia Stewart. New York: E. Weyhe, 1935, pp. 101–6.

———. "Martha Graham Is Interviewed by Pierre Tugal." *Dancing Times* (October 1950): 21–22.

———. "A Dancer's World." Transcript of the film *A Dancer's World*. *Dance Observer* (January 1958): 5.

———. "Martha Graham Speaks." *Dance Observer* (April 1963): 53–54.

———. "How I Became a Dancer." *Saturday Review* 48, no. 35 (August 28, 1965): 54.

———. *The Notebooks of Martha Graham*. New York: Harcourt Brace Jovanovich, 1973.

Grand Union. "The Grand Union." *Dance Scope* 7 (Spring–Summer 1973): 28–32.

———. "There Were Some Good Moments." *Avalanche* no. 8 (Summer–Fall 1973): 40–47.

Gross, Rev. J. B. *The Parson on Dancing* (1879). New York: Dance Horizons, n.d.

Guest, Ivor. *The Romantic Ballet*. Middletown, Conn.: Wesleyan University Press, 1966.

Hall, Edward. *The Hidden Dimensions*. Garden City, N.Y.: Anchor Press, 1965.

———. *The Silent Language*. Garden City, N.Y.: Anchor Press, 1973.

Hanna, Judith Lynn. "Movements toward Understanding Humans through the Anthropological Study of Dance." *Current Anthropology* 20, no. 2 (June 1979): 313–24, 330–39.

———. *To Dance Is Human*. Austin: University of Texas Press, 1979.

———. "Towards Semantic Analysis of Movement Behavior." *Semiotica* 25½: 77–110.

Hay, Deborah. "Dance Talks." *Dance Scope* 12, no. 1 (Fall–Winter 1977–78): 18–22.

———. "Deborah Hay." In *Contemporary Dance*, edited by Anne Livet. New York: Abbeville Press, 1978, pp. 120–33.

Hay, Deborah, and Donna Jean Rogers. *Moving through the Universe in Bare Feet: Ten Circle Dances for Everybody*. 1974. Reprint. Chicago: Swallow Press, 1975.

Hay, Deborah, with Tina Girouard and Pauline Oliveros. *Tasting the Blaze*. Austin, Tex.: Futura Press, 1985.

H'Doubler, Margaret N. *Dance*. Madison: University of Wisconsin Press, 1962.

Hecht, Robin Silver. "Reflections on the Career of Yvonne Rainer and the Value of the Minimal Dance." *Dance Scope* 8, no. 1 (Fall–Winter 1973–74): 12–25.

Helpern, Alice. "The Evolution of Martha Graham's Dance Technique." Ph.D. diss., New York University, 1981.

Hewitt, Barnard. *The Renaissance Stage*. Coral Gables, Fla.: University of Miami Press, 1958.

Hilton, Wendy. *Dance of Court and Theatre: The French Noble Style, 1690–1725*. Princeton, N.J.: Princeton Book Company, 1981.

Horst, Louis, and Carroll Russell. *Modern Dance Forms*. Brooklyn: Dance Horizons, 1961.

Huet, Michel. *The Dance Art and Ritual of Africa*. Translated from the French. New York: Pantheon Books, 1978.

Humphrey, Doris. *The Art of Making Dances*. New York: Grove Press, 1959.
———. *Doris Humphrey: An Artist First*. Edited by Selma Jeanne Cohen. Middletown, Conn.: Wesleyan University Press, 1972.

Hunt, Valerie. "Movement Behavior: A Model for Action." *Quest* Monograph 2 (April 1964): 69–91.
———. "The Biological Organization of Man to Move." *Impulse*. San Francisco: Impulse Publishers, 1968, pp. 51–63.

Jaques-Dalcroze, Émile. *Rhythm, Music, and Education*. Translated by Harold F. Rubinstein. New York and London: G.P. Putnam, 1921.

Jeffers, Bill. "Leaving the House: The Solo Performance of Deborah Hay." *The Drama Review* 23, no. 1 (March 1979): 79–86.

Johnston, Jill. *Marmalade Me*. New York: Dutton, 1971.

Jowitt, Deborah. *Dance in the Mind: Profiles and Reviews, 1977–83*. Boston: Godine, 1984.

Kaeppler, Adrienne. "Method and Theory in Analyzing Dance Structure with an Analysis of Tongan Dance." *Ethnomusicology* 16, no. 2 (May 1972): 173–217.

Karsavina, Tamara. *Classical Ballet: The Flow of Movement*. New York: Theater Arts Books, 1973.

Kealiinohomoku, Joanne. "An Anthropologist Looks at Ballet as a Form of Ethnic Dance." *Impulse* (1969–70): 24–33.

Kendall, Elizabeth. "Grand Union: Our Gang." *Ballet Review* 5, no. 4 (1975–76): 44–45.
———. *Where She Danced*. New York: Knopf, 1979.

Kinkeldy, Otto. *A Jewish Dancing Master of the Renaissance: Guglielmo Ebreo*. Brooklyn: Dance Horizons, 1929.

Kirby, Michael. *The Art of Time*. New York: Dutton, 1969.

Kirstein, Lincoln. *Dance: A Short History of Classical Theatrical Dancing*. New York: Dance Horizons, 1935.

———. *Movement and Metaphor*. New York: Praeger, 1970.

———. *The New York City Ballet*. New York: Knopf, 1973.

Klosty, James, ed. *Merce Cunningham*. New York: Saturday Review Press, 1975.

Koegler, Horst. *The Concise Oxford Dictionary of Ballet*. London: Oxford University Press, 1977.

Kostelanetz, Richard, ed. *The New American Arts*. New York: Horizon Press, 1965.

Kraus, Rosalind. *Passages in Modern Sculpture*. London: Thames & Hudson, 1977.

Kriegsman, Sali Ann. *Modern Dance in America: The Bennington Years*. Boston: G. K. Hall, 1981.

Kurath, Gertrude. "Panorama of Dance Ethnology." *Current Anthropology* 1, no. 3 (May 1960): 233–54.

Laban, Rudolf von. *The Mastery of Movement*. London: Macdonald and Evans, 1960.

———. *Choreutics*. London: Macdonald and Evans, 1966.

———. *Modern Educational Dance*. London: Macdonald and Evans, 1968.

———. *A Life for Dance*. Translated by Lisa Ullman. New York: Theater Arts Books, 1975.

Laban, Rudolf von, and F. C. Lawrence. *Effort*. London: Macdonald and Evans, 1947.

Lamb, Warren. *Posture and Gesture*. London: Duckworth, 1965.

———. *Body Code*. Boston: Routledge & Kegan Paul, 1979.

Lambranzi, Gregorio. *New and Curious School of Theatrical Dancing* (1716). Translated by Derra de Moroda. New York: Dance Horizons, 1966.

Lang, Father Franciscus. *Dissertatio de actione scenica*. Monachii Typis Mariae Magdalenae Riedlin, 1727.

Langer, Suzanne. *Feeling and Form: A Theory of Art*. New York: Scribner, 1953.

———. *Philosophy in a New Key*. Cambridge: Harvard University Press, 1957.

deLauze, Ferdinand. *Apologie de la danse* (1623). London: Frederick Muller, 1952.

Lawler, Lillian. *The Dance in Ancient Greece*. Middletown, Conn.: Wesleyan University Press, 1964.

Lawrenson, Thomas E. *The French Stage in the Seventeenth Century*. Manchester: University of Manchester Press, 1957.

Leatherman, LeRoy. *Martha Graham: Portrait of the Lady as an Artist*. New York: Knopf, 1966.

Lee, Richard. "The Sociology of !Kung Bushmen Trance Performances." In *Trance and Possession States*, edited by Raymond Prince. Montreal: R. M. Bucke Memorial Society, 1968, pp. 35–54.

Leenhardt, Maurice. *Do Kamo*. Translated by Basia Miller Gulati. Chicago: University of Chicago Press, 1979.

Légendre, Pierre. *La Passion d'être un autre: étude pour la danse*. Paris: Seuil, 1978.

Levi, Anthony. *French Moralists: The Theory of the Passions, 1585–1649*. Oxford: Clarendon Press, 1964.

Levin, David Michael. "The Embodiment of Performance." *Salmagundi* no. 31–32 (Fall 1975–Winter 1976): 120–42.

Lippard, Lucy. *Six Years: The Dematerialization of the Art Object from 1966–1972*. New York: Praeger, 1973.

Livet, Anne, ed. *Contemporary Dance*. New York: Abbeville Press, 1978.

Lomax, Alan. *Folk Song Style and Culture*. Washington, D.C.: American Association for the Advancement of Science, 1968.

Lorber, Richard. "The Problem with Grand Union." *Dance Scope* 7, no. 2 (Spring–Summer 1973): 33–34.

Lough, John. *Paris Theater Audiences in the Seventeenth and Eighteenth Centuries*. London: Oxford University Press, 1957.

Lowen, Alexander. *The Betrayal of the Body*. New York: Collier Macmillan, 1967.

Lucian of Samosata. *The Works of Lucian of Samosata*. Translated by H. W. Fowler and F. G. Fowler. Oxford: Clarendon Press, 1905.

Lyle, Cynthia. *Dancers on Dancing*. New York: Drake Publishing, 1977.

Lynham, Deryck. *The Chevalier Noverre*. London: Chameleon Press, 1972.

McDonagh, Don. *The Rise and Fall and Rise of Modern Dance*. New York: Mentor, 1970.

———. *Martha Graham: A Biography*. New York: Praeger, 1973.

———. *The Complete Guide to Modern Dance*. New York: Doubleday, 1976.

McGowan, Margaret. *L'Art du ballet de cour en France 1581–1643*. Paris: Éditions du Centre National de la Recherche Scientifique, 1963.

McNamara, Brooks. "*Vessel*: The Scenography of Meredith Monk (interview)." *The Drama Review* 16, no. 1 (T-53, March 1972): 87–103.

Magriel, Paul. *Nijinsky*. New York: Henry Holt & Company, 1946.

———. *Isadora Duncan*. New York: Henry Holt & Company, 1947.

Mallarmé, Stéphane. "Crayonné au théâtre." *Ouvres complètes*. Paris: Gallimard, 1945.

duManoir, G. *Le Mariage de la musique avec la danse*. Paris, 1664.

Marks, Joseph E. *America Learns to Dance: A Historical Study of Dance Education in America before 1900*. New York: Exposition Press, 1957.

———. *A Pictorial History of the Dance*. San Francisco: Contemporary Dancers Foundation, 1962.

Marshall, Lorna. "The Medicine Dance of the !Kung Bushmen." *Africa* 39 (1969): 347–81.

Martin, Gyorgy, and Erno Pesovar. "A Structural Analysis of the Hungarian Folk Dance (A Methodological Sketch)." *Acta Ethnographica* 10 (1961): 1–40.

Martin, John. *The Dance*. New York: Tudor, 1946.

———. *Introduction to the Dance*. 1939. Reprint. New York: Dance Horizons, 1968.

Massine, Léonide. *Massine on Choreography*. London: Faber, 1976.

Mazo, Joseph. *Dance Is a Contact Sport*. New York: Saturday Review Press, 1974.

Mead, Margaret. *Growth and Culture*. New York: Putnam, 1951.

Mead, Margaret, and Gregory Bateson. *Balinese Character*. New York: New York Academy of Sciences, 1942.

Meagher, John C. "The Dance and the Masques of Ben Jonson." *Journal of the Warburg and Courtauld Institutes* 25 (1962): 258–300.

Menestrier, Claude François. *Remarques pour la conduite des ballets*. Lyon: J. Molin, 1668.

———. *Des ballets anciens et modernes. Selon les règles du théâtre*. Paris: Chez R. Quignard, 1682.

Michel, Artur. "The Earliest Dance Manuals." *Medievalia et Humanistica* no. 3 (1945): 117–31.

Michelson, Annette. "Yvonne Rainer, Part One: The Dancer and the Dance." *Artforum* 12 (January 1974): 57–63.

Miller, James. "The Philosophical Background of Renaissance Dance." *York Dance Review* no. 5 (Spring 1976): 3–15.

Monk, Meredith. "Comments of a Young Choreographer." *Dance Magazine* (June 1968): 60–64.

Morris, Robert. "Notes on Dance." *Tulane Drama Review* no. 10 (T-30, Winter 1965): 179–86.

Nadel, Myron, and Constance Nadel. *The Dance Experience.* New York: Praeger, 1970.

Nagler, A. M. *Theatre Festivals of Medici.* New Haven, Conn.: Yale University Press, 1964.

Nahumck, Nadia. *Introduction to Dance Literacy: Perception and Notation of Dance.* Transvaal, South Africa: International Library of African Music, 1978.

Negri, Cesar. *Le gratie d'amore.* Milan: Pacifico Pontio and Giovanni Battista, 1602.

———. *Nuove inventioni di balli.* Milan: Pacifico Pontio and Giovanni Battista, 1602.

Nijinsky, Romola. *Nijinsky.* New York: Simon & Schuster, 1934.

———, ed. *The Diary of Vaslav Nijinsky.* Berkeley and Los Angeles: University of California Press, 1968.

North, Marion. *Personality Assessment through Movement.* Boston: Plays, Inc., 1975.

Noverre, Jean Georges. *Letters on Dancing and Ballets* (1760). Translated by Cyril W. Beaumont. Brooklyn: Dance Horizons, 1966.

O'Dea, William. *The Social History of Lighting.* London: Routledge & Kegan Paul, 1958.

Olson, Charles. *Selected Writings of Charles Olson.* Edited by Robert Creeley. New York: New Directions, 1970.

Orgel, Stephen. *The Jonsonian Masque.* Cambridge: Harvard University Press, 1965.

———. "The Poetics of Spectacle." *New Literary History* 2, no. 3 (Spring 1971): 367–89.

———. *The Illusion of Power.* Berkeley and Los Angeles: University of California Press, 1975.

Parabola. "Sacred Dance." 4, no. 2 (May 1979).

Paxton, Steve. "*Satisfyin' Lover.*" *0 to 9* no. 4 (June 1968): 27–30.

———. "The Grand Union: Improvisational Dance." *The Drama Review* 16 (T-55, September 1972): 128–34.

Pemberton, Ebenezer. *An Essay for the Further Improvement of Dancing.* London: J. Walsh, 1711.

Penzel, Frederick. *Theatre Lighting before Electricity.* Middletown, Conn.: Wesleyan University Press, 1978.

Playford, John. *The English Dancing Master* (1651). New York: Dance Horizons, 1933.

Polhemus, Ted, and J. Benthall, eds. *The Body as a Medium of Experience.* London: A. Lane, 1975.

Preston-Dunlop, Valerie. *A Handbook for Modern Educational Dance.* London: Macdonald and Evans, 1963.

Rainer, Yvonne. "Some Retrospective Notes. . . ." *Tulane Drama Review* no. 10 (T-30, Winter 1965): 168–78.

———. *Work 1961–73.* Halifax and New York: Press of the Nova Scotia College of Art and Design and New York University Press, 1974.

———. "Film about a Woman Who. . . ." *October* 2 (Summer 1976): 39–67.

Rainer, Yvonne, with Willoughby Sharp and Liza Béar. "The Performer as a Persona: An Interview with Yvonne Rainer." *Avalanche* no. 5 (Summer 1972): 46–59.

Rainer, Yvonne, with Camera Obscura Collective. "Yvonne Rainer: Interview." *Camera Obscura* 1 (1976): 76–96.

Rameau, Pierre. *The Dancing Master* (1725). Translated by Cyril W. Beaumont. New York: Dance Horizons, 1970.

Reiss, Françoise. *Nijinsky.* Translated by Helen Haskell and Stephen Haskell. London: Adam and Charles Black, 1960.

Reynolds, Nancy. *Repertory in Review: Forty Years of the New York City Ballet.* New York: Dial Press, 1977.

Robertson, Michael. "Fifteen Years: Twyla Tharp and the Logical Outcome of Abundance." *Dance Magazine* 54 (March 1980): 66–74.

Rosenthal, Robert, et al. *Sensitivity to Nonverbal Communication.* Baltimore: Johns Hopkins University Press, 1979.

Rosner, Stanley, and Lawrence E. Abt, eds. *The Creative Experience.* New York: Grossman Publishers, 1970.

Rouch, Jean. "On the Vicissitudes of the Self: The Possessed Dancer, the Magician, the Sorcerer, the Filmmaker, and the Ethnographer." *Studies in the Anthropology of Visual Communication* 5, no. 1 (1978): 208.

Rouché, Jacques. *L'Art théâtrical moderne.* Paris: Librairie Bloud et Gay, 1924.

Royce, Anya Peterson. *The Anthropology of Dance.* Bloomington: Indiana University Press, 1977.

Ruyter, Nancy Lee Chalfa. *Reformers and Visionaries: The Americanization of the Art of Dance.* New York: Dance Horizons, 1979.

Sachs, Curt. *World History of the Dance.* 1937. Reprint. New York: W. W. Norton and Company, 1963.

St. Denis, Ruth. *An Unfinished Life.* New York: Harper & Brothers, 1939.

Saint-Hubert, M. de. "How to Compose a Successful Ballet" (1641). *Dance Perspectives* no. 20 (Winter 1966). Translated by Andrée Bergens and edited by A. J. Pischl.

Salmagundi. Special Dance Issue. no. 33–34 (Spring–Summer 1976).

Scheflen, Albert. *Body Language and Social Order.* Englewood Cliffs, N.J.: Prentice-Hall, 1972.

———. *How Behavior Means.* Garden City, N.Y.: Anchor Press, 1974.

Scheyer, Ernst. "The Shapes of Space." *Dance Perspectives* no. 41 (Spring 1970).

Schieffelen, Edward. *The Sorrow of the Lonely and the Burning of the Dancers.* New York: St. Martin's Press, 1976.

Schilder, Paul. *The Image and Appearance of the Human Body.* New York: International University Press, 1950.

Schlemmer, Oscar, et al. *The Theatre of the Bauhaus.* Translated by Arthur S. Wensinger. Middletown, Conn.: Wesleyan University Press, 1961.

Schlundt, Christina L. "Into the Mystic with Miss Ruth." *Dance Perspectives* no. 46 (Summer 1971).

Scully, Vincent. *Pueblo Village, Mountain Dance.* New York: Viking Press, 1975.

Seldon, Elizabeth. *The Dancer's Quest.* Berkeley and Los Angeles: University of California Press, 1935.

Seroff, Victor. *The Real Isadora.* New York: Avon, 1971.

Shawn, Ted. *Gods Who Dance.* New York: Dutton, 1929.

———. *Every Little Movement: A Book about François Delsarte.* Pittsfield, Mass.: Eagle Printing, 1954.

———. *Thirty-Three Years of American Dance, 1927–59.* Pittsfield, Mass.: Eagle Printing, 1959.

Sheets, Maxine. *The Phenomenology of Dance.* Madison: University of Wisconsin Press, 1966.

Shelton, Suzanne. *Divine Dancer: A Biography of Ruth St. Denis.* Garden City, N.Y.: Doubleday, 1981.

Sherman, Jane. *The Drama of Denishawn Dance.* Middletown, Conn.: Wesleyan University Press, 1979.

Siegel, Marcia. *At the Vanishing Point.* New York: Saturday Review Press, 1972.

———. *Watching the Dance Go By.* Boston: Houghton Mifflin, 1977.

———. *The Shapes of Change.* Boston: Houghton Mifflin, 1979.

Skeaping, Mary. "Ballet under the Three Crowns." *Dance Perspectives* no. 32 (Winter 1967).

Snyder, Allegra Fuller. "The Dance Symbol." Committee on Research in Dance. Research Annual VI. *New Dimensions in Dance Research: Anthropology and Dance—The American Indian*. The Proceedings of the Third Conference on Research in Dance. Edited by Tamara Comstock. New York: New York University, 1972, pp. 213–25.

Sommer, Sally R. "Equipment Dances: Trisha Brown." *The Drama Review* 16 (T-55, September 1972): 135–41.

———. "Trisha Brown Making Dances." *Dance Scope* 11, no. 2 (Spring–Summer 1977): 7–18.

Sorell, Walter, ed. *The Dance Has Many Faces*. New York: World Publishing, 1951.

———. *The Mary Wigman Book*. Middletown, Conn.: Wesleyan University Press, 1975.

Spicker, Stuart. *The Philosophy of the Body: Rejections of Cartesian Dualism*. Chicago: Quadrangle, 1970.

Stanislavsky, Konstantin. *Building a Character*. Translated by Elizabeth Reynolds Hapgood. New York: Theater Arts Books, 1949.

———. *Stanislavsky on the Art of the Stage*. Translated by David Magarshack. 1950. Reprint. New York: Hill & Wang, 1961.

Stebbins, Genevieve. *Delsarte System of Expression* (1902). Brooklyn: Dance Horizons, 1977.

Stefan, Paul, ed. *Dance in Our Time*. Vienna and New York: Universal Edition, 1922.

Stodelle, Ernestine. *The Dance Technique of Doris Humphrey and Its Creative Potential*. Princeton, N.J.: Princeton Book Company, 1978.

Stravinsky, Igor. *Poetics of Music*. Cambridge: President and Fellows of Harvard College, 1947.

Stravinsky, Igor, and Robert Craft. *Themes and Episodes*. New York: Knopf, 1966.

Strong, Roy. *Splendor at Court*. Boston: Houghton Mifflin, 1973.

Svetloff, V. *Anna Pavlova*. New York: Dover, 1974.

Sweigard, Lulu. *Human Movement Potential: Its Ideokinetic Facilitation*. New York: Harper & Row, 1974.

Swift, Mary Grace. *A Loftier Flight: The Life and Accomplishments of Charles Louis Didelot, Balletmaster*. Middletown, Conn.: Wesleyan University Press, 1973.

Taper, Bernard. *Balanchine: A Biography*. New York: Macmillan, 1974.

Terry, Walter. *Isadora Duncan: Her Life, Her Art, Her Legacy*. New York: Dodd, Mead, 1963.

Tobias, Tobi. "Twyla Tharp." *Dance Scope* 4, no. 2 (Spring 1970): 6–17.

Todd, Mabel Ellsworth. *The Thinking Body*. Brooklyn: Dance Horizons, 1937.

Tomkins, Calvin. *The Bride and the Bachelors*. New York: Viking Press, 1965.

Tomlinson, Kellom. *The Art of Dancing Explained by Reading and Figures* (1735). London: Gregg International, 1970.

Toulouze, Michel. *L'Art et instruction de bien danser*. Paris: 1486. Facsimile, London: Emory Walker, 1936.

Tuccaro, Archange. "Trois dialogues de l'exercise de sauter et voltiger en l'air." Paris, 1599.

Turner, Victor. "Symbols in African Ritual." *Science* 179, no. 4078 (March 1973): 1100–5.

Tzara, Tristan. *Seven Dada Manifestations and Lampisteries*. Translated by Barbara Wright. London: J. Calder, 1977.

Van Praagh, Peggy, and Peter Brinson. *The Choreographic Art*. New York: Knopf, 1963.

Van Tuyl, Marian, ed. *Anthology of Impulse*. Brooklyn: Dance Horizons, 1969.

Van Vechten, Carl. *The Dance Writings of Carl Van Vechten*. Edited by Paul Padgette. Brooklyn: Dance Horizons, 1974.

Van Zile, Judy, ed. *Dance in Africa, Asia, and the Pacific: Selected Readings*. New York: MMS Information Corporation, 1976.

von Kleist, Heinrich. "On the Marionette Theatre." *Times Literary Supplement* (October 20, 1978): 121–23.

Vuillier, Gaston. *A History of Dancing* (1898). Boston: Millford House, 1972.

Wagner, Ann. "Dance as Virtue: An Analysis from the Sixteenth Century Courtesy Literature." *Proceedings of the Society of Dance History*. Christena Schlundt, comp. (Riverside, Ca.: University of California 1983), pp. 37–47.

———. "Dance as Vice: An Analysis from the Sixteenth Century Courtesy Literature." *Proceedings of the Society of Dance History*. Christena Schlundt, comp. (Riverside, Ca.: University of California 1984), pp. 84–95.

Weaver, John. *An Essay Towards an History of Dancing*. London: Jacob Tonson, 1712.

———. *The Loves of Mars and Venus*. London: W. Mears, 1717.

———. *Anatomical and Mechanical Lectures upon Dancing*. London: Jacob Tonson, 1721.

———. *The History of the Mimes and Pantomimes*. London: Jacob Tonson, 1728.

Weschler, Lawrence. *Seeing Is Forgetting the Name of the Thing One Sees*. Berkeley and Los Angeles: University of California Press, 1982.

Wigman, Mary. "On Composition." Dresden: Mary Wigman School of the Dance, n.d.

———. "Composition in Pure Movement." *Modern Music* 8, no. 2 (January–February 1931): 20–22.

———. "My Teacher Laban." *Dance Magazine* (November 1956): 26–28.

———. *The Language of Dance*. Translated by Walter Sorell. Middletown, Conn.: Wesleyan University Press, 1966.

———. "Reminiscences of Mary Wigman: Dance Scene in the Late 1920's." *Dance News* (June 1973): 4.

Wigman, Mary, et al. *Modern Dance*. New York: Carnegie, 1935.

Wood, Melusine. *Advanced Historical Dances*. London: Imperial Society of Teachers of Dancing, 1960.

———. *Historical Dances*. London: Imperial Society of Teachers of Dancing, 1972.

Wynne, Shirley. "Background Research in Dance, Music and Costume. Support Materials for Use by Teachers and Students Viewing Baroque Dance. 1675–1725." Under the sponsorship of the Department of Dance, UCLA, funded by NEH EH-25011-76-859 at UCLA 1977.

———. "Complaisance, An Eighteenth-Century Cool." *Dance Scope* 5, no. 1 (Fall 1970): 22–35.

———. *Frontiers of Life: The Life of Martha Graham*. New York: Thomas Y. Crowell, 1975.

Yates, Frances A. *The French Academies of the Sixteenth Century*. London: The Warburg Institute, University of London, 1947.

Zorn, Friedrich Albert. *Grammar of the Art of Dancing*. Translated by Benjamin P. Coates. Brooklyn: Dance Horizons, 1976.

Zorn, John W., ed. *The Essential Delsarte*. Metuchen, N.J.: Scarecrow Press, 1968.

INDEX

Accumulation, 213; and movement order, 95

Adam and Eve, mythic story of, 73

African dance, 88

Ailey, Alvin, 88

Aleatory techniques, xvii, 37, 94–95; compared with improvisation, 95. *See also* Chance procedures

Allegorical dance in the late Renaissance, 100–121. *See also* Renaissance dance

Allemande, 119

Allen, Maud, 147, 149

Amants magnifiques, Les, 134, 136

American Dance Festival, xiii

Anger, representation of, 94, 129, 157, 158. *See also* Emotion

Announcements of dance concerts, 59–60

Anthropological research on the body and subject, 273 n3

Anthropological studies of dance, 233 n11

Arbeau, Thoinot, 115, 130, 131, 133, 252 n25

"Archeology of dance," 248 n2

Archetypes: figures, 206; psychological events, 27; vignettes of American life, 191, 193

Architectural context of dance performances, 191; influence of, 60–62; innovations in, 121, 149, 169, 171. *See also* Proscenium theater; Theater-in-the-round

Arena, Antonius de, 115

Arnold, Becky, 261 n9

Art. *See* Life and art; Visual arts

Audience: attitudes of dancers toward, 63–64; democratization of, 169, 171; of expressionist dance, 149–50, 167; in Graham's choreographic conception, 27, 31–32, 53–54; in Hay's choreographic conception, 5, 6, 13–14, 46, 54, 55–56; and improvisation, 194–95, 223; influence of the architectural setting on, 60–61 (*see also* Frames); in Monk's choreographic style, 209, 223; movement and seat changes by, 61, 169, 171,

Audience (*continued*)
225; of neoclassical dance, 122, 125,
126; of objectivist dance, 169, 171,
174; participation by, 224–26; of
Renaissance dance, 102, 104, 107,
249*n*5; in Tharp's choreographic
style, 223–24. *See also* Viewers

Balanchine, George, xvii–xviii, 2, 14–
23; *Apollo* by, 15, 22, 68; attitudes
toward the body, 49, 83; attitudes toward life and art, 19, 60; beauty as a
choreographic goal of, 21–22, 55,
122; career of, 238*n*12; character
portrayal in choreography of, 52;
choreography of compared with
eighteenth-century neoclassical
dance, 121, 122, 125–26, 129–30,
131, 134–35, 141, 143, 144; compared with Cunningham, 34–35,
44–45; compared with Graham, 25,
27, 41–42, 47–48, 84, 93, 148;
compared with Hay, 16, 19, 52;
compared with Tharp, 212; creative
process of, 16–17, 19–20, 44; on
dance rehearsals, 19–20, 47; on
dance training and classes, 19, 47,
48; death of, 1; and expression, 44,
53; frames used by, 121; gaze of
dancers in choreography by, 16, 64;
imitative representation used by, 122;
lexicon of, 91, 121; modes of representation used by, 68, 69, 122;
on movement and dance theory, 17,
19; *Orpheus and Eurydice* by, 62,
245*n*3; relation of music to choreography of, 14, 16, 19, 21, 23, 93, 141,
143, 239*n*13; relative to other choreographers, 41–56; rhetorical and
pantomimic gestures used by, 129–
30; story dances by, 14, 21; style of,
83, 84, 87, 91; subject matter used
by, 134; syntax used by, 93; technical
skills of dancers required by, 16, 17,
19, 23, 121, 143; viewers in the cho-

reographic conception of, 16, 21, 23,
54–55; on visual perception and
choreographic movement, 19; vocabulary of, 19, 91
Ballet: Balanchine's approach to, 17, 19,
21, 44; Balanchine's influence on,
239*n*12; and body parts used with
specific movement qualities, 83;
compared with modern dance, xiii,
xx, 87; composed by "modern" dancers, 212, 213; intermixed with tap
dance and fox-trot, 211; lexicon of,
19, 90, 91, 144, 213; modes of representation in, 68–69; pantomime
used in, 128; stylistic innovations in,
165; syntax used in, 93; tradition of,
87; training for, 19
Ballet de Monsieur de Vendosme, Le,
107, 108, 112–13, 114
Ballroom dancing, parodies of, 216–17,
219
Baron, John H., 250*n*12
Baroque period in dance history, 258*n*2
Barthes, Roland: on the "I," 236*n*3; and
interpretations of Graham's choreography, 240*n*26; on the Japanese system of signification, 236*n*2; on
"natural" and "naturalness," 229*n*3,
254*n*41; and sign theory, 233*n*11;
on style, 246*n*9; on the subject and
the body, 237*n*3; and theory on representation in dance, xix–xx; on
"writerly" vs. "readerly" texts,
240*n*26, 259*n*7
Baryshnikov, Mikhail, 77, 78
Beauchamp, Pierre, 135, 140, 253*n*30
Beckett, Samuel, 258*n*90
Beginnings of dance performances, 62–
63, 92
Behrman, David, 241*n*36
Bejart, Maurice, 88
Bettis, Valerie, 167
Black Mountain College, 167
Body: attitudes toward, compared, 43,
49–50, 84–85; Balanchine's atti-

tudes on, 49, 83, 84; cellular consciousness of, 9, 11–12, 13, 48, 49, 118; center of, 25, 28, 73, 78; cultural codes of, 79; in Cunningham's choreography, 32, 35–36, 41, 49, 84–85; in daily life and movement, 6–8, 9, 48, 105; in Duncan's choreographic style, 79, 81, 83; in Graham's theory on dance and movement, 25, 28, 49–52, 79, 81, 83, 84; in Hay's choreographic style, 8, 9, 84–85; ideological message of, 259*n*3; interaction with the mind, 35–36; interpreted by Roland Barthes, 237*n*3; jointedness of, 32; and literary tropes applied to dance, 235*n*1; new vision of, 227; in objectivist dance, 174–81; right and left sides of, 79; role in choreographic styles, 79–85; solar plexus, 79; symbolic significance of, 3; and theory on dance representation, xx; in twentieth-century choreography, xvi; weight of, 36, 165, 174–75, 198; and writing dancing, 227

Body and subject, xvii, 41–56, 181, 220, 258*n*89; in Balanchine's choreography, 52; in Cunningham's choreography, 52, 53; Graham's concepts of, 50–51; in Grand Union performances, 220, 221; in Hay's choreography, 51–52; in Monk's choreography, 220, 221; in objectivist dance, 181; Tharp's attitudes toward, 220, 222, 223, writing of, 220–27

Body parts: abdomen, 79, 81; arms, 16, 29, 32, 71, 72, 79, 81, 83, 91, 117, 130, 131, 163; chest, 79, 83; in choreographic styles, 78–85; in comparison of Balanchine's and eighteenth-century dance choreography, 131; in contemporary ballet, 83–84; in Delsartian theory, 156; in eighteenth-century neoclassical dance, 130–31; in expressionist

dance, 163, 165–66; feet, 79, 84, 91, 117; fingers, 71, 81, 163; hand, 163; head, 32, 71, 79, 81, 83–84, 109, 156; joints, 32, 168; knees, 72, 91; legs, 32, 71, 79, 84; limbs, 16, 183; in objectivist dance, 174–81; pelvis, 73, 79, 81, 83, 156; in Renaissance dance, 117; rib cage, 91; shoulders, 91; solar plexus, 79; spine, 83, 90, 117; symbolic associations of, 78–79, 81, 83–84; torso, 16, 32, 73, 79, 83, 84, 88, 156, 165, 168; and variation, 96; in vocabularies of movement, 90–91

Bournonville, Auguste, 144
Bourrées, 2
Boxing, 213
Boxlike stages, 61
Brach, Pierre de, 250*n*13
Branle, 116, 118
Breathing, 8, 90, 154; natural cycle of, 158
Bricolage, 179; in Cunningham's choreography, 34, 37; of expressive forms in Grand Union performances, 222; used by the Judson Church group, 169
Brown, Carolyn, frontispiece, 38–39, 41
Brown, Trisha, xx, xxi, 170, 261*n*9; *Accumulation (1971) With Talking (1973) Plus Watermotor (1977)* by, 182, 183; approach to movement organization and dance structure, 95, 176–77; choreography by, 172, 176–77, 178, 182; *Equipment Pieces* by, 257*n*82; *Line Up* by, 182; *Locus* by, 176–77, 180; reflexivity used by, 182; *Rummage Sale and the Floor of the Forest* by, 172, 174; spoken dialogue incorporated by, 182, 184
Bulwer, John, 253*n*36
Bunraku puppet theater, 237*n*3
Burke, Kenneth, and literary tropes, 234*n*1

Courante, 119

Court ballet choreographers, 166

Court performances, 100–102; compared with eighteenth-century choreography, 143, 145; compared with proscenium ballet, 143–44. *See also* Renaissance dance

Cranko, John, 88

Creative process of choreographers, xvii, 2–3; of Balanchine, 16–17, 19–20, 44, 45; of Cunningham, 34–38, 44–45; in expressionist dance theory, 162–63; of Graham, 27–28, 43–44; of Hay, 6–9, 16, 45, 110; of Monk, 221; "natural" approach to, xv; of Tharp, 212

Culler, Jonathan, 243 n56

Cultural criticism, xix–xx

Culture, American, 244 n1; archetypal vignettes of, 191, 193

Cunningham, Merce, xiii–xiv, xvii–xix, 3, 32–41, 167–69, 244 n2, 247 n1; aleatory syntax used by, 37, 95; approach to dance composition, xvi–xvii, 34–35, 37, 167–68, 231 n8; attitudes on expression, 53, 167, 168; body and movement in choreography by, 32, 34–36, 41, 49, 84–85, 168–69; body and subject in choreography by, 52; career of, 3, 167–68, 241 n36; chance procedures used by, xiv, 37, 45, 95, 168, 169; *Changes: Notes on Choreography* by, 229 n2; collaboration with John Cage, xiii, 33, 167, 241 n36; compared with Balanchine, 34–35, 44–45; compared with Graham, 35, 47; compared with Hay, 48, 84–85; compared with other choreographers, 44–56; creative process of, 34–35, 44–45, 167–68; on dance classes, 36, 46–47, 48; dance company of, xiii, 238 n4; in dance performances, 3, 85; on dance rehearsals,

46–47; expressionist dance challenged by, 167–68; *Field Dances* by, xiii; frames used by, 167–68; and the gaze of dancers, 64; and interdisciplinary approach to dance composition, 187; and the Judson Church group, 169; on life and art, 48; modes of representation used by, 75–76, 167; movement theory of, 167–69; movement vocabulary of, 3, 168; *Pictures* by, 1; reflective mode of representation used by, 167; responsibilities of the dancers directed by, 3, 38–39, 41; revolutionary influence of, xviii, xx; role of music in choreography by, xiv, 34, 37–38, 168, 169; role of viewers in choreography by, 55, 168; style of, 3, 84–85, 167–68; *Suite by Chance* by, xiv, 229 n2; in *Suite for Five*, frontispiece; syntax of, 95; vocabulary of, 3, 168

Daily life, movement in, 6–8, 9, 48, 105. *See also* Life and art

Dance: and the artistic boundaries of the dance medium, 225; in the choreographic sources of expressionist dance, 153–54; in Graham's creative process, 27; and martial art forms, 8, 213; relationship with other arts, 3; in the Renaissance period, 112, 119–20; and visual art forms, 171–72. *See also* Interdisciplinary approach to dance composition; Music

Dance classes, xvii, 3; Balanchine's approach to, 19, 47, 48; for ballet, 19; comparative approaches to, 46–48; Cunningham's approach to, 36–37, 46–47; Graham's approach to, 28–30, 47, 48; Hay's approach to, 11–12, 46, 48; literacy in dance acquired by, 58–59; relative to performance, 46–48

Dance composition, xvii, 58–98; Balanchine's approach to, 19–20, 41–42; Cunningham's approach to, xvi–xvii, 34–35, 37–38, 167–69, 231*n*8; historical approach to, xviii–xix, 99–100, 186–87, 248*n*2, 258*n*1; Humphrey's theory on, xv, 158; interdisciplinary approach to, 187–88, 220–21, 222, 225, 226, 261*n*11 (*see also* Interdisciplinary approach to dance composition); "natural" approach to, xv; paradigmatic types of, 1–3, 234*n*1; role of dancers in, 17, 19–20, 28, 194–95, 197, 225; Tharp's approach to, 211–13. *See also* Creative process of choreographers

Dance for Three People and Six Arms, 62, 245*n*3

Dance of the universe, 8, 105

Dance rehearsals, 3, xvii; Balanchine's attitudes on, 19–20, 42, 47; Cunningham's attitudes on, 46–47; Graham's attitudes on, 28, 47; by Grand Union performers, 198; Hay's approach to, 46; relative to performance, 46–48

Dancers: in the beginnings and endings of performances, 63; cellular consciousness of, 9, 11–12, 13, 48, 49, 118; changing personae of, 195, 198; facial expressions of, 23, 34, 84; and feelings in expressionist choreography, 150, 166–67; gaze and focus of, 14, 16, 27, 63–64, 68, 90, 97, 174, 176; in Graham's choreography, 27, 28; in Grand Union performances, 194–95, 197, 198, 224, 225; in Hay's compositions, 8–9, 11–13; innate talent and dedication of, 48; male and female roles of, 84, 85; in objectivist compositions, 169, 171, 179–80, 181; participation in composition and choreography, 17, 28, 194–95, 197, 225; professional

status of, 121; requirements in expressionist dance, 166–67; responsibilities in Cunningham's dance company, 3, 38–39, 41; "self" of, 13, 43, 50–52, 181, 236*n*3 (*see also* Subject); style of, 77, 78, 179, 213, 215; technical expertise and responsibilities in Balanchine's choreography, 16, 17, 19, 23, 121; in Tharp's compositions, 213, 215; training of, xvi, 19, 28–30, 46–48; untrained, 169, 171, 209

Dance theory, xiv–xvii; Langer's approach to, xvi, 230*n*7; on the origins of dance, xvi, 211; role of signs in, 232*n*11

Dance traditions: Balanchine's attitudes on, 23; and choreographic styles, 87–88; and modern dance, 87, 90; parodies of, 219; and principles on the generation of steps, 90–91; and Tharp's use of reflexivity, 219, 226

Davies, John, 105; galliard described by, 119, 253*n*28

"Death of the author," in literary theory, 242*n*43

Decoding, 219

De la Renta, Oscar, 219

Deliverance de Renaud, La, 113

Delsarte, François: expressionist choreographers influenced by, 158–59, 168; system on movement analysis developed by, 156, 157–59

Denby, Edwin, 22

Denishawn school, 158, 239*n*24

Derrida, Jacques, 233*n*11

Diderot, Denis, *The Paradox of Acting* by, 134, 255*n*47

Dilley, Barbara, 194

Discourse, 100, 143; forms of, xv

Dramatic theater, 200, 203

Duncan, Isadora, 68, 155, 169; compared with Cunningham, 168; compared with Graham, 81; and Greek dance, 88, 145; influence of Greek

art on, 88, 145, 153, 180; *La Marseillaise* by, 146, 147; modes of representation used by, 70–72, 79, 147;
Mother by, 151; on natural movement, 154; *Revolutionary Etude* by,
71; revolutionary impact of, 79, 145,
168; solo performances by, 145, 147;
on spirituality and dance movement,
150, 151; style of, 79, 81, 87, 88,
165–66; vocabulary of, 90; *Waltzes*
by, 71
Dunn, Douglas, xx, 194, 261*n*9; syntax
and vocabulary used by, 178
Dunn, Robert Ellis, 169; composition
classes taught by, 257*n*79
Dylan, Bob, 197

Ebreo, Guglielmo, 115, 252*n*26
Eco, Umberto, 233*n*11, 259*n*4
Egyptian symbolism, 151–52, 250*n*14
Eighteenth-century dance, 154. *See also*
Neoclassical dance in the eighteenth
century
Elyot, Thomas, 115–17, 129
Emotion: associated with the chest, 79;
in Cunningham's choreography, 38;
in Duncan's choreography, 71–72;
in eighteenth-century neoclassical
dance, 128–29; in expressionist
dance, 150; in Graham's choreography, 2, 23, 25, 27, 30–32, 50–
51, 53–54, 73, 93–94; in objectivist
dance, 181; representational modes
of, 71–73. *See also* Feeling
English masques, 100–101
English Renaissance dance, 115–17,
129. *See also* Renaissance dance
Erasmus, 254*n*46
Ethnography, 236*n*2
European court spectacles, 100–102,
143, 145. *See also* Renaissance dance
Expression, 52–53; Balanchine's attitudes on, 44, 53; comparative concepts of, 43; in Cunningham's choreography, 34, 44, 53; in eighteenth-

century choreography, 128–29;
of feeling, 71–72, 157–58; in
Graham's choreography, 30–31,
43–44, 53; in Hay's choreography,
53; relationship with the body, 128–
29, 220
Expressionist dance, 145–67; audience
of, 149–50, 167; challenged by Cunningham, 167–68; compared with
objectivist dance, 169, 175–76; correlated with the literary trope of synecdoche, 236*n*1; frames of, 149;
influence of Delsarte's movement theory on, 156–59; lighting used in,
149, 159; music in, 163, 165; organic principles in, 151, 163, 166,
168, 176; on the relationship between individuals and society, 161;
representation based on replication
in, 151, 153, 159, 163; requirements
of the performers in, 166–67; response of the Judson Church group
to, 169; role of body parts in, 163,
165–66; role of the natural body
and natural movement in, 153–54;
style of, 165–67; subject matter of,
153, 159, 161–62, 163; syntax in,
163, 165

Feeling, 152; correspondence with movement, 128–29, 157; in expressionist
compositions, 150, 166–67; in
Graham's choreography, 93–94; in
Langer's theory on dance composition, 230*n*7; in the "natural" approach to choreography and movement, xiv–xv; and the objectification
of dance movement, xiv; in objectivist dance, 181; organic connection
with form, 168. *See also* Emotion
Fées des forests de S. Germain, Les, 109,
250*n*12, 251*n*20
Feminist analysis of dance, 244*n*1
Feuillet, Raoul Auger, 140, 254*n*42
Figure skating, 212

Flow, and movement quality, 77–78
Form, 1–2; analyzed by Curt Sachs, 231*n*7; in Balanchine's choreography, 17, 23; in expressionist dance, 151; organic connection with self-expression and feeling, 151, 168
Formalist strategy, 243*n*1, 244*n*1
Forms of dance, 211, 213, 216. *See also* Steps
Foster, Hal, 260*n*8
Foucault, Michel, 245*n*2; on history and epistemic periods, 248*n*2; influence on Foster's approach to dance history, 248*n*2, 249*n*4; and literary tropes, 234*n*1; *The Order of Things* by, 248*n*2, 249*n*4; on resemblance and similitude, 249*n*4; on style, 246*n*9; and theory on representation in dance, xix–xx; work of, interpreted by Hayden White, 248*n*2
Fox-trot, 211, 216
Frames, 59–65, 97; in announcements and advertising graphics, 59–60; of Balanchine's compositions, 121; in the beginnings and endings of dances, 62–63; of Cunningham's compositions, 167–68; defined, xviii, 59; of expressionist dance, 149–50; in the gaze or focus of dancers, 63–64, 68, 90, 97, 125; of Grand Union performances, 191; of Hay's compositions, 5, 101–2, 104; of Judson Church group performances, 169, 171; of Monk's compositions, 200, 223, 225; and the performance space, 60–62; in program notes, 62, 97; in the Renaissance period, 102, 104; of Tharp's compositions, 209, 215, 216, 222
Franko, Mark, xxi, 254*n*46; on Renaissance dance, 253*n*29
French *ballets de court*, 100, 249*n*3
French Revolution, 147
Fuller, Loie, 147; and expressionist dance, 148–49; on the primordial relationship between movement and light, 153; and spirituality, 151

Galliard, 119, 129
Game structures, 37, 95, 169
Gamson, Annabelle, 246*n*8
Gavotte, 119, 130
Gaze of dancers, 14, 16, 27, 63–64, 68, 90, 97, 125
Geometry: in allegorical Renaissance dance, 107; and movement order, 95, 107. *See also* Mathematical principles
Gestures, 85, 90, 129–30; in Balanchine's choreography, 129–30; and character portrayal in Monk's compositions, 200, 203, 208; in Cunningham's choreography, 3; in eighteenth-century dance, 127, 129–30; in Grand Union choreography, 195, 197, 200, 221–22; in objectivist dance, 174; pedestrian, 168 (*see also* Pedestrian movement); and tension between traditional sex roles, 217
Giselle, 144
Gluck, Christoph, 141
Gombrich, E. H., 246*n*9; on visual schemata, 246*n*6
Gordon, David, xx, 193, 261*n*9; approach to narrative, 188–89; game structures applied by, 95; *Random Breakfast* by, 188–89
Graham, Martha, xvii–xviii, 23–32; *Acts of Light* by, 2; *Appalachian Spring* by, 27, 88; body and dance movement in the theory of, 25, 28, 49–51, 79, 81, 83, 90; career of, 2, 148, 158, 239*n*24; *Cave of the Heart* by, 25, 27, 62, 240*n*25; character portrayal in compositions by, 27, 30–31, 47, 51, 73, 81, 241*n*34; collaboration with Balanchine, 41–

Hay, Deborah (*continued*)
used by, 78; modes of representation used by, 69–70; on movement and dance in daily life, 6–8, 9, 105; movement sequence used by, 11–13; movement vocabulary of, 5; *Moving Through the Universe with Bare Feet* by, 8; music in compositions by, 119; relative to other choreographers, 45–56, 84–85; role of the audience in dance theory of, 5, 6, 13–14, 46, 54, 55–56; role of body parts in choreographic style of, 84–85; and social dance, 8–9, 117–18; solo performances by, 5, 6; subject in compositions by, 114–15; syntax used by, 92, 95; techniques and attitudes of the dancers directed by, 8–9, 11–13, 14; theater-in-the-round utilized by, 101, 105

Henry IV, 112–13

Hilferding van Wewen, Franz Anton, 138

Hilton, Wendy, 254*n*44

Hindu mythology, 151, 153, 159

History of dance, 99–185; approach to, xviii–xix, 99–100, 186–87, 248*n*2, 258*n*1; correlated with literary tropes, 236*n*1

Holm, Hanya, 75

Honor, and Renaissance dance, 115, 129

Horst, Louis, 239*n*34

Human condition, 168, 174; in expressionist dance, 150, 159, 167; in Graham's choreography, 23, 25, 32

Human identity, changes in, 195, 198

Humphrey, Doris, 147, 167; *The Art of Making Dances* by, xv; choreographic style of, 87, 88; creative process of, 161; on dance composition, xv, 158; *The Life of the Bee* by, 75; on movement in proscenium stages, 86; on music and dance, 163; *New Dance* by, 161–62; on the principles of movement, 158, 161; *The Shakers*

by, 88, 89; on the subject matter of dance, 161–62; on technical competence of dancers, 154; on twentieth-century dance theory, 230*n*6; vocabulary of, 90–91, 154

Iconic relations, 233*n*11

Imitation, representational mode of, xviii, 120; in Balanchine's choreography, 68, 69, 122; combined with reflection, 68–70, 75; combined with replication, 75; and dance traditions, 88; described, 65–66; in Duncan's choreography, 72; in eighteenth-century neoclassical dance, 121, 122, 126–27, 128, 154; in Graham's choreography, 72–73; in nineteenth-century ballet, 68–69; and props, 195; as related to metonymy, 245*n*5; of running, 70

Improvisation: compared with chance procedures, 95; by the Grand Union, 194–95, 197, 198, 200, 222, 223; in Monk's choreography, 225; and viewer collaboration in performance interpretations, 222, 223; and viewer participation in dance composition, 194–95

Indes galantes, Les, 138

Indexical relations, 233*n*11

Interdisciplinary approach to dance composition, 187–88; and boundaries of the dance medium, 171–72, 225; Cunningham's attitudes toward, 187; by the Grand Union, 187, 193–94, 195, 220–21, 226; by the Judson Church group, 171–72; in Monk's choreography, 187, 204, 206, 208, 220–21, 225, 226, 261*n*11; in Tharp's choreography, 187, 211, 222

Interpretive methodologies, 243*n*1; on the history of dance, 248*n*2, 249*n*3; and the structuralist approach to dance organization, 88, 90, 247*n*13

Irony, literary trope of: applied to dance, 234n1; and Cunningham's choreography, 236n1; in twentieth-century history, 248n2
Irwin, Robert, 238n9
Italian intermezzi, 100

Jakobson, Roman, 233n11; on author-text-viewer interaction, 231n9
Japan, and signification, 236n2
Jazz, 88, 213
Jealousy, representation of, 129, 254n41
Johns, Jasper, 241n36
Johnson, Jill, on the Judson Church group, 257n86
Jointedness of the body, 32
Joyce, James, 258n90
Judson Church group, 169–74, 189, 191; body movement interpreted by, 174–76; on the continuum between art and ordinary life, 169, 171; defined, 169; experimentation by, 169–72, 244n2; participation of Monk in, 200; and representational modes, 188; untrained performers utilized by, 169, 171; visual arts integrated by, 171–72

Kinship, 200, 209
Kirstein, Lincoln, 232n10, 255n48
Koner, Pauline, 167

Laban, Rudolf von, 147; influence on Mary Wigman, 91, 154, 158–59; movement quality systematized by, 77–78
Lacan, Jacques, 237n3
Lambranzi, Gregorio, 140
Langer, Suzanne, xvi, 230n7
Lanham, Richard, 235n1
Lévi-Strauss, Claude, 232n11
Lewis, Nancy, 193–94
Lexicon: in Balanchine's compositions, 91, 121; of ballet, 19, 90, 91, 144;

expanded by the Judson Church group, 169; expanded by Tharp, 213; of eighteenth-century dance, 121, 130–31, 144; of expressionist dance, 153; in Graham's choreography, 2; of Renaissance social dance, 117–18; stylistic treatment of, 91. *See also* Vocabulary
Life and art, 60, 63; and autobiographical references in Tharp's choreography, 211, 212; Balanchine's attitudes on, 19, 60; in Graham's choreography, 31, 60; Hay's approach to, 6–9, 46, 48, 60; interpreted by the Judson Church group, 169, 171; in objectivist dance, 169, 171, 180
Lighting, 37; in the beginnings and endings of dance performances, 63, 92; equipment for, 61; in expressionist compositions, 149, 159
Limón, José, 75, 91, 167; *The Moor's Pavane* by, 75
Literacy in dance, 56, 58
Literary theory: and art references to worldly events, 245n4; "death of the author" in, 242n43; "writerly" vs. "readerly" texts in, 240n26, 259n7
Literary tropes: applied to dance composition, 234n1; compared with epistemic periods in history, 248n2; correlated with modes of representation, 235n1, 236n1, 245n5. *See also* Irony, literary trope of; Metaphor; Metonymy, Synecdoche
Lloyd, Barbara, 261n9
Lofts, dance performances in, 60, 61, 167, 169
Lotman, Yuri, 247n16
Louis XIII, 113, 250n9
Louis XIV, 135–36, 253n30
Loves of Mars and Venus, The, 128–29, 136–38
Lully, Jean-Baptiste, 135

McGowan, Margaret, 248–49n3, 250n9, 251n18, 251n19

McNamara, Brooks, 261n12, 261n13, 261n15

Martial arts, 8, 213

Martin, Jean-Baptiste, costumes designed by, 124, 125

Martin, John: dance theory of, xvi, 230n7, 243n1; on expressionist dance, 150–51; on "inner mimicry," 230n7, 256n76

Masks, 125, 136

Masquerade du triomphe de Diane, Le, 110, 250n13

Mathematical principles: applied to movement order and dance structure, 95; used by the Judson Church group, 169; used by Childs, 177, 178; used by Tharp, 209

Meaning in dance, xvii, 189; and beauty in Balanchine's compositions, 21–22; and choreographic conventions, xviii; criteria for the interpretation of, 56; derived from movement, 35; in objectivist compositions, 168, 185; revealed by reflexivity, 189, 198, 212; and semiological studies, 233n11; structural guidelines for, 97; and Tharp's reflexive choreography, 211–12

Menestrier, Claude François, 251n15

Metacommentary: defined, 194; used by the Grand Union, 193–94, 195, 200, 208, 222; and viewer collaboration in dance interpretation, 222. *See also* Reflexivity

Metaphor, literary trope of: applied to dance, 234n1; correlated with the representational mode of resemblance, 236n1, 245n5; in the late Renaissance, 236n1, 248n2

Metonymy, literary trope of: applied to dance, 234n1; and Balanchine's relationship to eighteenth-century dance,

247n1; in the classical age, 248n2; correlated with the representational mode of imitation, 236n1, 245n5

Mimesis, syntactic principle of, 93, 95

Minimalist art, 174, 179, 257n83

Minimalist version of social dance, 197

Minuet, 130

Models of dance, 2; and choreographic conventions, xvii–xviii; comparisons of, 3, 42–56 *passim*; correlated with literary tropes, 234n1; historical precedents of, 100; and the interdisciplinary approach to composition, 187–88; on natural movement and the natural body, xiv–xvi, xviii; and viewer participation in dance composition, xix; and "writing dancing," xix, 187

Modern dance: compared with ballet, xx, 87, 90; in dance history, 258n2; modes of representation in, 75; and Tharp's compositions, 88, 213; tradition of, 87, 90; and vocabularies of movement, 90–91

Molière, 135

Monk, Meredith, xix, xx, 200–209; and boundaries of the dance medium, 225; career of, 200, 261n11; chanting utilized by, 206; compared with the Grand Union, 200, 208–9, 220–21, 222–23, 225–27; creative process of, 221; dance company of, 200; dramatic theater in compositions by, 200, 203; *Education of the Girlchild* by, 202, 203, 204–6, 208; frames used by, 200, 223, 225; interdisciplinary approach of, 187, 204, 206, 208, 220–21, 225, 226, 261n11; *Juice* by, 62, 245n3; and multiple interpretations by viewers, 209; *Paris* by, 201, 203; and participation of dancers in creating compositions, 225; reflexive techniques used by, 189, 200, 203–4; ritual and ceremony in choreography by, 200, 204, 206, 208, 223; role of audience in choreographic style of, 209, 223; solo performances by, 204, 205; on the sound of performance structure, 221; and the subject-body relationship, 220, 221; themes explored by, 200, 209; *Venice/Milan* by, 208; *Vessel* by, 206, 207, 208, 221, 225; and viewer participation in dance interpretation, xix, 222–23, 225–26

Morris, Robert, 171

Movement: in Balanchine's dance theory, 17, 19; and choreographic style relative to performance space, 85–87; in Cunningham's dance theory, 32, 34; in daily life, 6–8, 9, 105; Delsartian theory of, 157–59; in Graham's dance theory, 25, 28–30; in Grand Union choreography, 195, 197–98; in Humphrey's dance theory, 158, 161; materialization of, 168; in objectivist dance, 174–81; origins of, 153–54; patterns of, viewed as subject matter, 176–77; quality of, 77–78; in scientific theory of the nineteenth century, 154; sequences in Tharp's choreography, 209, 211, 213, 219; sources of, 79, 81, 83; structuralist approach to, 88, 90, 247*n*13. *See also* Quality in movement; Vocabulary

Music: and Balanchine's choreography, xiv, 14, 16, 19, 21, 23, 93, 141, 143, 239*n*13; contrasted with the sound of performance structure, 221; and Cunningham's choreography, xiv, 34, 37–38, 168, 169; and eighteenth-century dance compositions, 141, 143; and expressionist choreography, 163, 165; and Graham's choreography, 25, 28; and Grand Union choreography, 197–98; and Hay's choreography, 5, 119; and instru-

ments played by dance performers, 208; and Renaissance dance, 118; and syntax, 93; and Tharp's choreography, 222

Nagrin, Daniel, 167

Narrative: in Monk's compositions, 200, 203–4; in Tharp's compositions, 215, 219; viewer participation in the interpretation of, 222–23. *See also* Story dances

Narrative structure: and the body's ideological message, 259*n*3; in dances composed by David Gordon, 188–89; and modes of representation, 75; and syntax, 93

Narrators, in Tharp's compositions, 211–12

Natural body, xvii, 156; in Delsartian theory, 156; in expressionist choreography, 153; theory of, xiv–xv; vs. the "de-naturalized" approach to dance composition, xviii, 229*n*3, 237*n*3

Natural choreographic style, xiv–xv

Natural movement, xiv; in Duncan's dance theory, 154; in expressionist choreography, 154

"Naturalness," 229*n*3; as a cultural category, 254*n*41

Neoclassical dance in the eighteenth century, 121–45; compared with Balanchine's choreography, 121, 122, 125–26, 129–30, 131, 134–35, 141, 143, 247*n*1; compared with expressionist dance, 154, 165, 166; compared with the literary trope of metonymy, 236*n*1; compared with objectivist dance, 185; compared with Renaissance dance, 125, 130–34, 143–44; frames of, 121, 122, 125; imitative representation in, 121, 122, 126–27, 128, 154; lexicon of, 121, 130–31, 144; pantomime in,

Sex roles: and choreographic styles, 84, 85; in Renaissance dance, 109, 116–17; traditional, 217, 219, 224

Sexuality, 73; pelvis associated with, 79, 81, 83

Shawn, Ted, 151, 239*n*24; on Delsartian theory and expressionist dance, 156–57, 256*n*67; students of, 147–48

Signification, 236*n*2; by the body, 227, 243*n*1; and modes of representation, 66–67

Sign theory: and Cunningham's approach to choreography, 242*n*43; writing and dancing in, xxi, 232*n*11, 234*n*1

Sinatra, Frank, 216–19

Social dance: in eighteenth-century choreography, 130; and Hay's compositions, 8–9, 117–18; minimalist version of, 197; and parodies of ballroom dancing, 216–17, 219; in Renaissance court dance choreography, 101, 115–17, 118–19, 130; and Tharp's vocabulary, 211, 213

Sociology of Culture, The (Raymond Williams), 244*n*1

Sociopolitical conditions, 176; in Duncan's compositions, 72; and Hay's choreography, 111; and the Judson Church group, 169; in Renaissance dance, 109, 112, 251*n*15

Sokolow, Anna, 167

Space: and the architectural setting of dance performances, 60–62; and choreographic style, 85–86; in concepts of the quality of movement, 77–78; in Cunningham's choreography, 32, 34; of Grand Union performances, 191; in objectivist dance, 171–72, 179; and syntactic principles, 94; in Wigman's dance theory, 158

Spatial grid, 85–87

Speech: and chanting, 206; in Grand Union performances, 193–94, 195, 197, 221–22; and metacommentary, 193–94, 195, 200, 209; in objectivist dance, 182; in Tharp's compositions, 211–12

Spirituality, 156; in Duncan's compositions, 79, 150, 151; in expressionist dance, 151–52, 159, 161, 162; vs. materialism, 159, 161, 162

Stages: in Graham's choreography, 27; and styles of choreography, 85–87; types of, 61

Stage sets, 37; for Balanchine's compositions, 14; created by St. Denis, 148; designed by Isamu Noguchi, 73; of eighteenth-century neoclassical dance, 125; of expressionist compositions, 149–50; and Monk's choreography, 200, 203; and Tharp's choreography, 216, 222

Stanislavsky, Konstantin, 166, 241*n*34

Stars and planets, movement of, 107, 109

Steps, 70; and analysis of compositional forms, 231*n*7; in ballet, 90; of ballroom dancing, 216; of eighteenth-century social dance, 130–31; in Grand Union performances, 197; in modern dance, 90–91; in Renaissance social dances, 116, 118, 119, 130; used by Cunningham, 3

Stop action, 200, 203

Story dances: composed by Balanchine, 14, 17, 21; modes of representation used in, 68–69; syntax in, 93. *See also* Narrative

Stravinsky, Igor, 21

Strong, Roy, 250*n*14, 251*n*17

Structure of dance: devices used for, 93; paratactic procedures for, 95–96; syntactic principles applied to, 92–97; and vocabularies of movement, 88, 90–92

Studio concerts, 60, 61

Sturrock, John, 237*n*3

Style, xviii, 59, 76–88; of Balanchine's

Style (*continued*)
choreography, 83, 84, 87; body parts
and their symbolic associations used
in, 77, 78–85; and characteristic use
of the performance space, 77, 85–
87; compared with vocabulary, 91;
in contemporary ballet, 83–84, 88;
of Cunningham's choreography, 84–
85; and dance traditions, 87–88; defined, 76–77, 88; of Duncan's choreography, 79, 81, 87; in expressionist choreography, 165–66; of
Graham's choreography, 81, 83, 84,
87, 88; of Grand Union choreography, 197–98; of Hay's choreography, 84–85; of Humphrey's choreography, 87, 88; of male and female dance roles, 84, 85; and movement quality, 77–78, 81, 83, 85;
of objectivist dance, 179–80; of
Tharp's choreography, 88, 213, 215;
of Wigman's choreography, 166
Subject: and character portrayal, 51;
comparative concepts of, 43; defined,
236*n*3; in Graham's dance theory,
50–51; in Hay's choreography, 13,
51–52, 114–15; identity with image, 13; in objectivist dance, 181;
understanding of, 49
Subject-body relationship, 181, 220,
258*n*89. *See also* Body and subject
Subject matter: compared in Balanchine's
compositions and eighteenth-century
dance, 122, 134–35; of eighteenth-
century dance, 122, 134–35; envisioned by Isadora Duncan, 79; of expressionist dance, 152–53, 159,
161–62, 163; and modes of representation, 67–68; of Monk's compositions, 209; of objectivist dance,
176–77, 181, 185; of Tharp's compositions, 219
Surrealist composition, 200, 204, 223
Swan Lake, 144; modes of representation

in, 68–69, 70; style of dancers in,
77; syntax used in, 92
Sylphide, La, 69, 144
Symbols: of parts of the body, 78–79, 81,
82–84; relative to dance classes and
rehearsals, 46; in Renaissance dance,
115–17; theories on, 233*n*11
Synecdoche, 247*n*1; applied to dance,
234*n*1; correlated with the representational mode of replication, 236*n*1,
246*n*5; defined, 235*n*1; and the romantic period of the nineteenth century, 248*n*2
Syntax, 92–97; in Balanchine's choreography, 93; in Cunningham's choreography, 95; defined, xviii, 59; in expressionist dance, 163, 165; in
Graham's choreography, 92, 93–94;
in Hay's choreography, 92, 95; mimesis in, 93, 95; in objectivist dance,
178–79; parataxis in, 92, 94–96;
pathos in, 92, 93–94, 97; in Renaissance dance, 112, 115, 252*n*26; role
of variation in, 96–97; in Tharp's
choreography, 209, 213; in Wigman's
choreography, 94

T'ai chi ch'uan, 8
Tango, 216
Tap dance, 88, 211, 213
Taper, Bernard, 16–17, 21
Taylor, Paul, 91, 167; choreographic style
of, 257*n*78
Technique: in Balanchine's compositions,
19–20; comparative views on, 42,
46, 55–56; Cunningham's attitude
on, 35–36; defined, 19; in expressionist dance, 154; in Graham's
dance theory, 28–30
Tension, 184; between areas of the body,
79, 81; between props and representational modes, 195; between psychological and physical space, 94;
between sensuality and asceticism,

159; in expressionist choreography, 162–63; in Graham's choreography, 25, 81; and the meaning of dance, xviii

Texts, "writerly" vs. "readerly," 240*n*26, 259*n*7

Tharp, Twyla, xix, 209–20; *The Bix Pieces* by, 209, 211–12; choreographic style of, 88, 189, 209, 211–13, 219–20, 222, 223–24, 226; commentary on the choreography included in compositions by, 211–12; compared with the Grand Union and Monk, 220–27; creative process of, 212; *Deuce Coup* by, 213, 214; *Fait Accompli* by, 260*n*8; frames and stage sets used by, 209, 215, 216, 222; interdisciplinary approach of, 187, 211, 222; lexicon of, 213; movement in compositions by, 209, 211, 213; narrators used by, 211–12; *Nine Sinatra Songs* by, 216–17, 219; parodies by, 216–17, 219; reflexivity used by, 189, 211–12, 219, 224, 226, 260*n*8; role of audience in choreography of, 223–24; self-referential statements by, 211–12, 219; solo performances by, 211; style of, 213, 215; and the subject-body relationship, 220, 222, 223; subject matter used by, 219; syntactic principles used by, 209, 213; *Tank Dive* by, 209; and the traditional boundaries between art mediums, 222; viewer interpretation of, 224, 226; and viewer observations on the development of movement, 209; vocabulary of, 209, 213, 215

Theater design, 149–50

Theater-in-the-round, 60, 61, 85, 167; and choreographic style, 86–87; Grand Union performances in, 191; Hay's compositions performed in, 60, 101, 105; influence of, 61; objec-

tivist compositions performed in, 171; in the Renaissance period, 102, 104; and viewers as part of performance, 225

Theme and variation, syntactic principle of, 209, 213

Themes of dance: Graham's approach to, 27; in Humphrey's dance theory, 158, 162. *See also* Subject matter

Thrust stages, 61

Time, 85; and movement quality, 77–78

Topics of dance: compared for Balanchine's compositions and eighteenth-century choreography, 134–35; compared for court dances and proscenium ballets, 136; in eighteenth-century compositions, 134–35, 136; and modes of representation, 75; in Monk's compositions, 200, 203, 204; in the Renaissance period, 111–14, 136

Toulouze, Michel, 115

Transcendental experience: of dancers, 150; of viewers, 167

Tuccaro, Archange, on dance and celestial movement, 107, 109, 250*n*10

Tudor, David, 241*n*36

Turc généreux, Le, 138, 139

Unconscious, the, 79; in expressionist dance, 152; in Graham's choreographic style, 81; in Graham's concept of the body, 50; and theory on the natural body and natural movement, xiv

Universal dance, 8, 105

Untrained performers, 169, 171, 209

Van Vechten, Carl, 147

Variation: of ballroom dance steps, 216; role in dance structure, 96–97; of spatial and temporal movement properties, 94; theme and, 209, 213

Vico, Giambattista, 234*n*1, 248*n*2

Viewers, 3, 53–56, 76, 186–227, 243*n*55; analysis of the experience of, 243*n*55; and Balanchine's approach to choreography, 16, 21, 23, 54–55; as choreographers, 186–227 *passim;* of contemporary dance, 191; criteria of, 55–56; critical capacity of, 125; and Cunningham's approach to choreography, 41, 54–55; effect of architecture and space on, 60–62; of eighteenth-century neoclassical dance, 122, 125, 126; expanded perceptual acuity of, 221; expectations of, 60, 168, 213; of expressionist dance, 167; and Graham's approach to choreography, 53–54; of Grand Union performances, 198, 200, 222–23; and Hay's approach to choreography, 6, 13–14, 54, 55; influence of dance announcements and advertisements on, 59–60; interaction with dancers, 63–64; ironic attitudes of, 224; literacy of, 56–57, 58–59; of objectivist dance, 172, 176, 184, 185; opportunities for multiple interpretations by, 188, 209; as participants in the performance and in the choreography, xix, 225–26; participation in performance interpretation by, 188, 209, 222–23; program notes for, 5–6, 62 (*see also* Program notes); reading of dance performances by, 56–57, 97–98, 226; of Renaissance dance, 102, 104, 107, 249*n*5; sense of community and kinship with the dancers experienced by, 200, 209; and Tharp's approach to choreography, 189, 212, 213, 220, 223–24, 226; transcendental experience of, 167; and understanding of the vocabulary of movement, 91–92; and writing dance, xix, 226–27. *See also* Audience

Vigarini, Gasparo, 135
Visual arts, integrated with dance performances, 171–72
Visual perception, theory of, 17
Vocabulary, 84, 88–92; applied by Trisha Brown, 178; in Balanchine's choreography, 19, 91; compared with style, 91; in compositions by Childs, 177; in Cunningham's choreography, 3, 168; defined, xviii, 59; in Duncan's choreography, 90; in expressionist dance, 153, 154; in Graham's choreography, 2, 28–29, 90; in Hay's choreography, 5; in Humphrey's choreography, 90–91; and parts of the body, 90–91; in Tharp's choreography, 209, 213, 215, 219; used by Wigman, 90, 91; viewer understanding of, 91–92
Voltaire, on competition among dancers, 253*n*34

Walking, 172, 177
Waring, James, dance company of, 238*n*4
Weaver, John: *The Loves of Mars and Venus* analyzed by, 128–29, 136–38; on pantomine in ballet, 128; on the representation of anger, 129, 157, 168; on the representation of passion, 128–29, 254*n*41
Weidman, Charles, 75, 161
Weight: of the body, 36, 165, 174–75, 198; in concepts of movement quality, 77–78; new approaches to, 172
White, Hayden: on Foucault's approach to epistemic periods, 248*n*2; and literary tropes, 234*n*1, 248*n*2; and theory of representation in dance, xix–xx
Wigman, Mary, 147, 167; compared with Doris Humphrey, 158; on dance composition, 152, 162; influence of Laban's movement theory on, 91,

154, 158–59; movement vocabulary of, 90, 91, 154; role of body parts in choreography by, 163; style of, 166; syntax in choreography by, 94; *Witch Dance* by, 75

Williams, Raymond, 244*n*1

Wolff, Christian, 241*n*36

Worldly events, 97; methods for representation of, 65–76; and new literary criticism, 245*n*4; and objectivist dance, 174

Writing: body movement as act of, 237*n*3; as metaphor for dance interpretation, xix–xx, 234*n*1; and sign theory, xxi, 232*n*11

Writing dancing, 186–227; defined, xix; and interdisciplinary approach to dance composition, 187; relevant to the body and subject, 220–27; by viewers, xix, 226–27

Wynne, Shirley, 253*n*33

Yates, Frances A., 249*n*3, 250*n*11

Yoga, 151, 153

Designer: Sandy Drooker
Compositor: G & S Typesetters, Inc.
Text: 10/13 Sabon
Display: Sabon Italic
Printer: Malloy Lithographing, Inc.
Binder: John H. Dekker & Sons